THE LAMB AND THE FÜHRER

KINGSTONE
COMICS

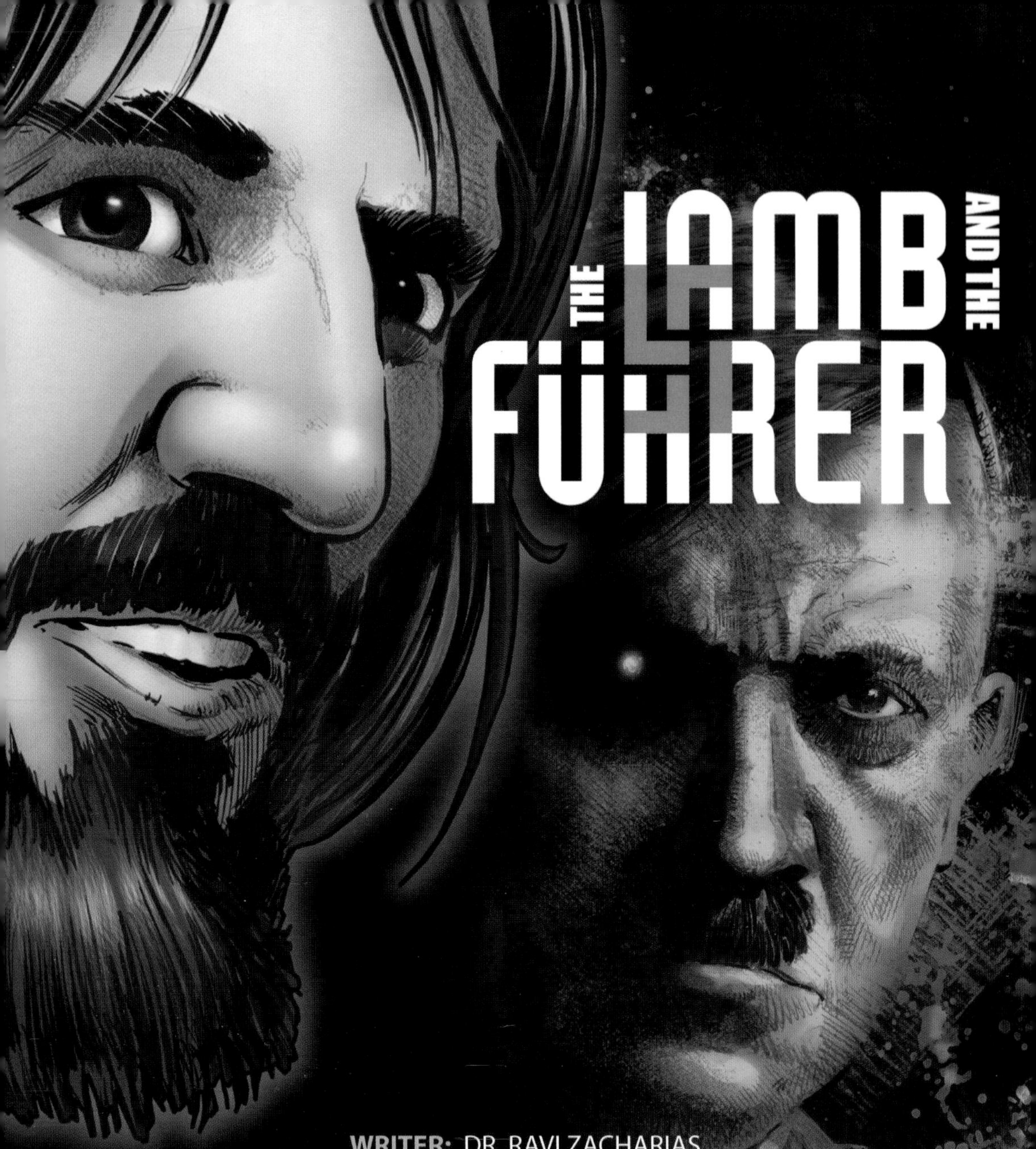
THE LAMB AND THE FÜHRER

WRITER: DR. RAVI ZACHARIAS

EDITOR: KELLY AYRIS

ARTISTS: JEFF SLEMONS & GEOF ISHERWOOD

COLORS: JOEL CHUA & TOM SMITH

LETTERS: ZACH MATHENY

DESIGN: NATE BUTLER, KEN RANEY & ZACH MATHENY

Published by Kingstone Comics
www.KingstoneMedia.com

Printed in USA

INTRODUCTION

✝

"I want to raise a generation of young people, imperious, relentless and cruel." With these words, Adolf Hitler spilled the blood of millions of people, his own as well as others, when he set himself as a god in the minds of his people. He pursued his dream and unleashed a hell upon the earth. As I traveled through the sites of the carnage of the Second World War, I was reminded afresh of the horror and the extent of human pain and suffering inflicted on so many by one man and those willing to follow him. The concentration camps, the Gestapo offices, and the gas ovens still speak today of the incalculable price that was paid. Any words that try to describe it become dwarfed because the story is so monstrous.

There is no name today more synonymous with power wickedness, and unprecedented violence than his. But nearly two thousand years before him, another walked this earth whose name is symbolic of love, peace, and life. His was a name also associated with the spilling of blood – His own, shed for the sake of the world. He endured hell to open the way to heaven. What would a conversation between these two be like? There were voices in Hitler's day that tried to stop him. One was Dietrich Bonhoeffer, a German pastor, who went so far as to be part of a plot to assassinate Hitler. Bonhoeffer believed that for the sake of the world, Hitler had to be removed, and he paid for that conviction with his life.

In this conversation that we imagine between Jesus and Hitler, Bonhoeffer joins in because he brings into focus the reality of the struggle that good men and women faced under national socialism. Violence, racism, power, lies, death, philosophy, evil are all given a face here. But then there is the face of love, individual worth, supreme goodness, power, truth, peace, and life in Jesus Christ. In the face of Bonhoeffer we see anguish, helplessness, and a will to change evil for good.

It was not difficult to find Hitler's own words of self-justification for his actions. It was not that difficult either to find Bonhoeffer's words that described the soul struggle he faced. But what would Jesus have said when ethics comes into conflict with an ethic that chose to kill to stop the killing? That part was harder, and it is in those words alone that the huge reality of those issues can be grasped.

So enter with me into Hitler's bunker and listen in as the Fuhrer, gun in hand, is about to end his life (synonymous in his mind with Germany itself), knowing that his Third Reich did not last a thousand years or bring a Final Solution, but in fact resulted in the destruction of his own country and much of Europe. How could good people have followed such an evil man? What is the origin of such violence? How does blood recompense for blood? Listen as Jesus, Hitler, and Bonhoeffer engage in a life-and-death discussion.

It is my earnest hope that, in a world now full of violence, the voice of Jesus will be heard again calling men and women to submit to His sacrifice so that we will not continue to sacrifice our own sons and daughters on the battlefields of human ego and ideological conflict.

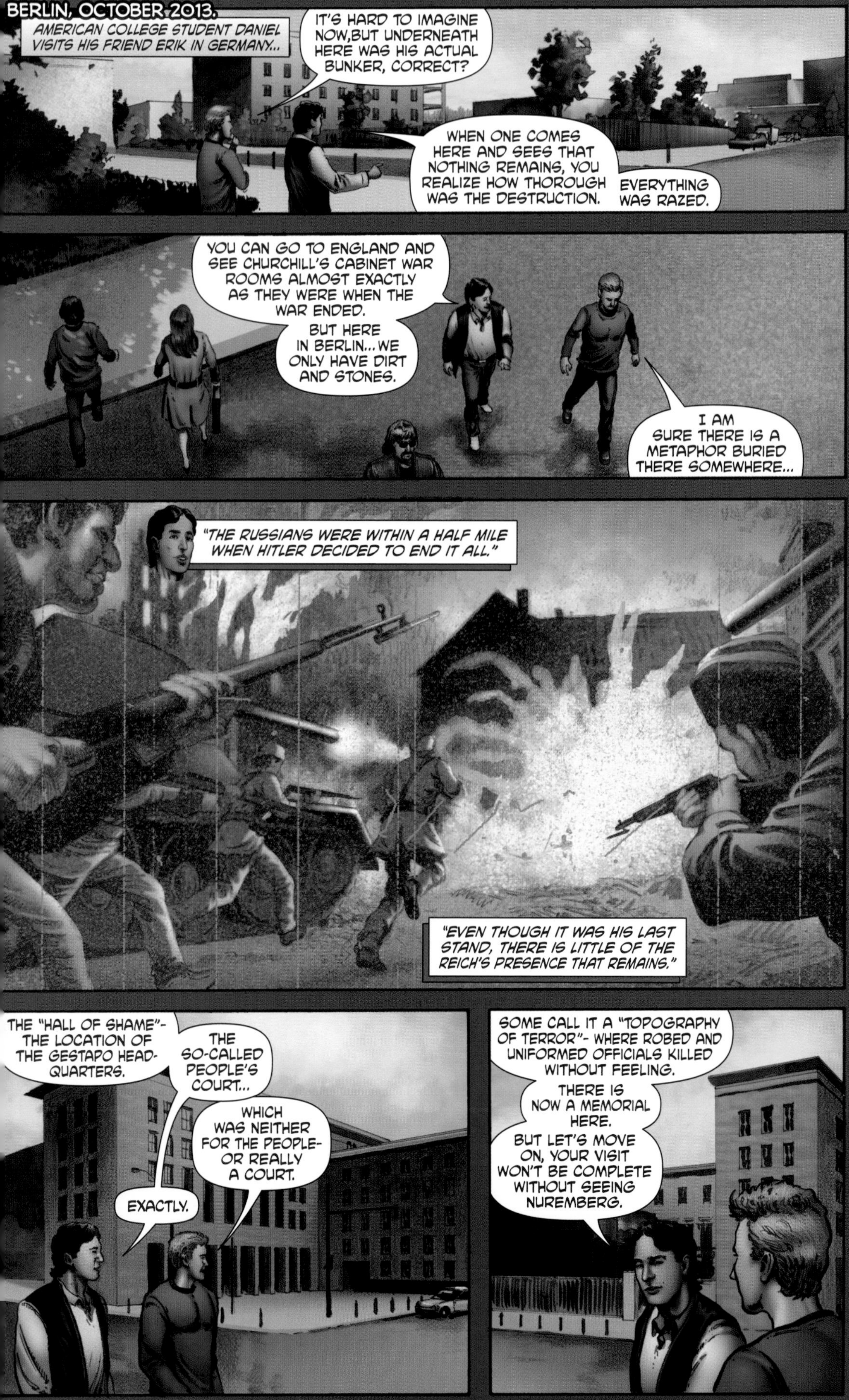
BERLIN, OCTOBER 2013.
AMERICAN COLLEGE STUDENT DANIEL VISITS HIS FRIEND ERIK IN GERMANY...
IT'S HARD TO IMAGINE NOW, BUT UNDERNEATH HERE WAS HIS ACTUAL BUNKER, CORRECT?
WHEN ONE COMES HERE AND SEES THAT NOTHING REMAINS, YOU REALIZE HOW THOROUGH WAS THE DESTRUCTION.
EVERYTHING WAS RAZED.
YOU CAN GO TO ENGLAND AND SEE CHURCHILL'S CABINET WAR ROOMS ALMOST EXACTLY AS THEY WERE WHEN THE WAR ENDED.
BUT HERE IN BERLIN... WE ONLY HAVE DIRT AND STONES.
I AM SURE THERE IS A METAPHOR BURIED THERE SOMEWHERE...
"THE RUSSIANS WERE WITHIN A HALF MILE WHEN HITLER DECIDED TO END IT ALL."
"EVEN THOUGH IT WAS HIS LAST STAND, THERE IS LITTLE OF THE REICH'S PRESENCE THAT REMAINS."
THE "HALL OF SHAME"- THE LOCATION OF THE GESTAPO HEAD-QUARTERS.
THE SO-CALLED PEOPLE'S COURT...
EXACTLY.
WHICH WAS NEITHER FOR THE PEOPLE- OR REALLY A COURT.
SOME CALL IT A "TOPOGRAPHY OF TERROR"- WHERE ROBED AND UNIFORMED OFFICIALS KILLED WITHOUT FEELING.
THERE IS NOW A MEMORIAL HERE.
BUT LET'S MOVE ON, YOUR VISIT WON'T BE COMPLETE WITHOUT SEEING NUREMBERG.

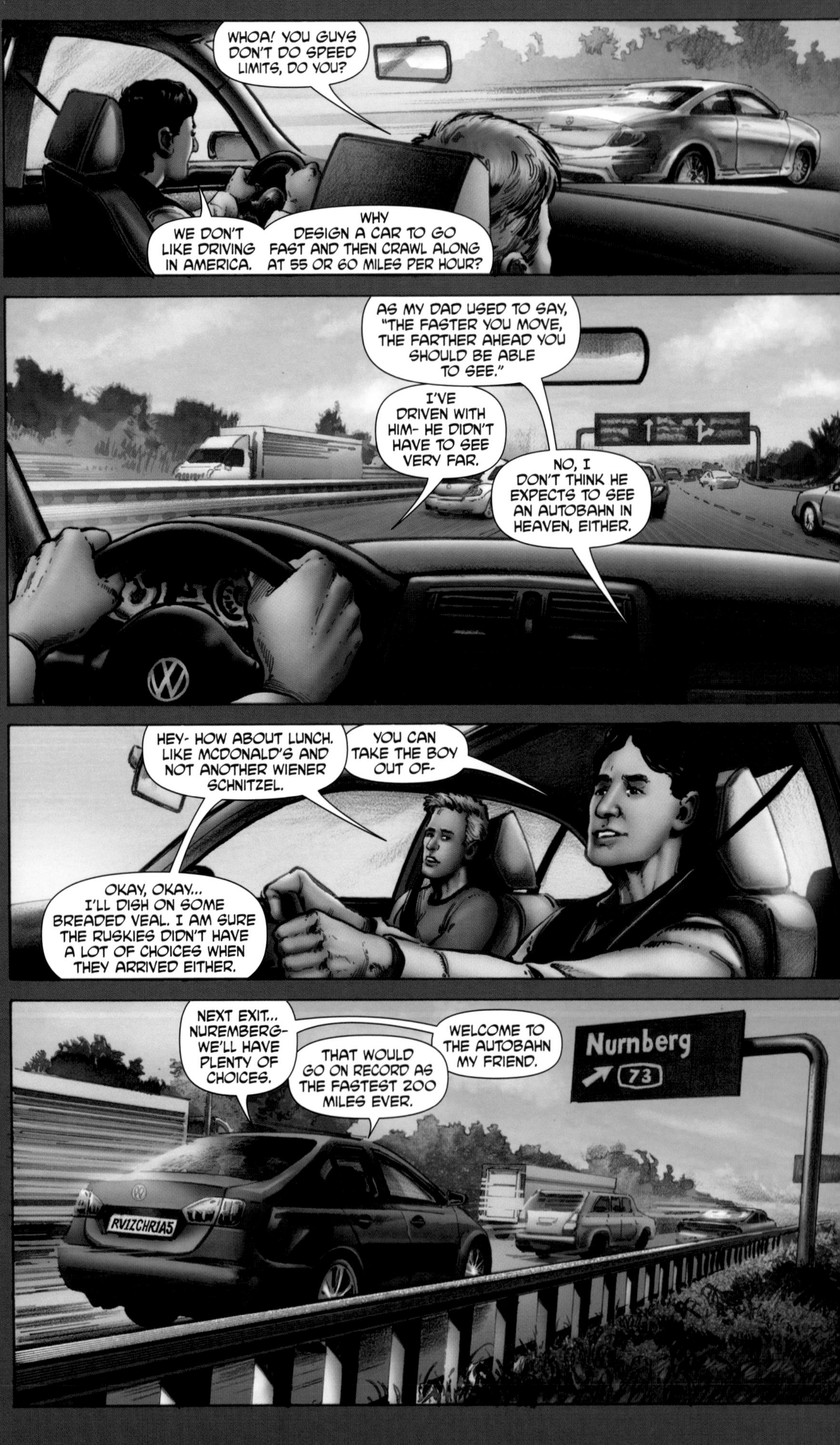
WHOA! YOU GUYS DON'T DO SPEED LIMITS, DO YOU?
WE DON'T LIKE DRIVING IN AMERICA.
WHY DESIGN A CAR TO GO FAST AND THEN CRAWL ALONG AT 55 OR 60 MILES PER HOUR?
AS MY DAD USED TO SAY, "THE FASTER YOU MOVE, THE FARTHER AHEAD YOU SHOULD BE ABLE TO SEE."
I'VE DRIVEN WITH HIM- HE DIDN'T HAVE TO SEE VERY FAR.
NO, I DON'T THINK HE EXPECTS TO SEE AN AUTOBAHN IN HEAVEN, EITHER.
HEY- HOW ABOUT LUNCH. LIKE MCDONALD'S AND NOT ANOTHER WIENER SCHNITZEL.
YOU CAN TAKE THE BOY OUT OF-
OKAY, OKAY... I'LL DISH ON SOME BREADED VEAL. I AM SURE THE RUSKIES DIDN'T HAVE A LOT OF CHOICES WHEN THEY ARRIVED EITHER.
NEXT EXIT... NUREMBERG- WE'LL HAVE PLENTY OF CHOICES.
THAT WOULD GO ON RECORD AS THE FASTEST 200 MILES EVER.
WELCOME TO THE AUTOBAHN MY FRIEND.
Nurnberg
73
RV1ZCHRIA5

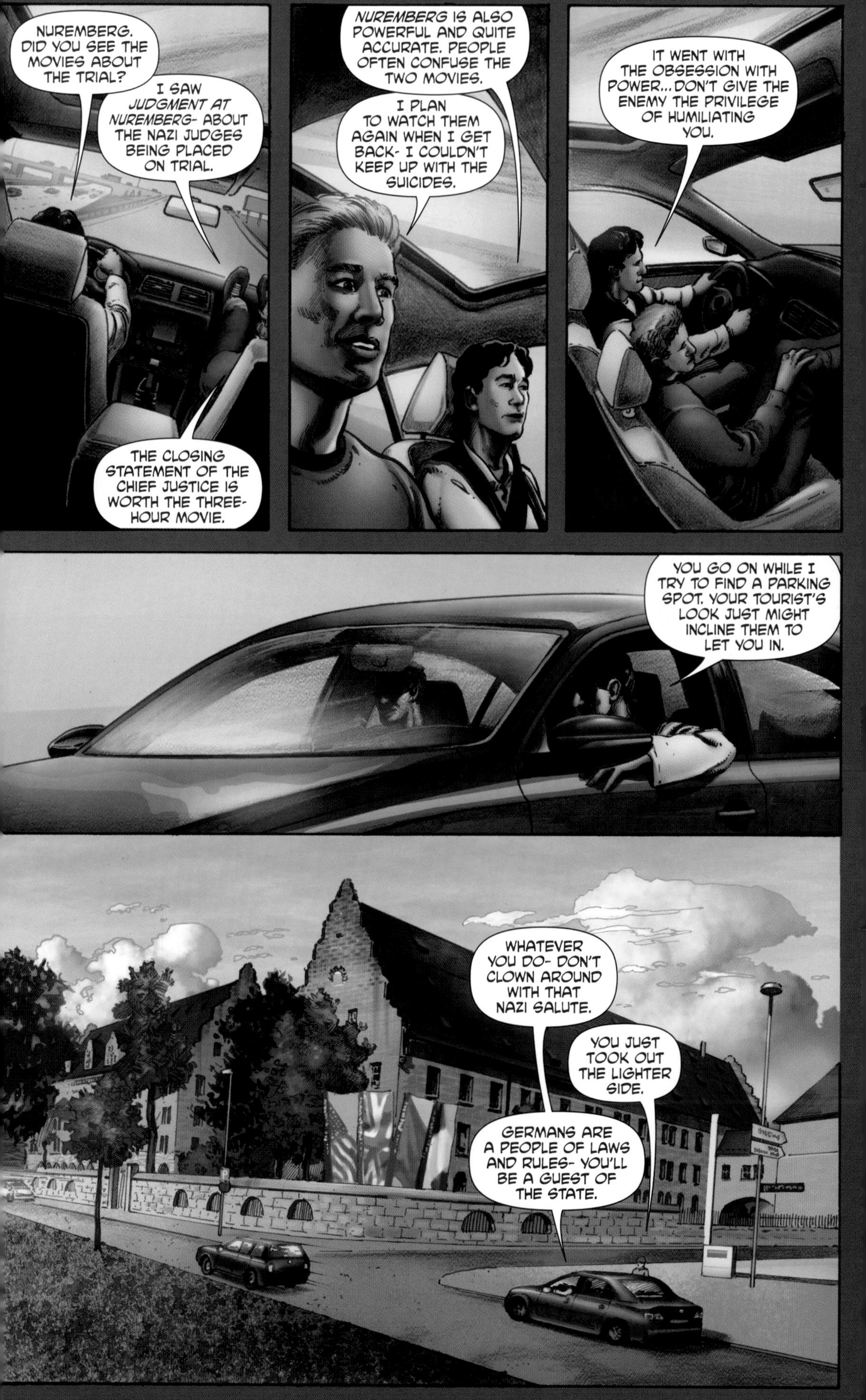

NUREMBERG. DID YOU SEE THE MOVIES ABOUT THE TRIAL?
I SAW *JUDGMENT AT NUREMBERG*- ABOUT THE NAZI JUDGES BEING PLACED ON TRIAL.
THE CLOSING STATEMENT OF THE CHIEF JUSTICE IS WORTH THE THREE-HOUR MOVIE.
NUREMBERG IS ALSO POWERFUL AND QUITE ACCURATE. PEOPLE OFTEN CONFUSE THE TWO MOVIES.
I PLAN TO WATCH THEM AGAIN WHEN I GET BACK- I COULDN'T KEEP UP WITH THE SUICIDES.
IT WENT WITH THE OBSESSION WITH POWER... DON'T GIVE THE ENEMY THE PRIVILEGE OF HUMILIATING YOU.
YOU GO ON WHILE I TRY TO FIND A PARKING SPOT. YOUR TOURIST'S LOOK JUST MIGHT INCLINE THEM TO LET YOU IN.
WHATEVER YOU DO- DON'T CLOWN AROUND WITH THAT NAZI SALUTE.
YOU JUST TOOK OUT THE LIGHTER SIDE.
GERMANS ARE A PEOPLE OF LAWS AND RULES- YOU'LL BE A GUEST OF THE STATE.

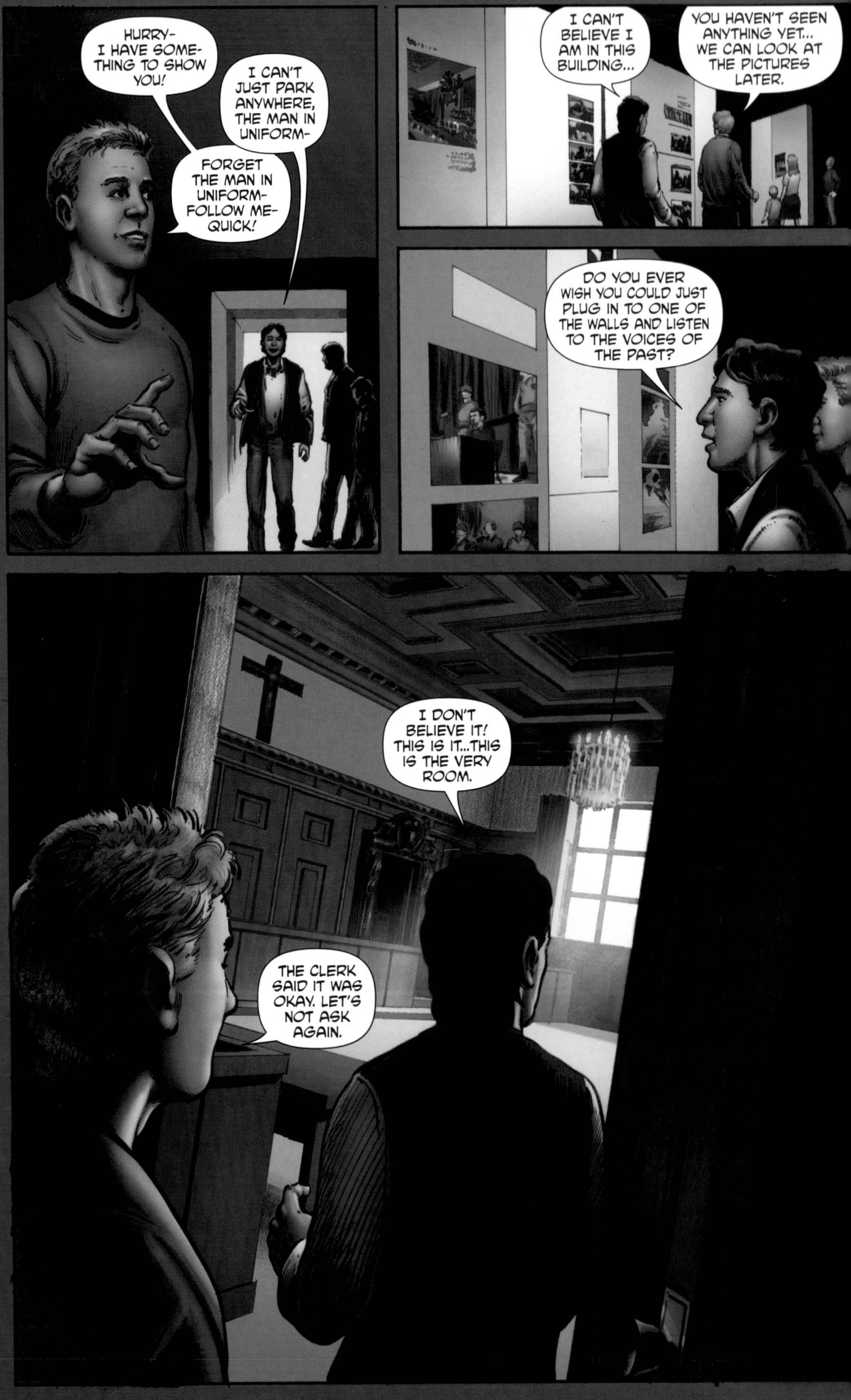
HURRY- I HAVE SOME-THING TO SHOW YOU!
I CAN'T JUST PARK ANYWHERE, THE MAN IN UNIFORM-
FORGET THE MAN IN UNIFORM- FOLLOW ME- QUICK!
I CAN'T BELIEVE I AM IN THIS BUILDING...
YOU HAVEN'T SEEN ANYTHING YET... WE CAN LOOK AT THE PICTURES LATER.
DO YOU EVER WISH YOU COULD JUST PLUG IN TO ONE OF THE WALLS AND LISTEN TO THE VOICES OF THE PAST?
I DON'T BELIEVE IT! THIS IS IT...THIS IS THE VERY ROOM.
THE CLERK SAID IT WAS OKAY. LET'S NOT ASK AGAIN.

WHAT SILENCE HAUNTS THIS ROOM. THERE WAS A DAY WHEN THE SCREAMS OF THE MURDERED WERE—

HEY— I AM NOT SURE WE ARE SUPPOSED TO BE IN HERE WITHOUT SOMEBODY IN AUTHORITY.

LET'S SIT DOWN AND *PRETEND* WE'RE HERE BY AUTHORITY.

I DON'T LIKE THAT WORD— PRETEND. THAT'S THE WAY THE WHOLE THING GOT STARTED.

IT WAS ALL A CHARADE— CEREMONY, GOOSE STEPPING, THE SALUTE.

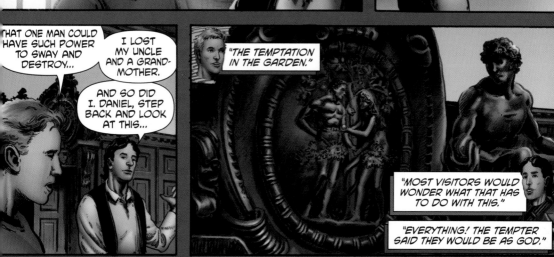

THAT ONE MAN COULD HAVE SUCH POWER TO SWAY AND DESTROY...

I LOST MY UNCLE AND A GRAND- MOTHER.

AND SO DID I. DANIEL, STEP BACK AND LOOK AT THIS...

"THE TEMPTATION IN THE GARDEN."

"MOST VISITORS WOULD WONDER WHAT THAT HAS TO DO WITH THIS."

"EVERYTHING! THE TEMPTER SAID THEY WOULD BE AS GOD."

CHILLING APPROPRIATENESS.

I BELONG TO THE CHURCH BUT I KNOW LITTLE ABOUT THE BIBLE.

THE STATE CHURCH SUCKS THE TRUE SPIRITUALITY OUT OF US.

BUT SOME MINISTERS STOOD IN THE WAY OF HITLER—SOME EVEN TRIED TO ASSASINATE HIM.

EVERY GERMAN KNOWS THE NAME OF DIETRICH BONHOEFFER.

THAT'S ANOTHER THING... CHURCH AND STATE.

LOOK ABOVE THE JUDGE'S CHAIR. THEY LOOK LIKE THE TEN COMMANDMENTS.

THERE ARE THREE COMMANDMENTS ON THE FIRST TABLET BUT SEVEN ON THE SECOND—IS THAT HOW THEY ARE USUALLY WRITTEN?

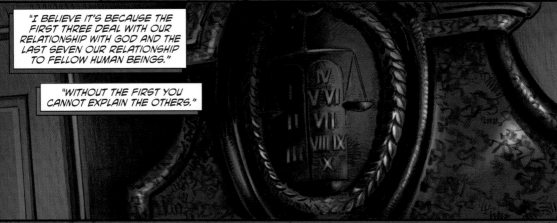

"I BELIEVE IT'S BECAUSE THE FIRST THREE DEAL WITH OUR RELATIONSHIP WITH GOD AND THE LAST SEVEN OUR RELATIONSHIP TO FELLOW HUMAN BEINGS."

"WITHOUT THE FIRST YOU CANNOT EXPLAIN THE OTHERS."

I WAS SIMPLY FOLLOWING THE LAW OF THE LAND.

THERE IS A LAW THAT STANDS SUPREME ABOVE ALL OTHER LAW!

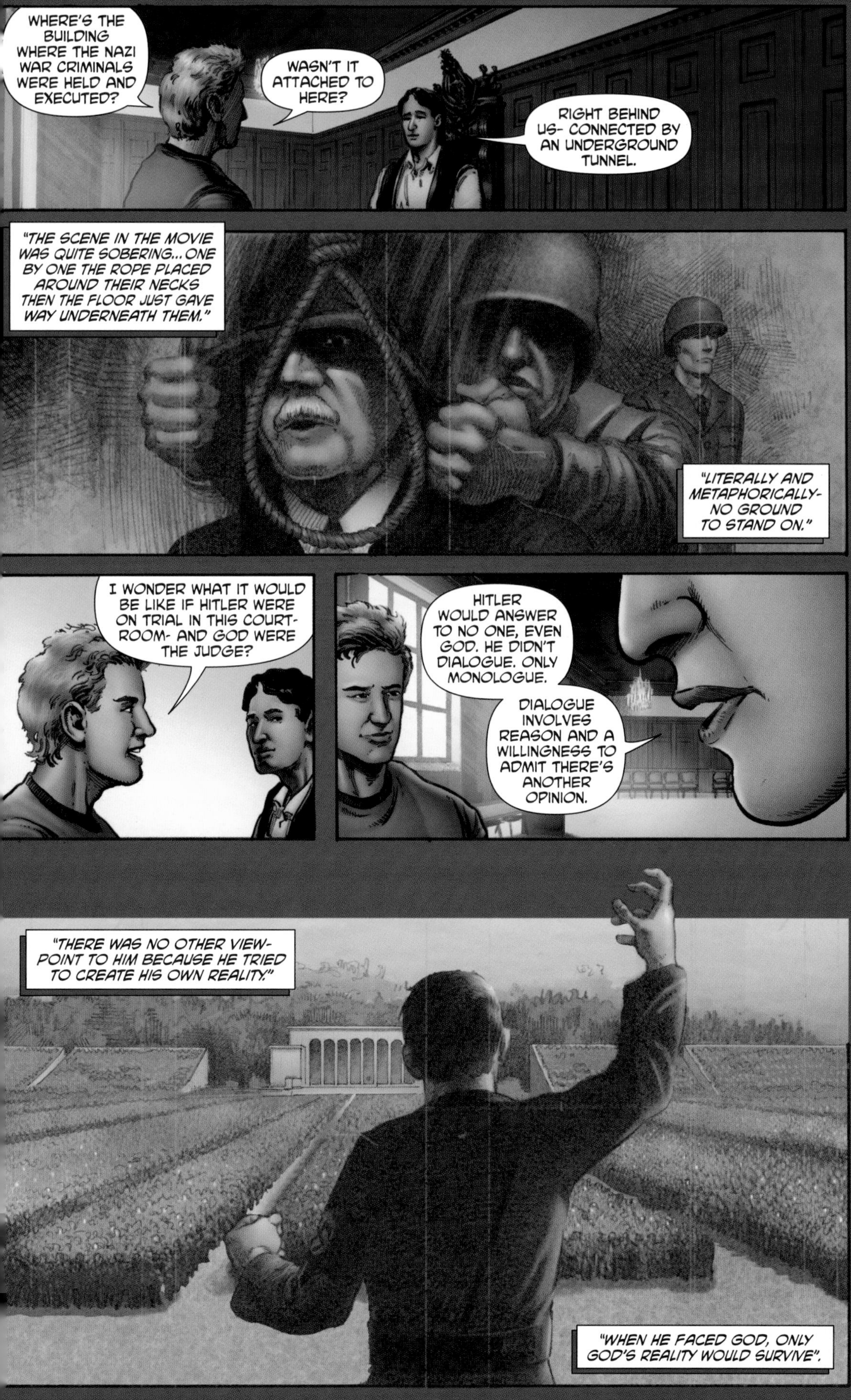
WHERE'S THE BUILDING WHERE THE NAZI WAR CRIMINALS WERE HELD AND EXECUTED?
WASN'T IT ATTACHED TO HERE?
RIGHT BEHIND US- CONNECTED BY AN UNDERGROUND TUNNEL.
"THE SCENE IN THE MOVIE WAS QUITE SOBERING...ONE BY ONE THE ROPE PLACED AROUND THEIR NECKS THEN THE FLOOR JUST GAVE WAY UNDERNEATH THEM."
"LITERALLY AND METAPHORICALLY- NO GROUND TO STAND ON."
I WONDER WHAT IT WOULD BE LIKE IF HITLER WERE ON TRIAL IN THIS COURT-ROOM- AND GOD WERE THE JUDGE?
HITLER WOULD ANSWER TO NO ONE, EVEN GOD. HE DIDN'T DIALOGUE. ONLY MONOLOGUE.
DIALOGUE INVOLVES REASON AND A WILLINGNESS TO ADMIT THERE'S ANOTHER OPINION.
"THERE WAS NO OTHER VIEW-POINT TO HIM BECAUSE HE TRIED TO CREATE HIS OWN REALITY."
"WHEN HE FACED GOD, ONLY GOD'S REALITY WOULD SURVIVE".

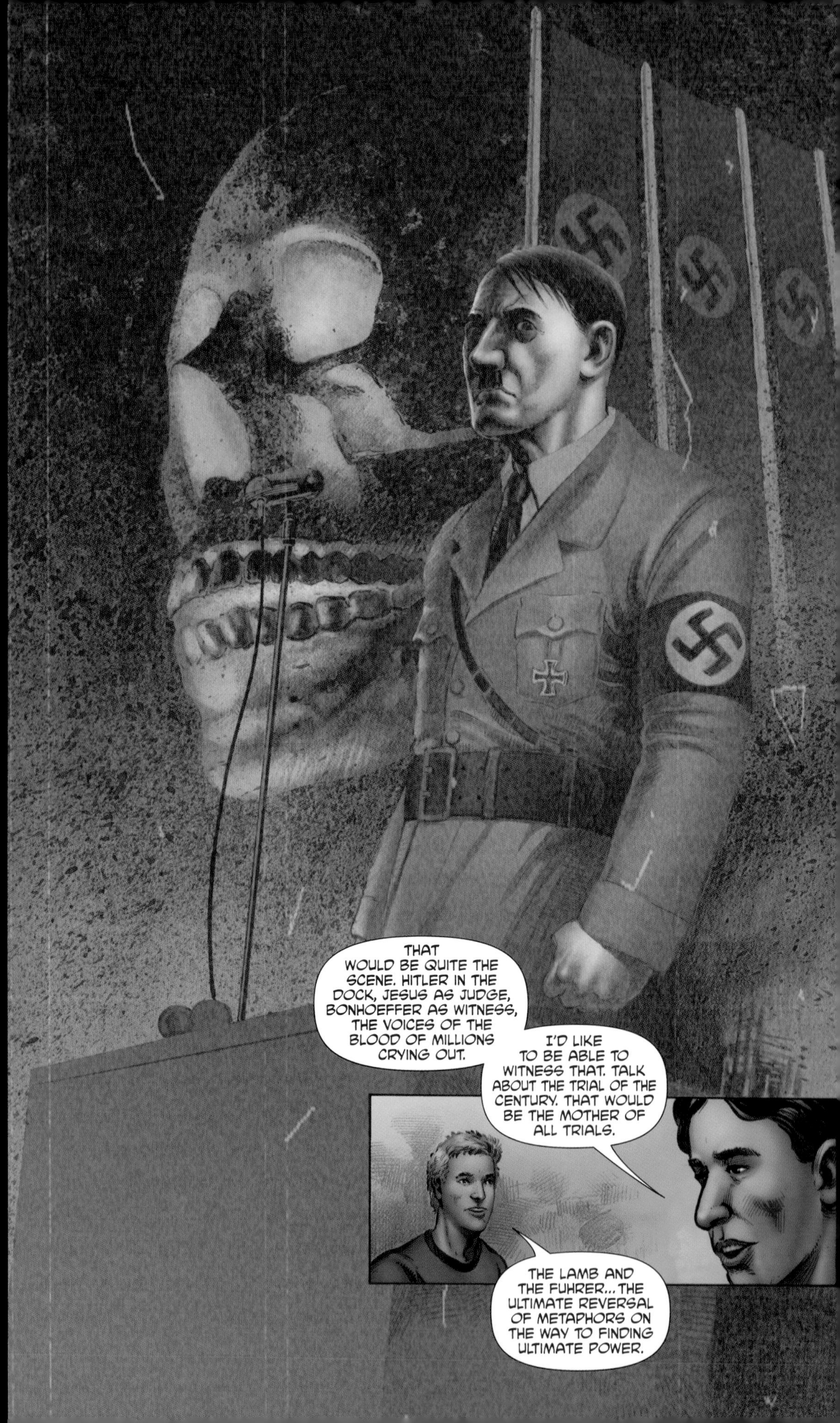
THAT WOULD BE QUITE THE SCENE. HITLER IN THE DOCK, JESUS AS JUDGE, BONHOEFFER AS WITNESS, THE VOICES OF THE BLOOD OF MILLIONS CRYING OUT.
I'D LIKE TO BE ABLE TO WITNESS THAT. TALK ABOUT THE TRIAL OF THE CENTURY. THAT WOULD BE THE MOTHER OF ALL TRIALS.
THE LAMB AND THE FUHRER... THE ULTIMATE REVERSAL OF METAPHORS ON THE WAY TO FINDING ULTIMATE POWER.

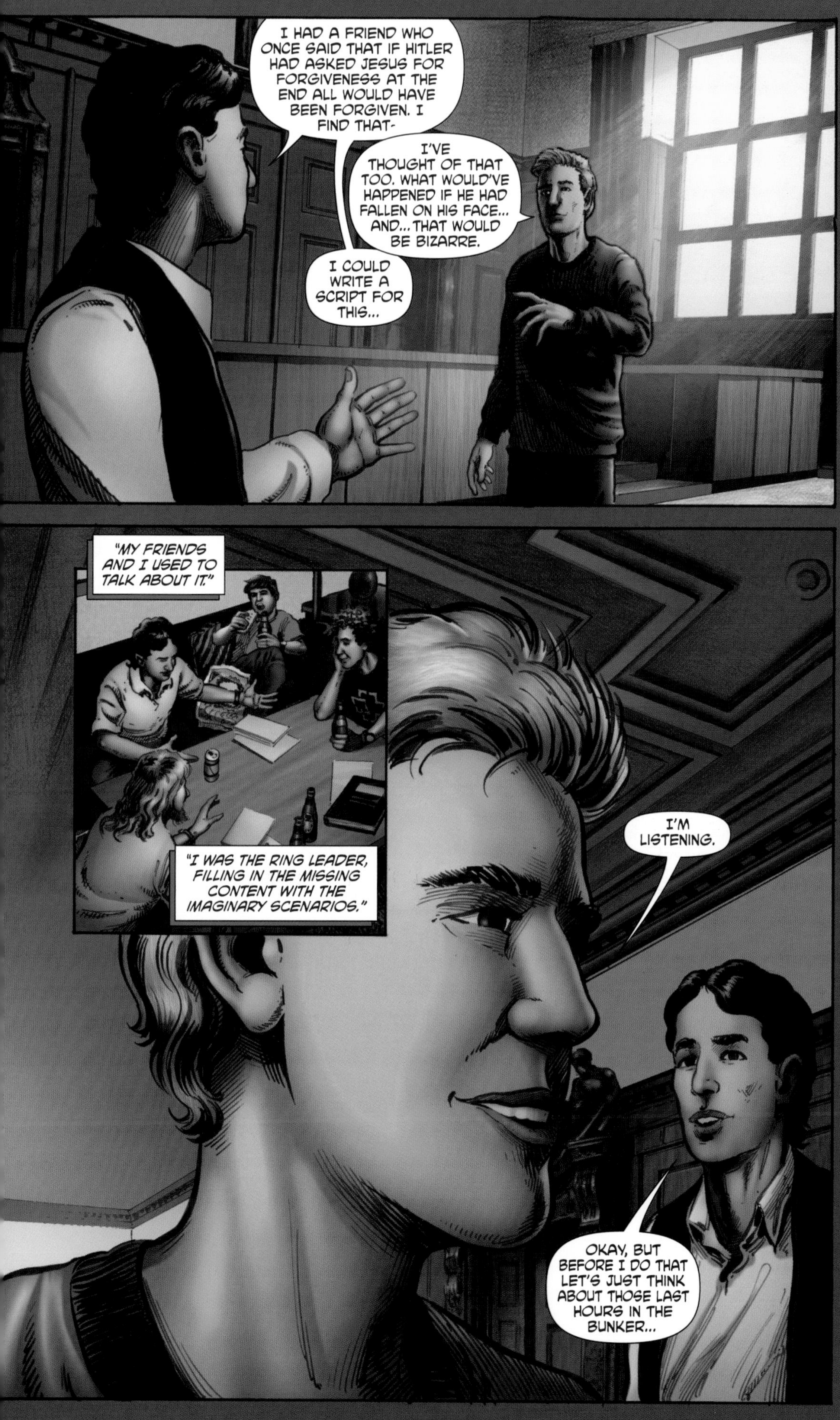
I HAD A FRIEND WHO ONCE SAID THAT IF HITLER HAD ASKED JESUS FOR FORGIVENESS AT THE END ALL WOULD HAVE BEEN FORGIVEN. I FIND THAT-
I'VE THOUGHT OF THAT TOO. WHAT WOULD'VE HAPPENED IF HE HAD FALLEN ON HIS FACE... AND... THAT WOULD BE BIZARRE.
I COULD WRITE A SCRIPT FOR THIS...
"MY FRIENDS AND I USED TO TALK ABOUT IT."
"I WAS THE RING LEADER, FILLING IN THE MISSING CONTENT WITH THE IMAGINARY SCENARIOS."
I'M LISTENING.
OKAY, BUT BEFORE I DO THAT LET'S JUST THINK ABOUT THOSE LAST HOURS IN THE BUNKER...

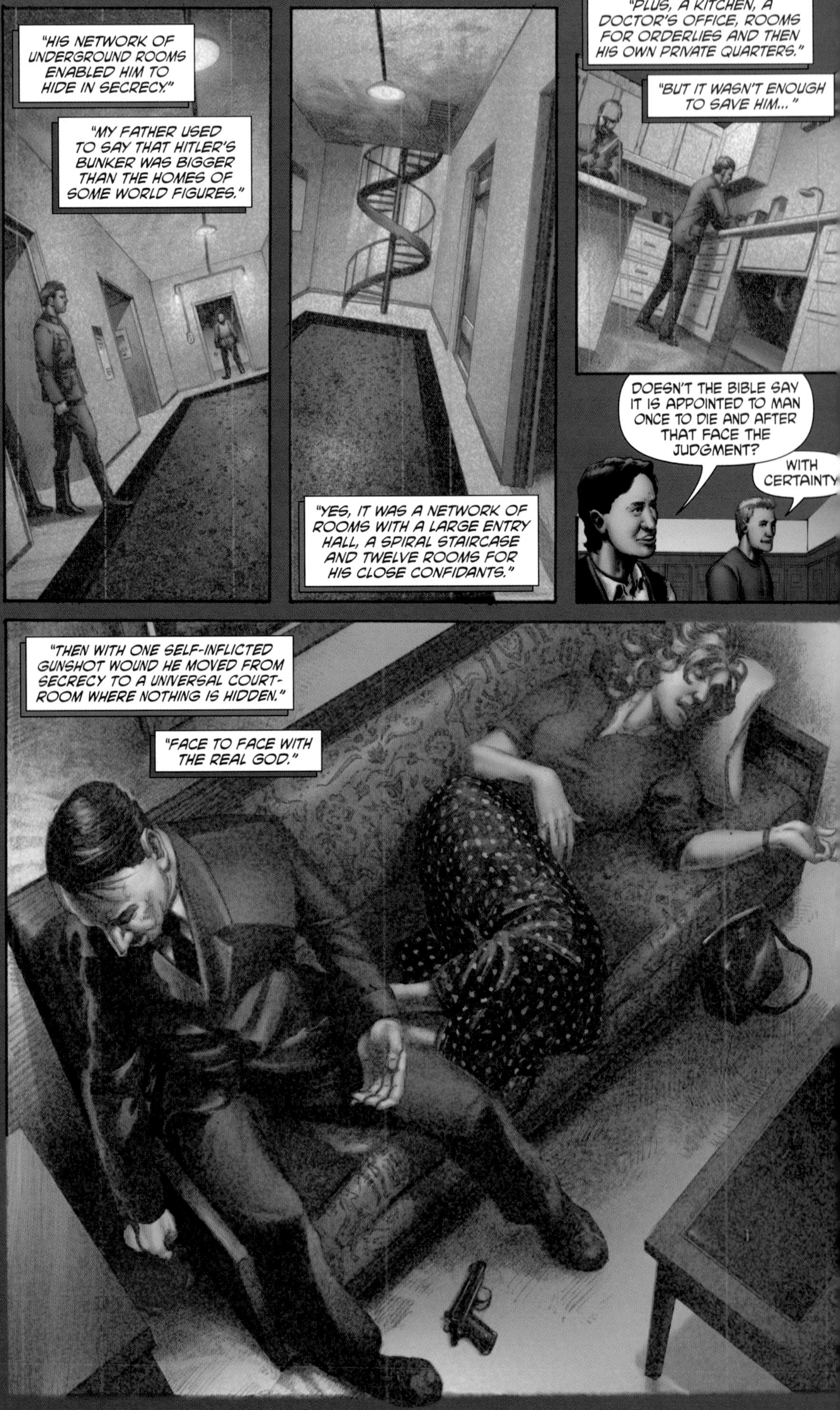
"HIS NETWORK OF UNDERGROUND ROOMS ENABLED HIM TO HIDE IN SECRECY."
"MY FATHER USED TO SAY THAT HITLER'S BUNKER WAS BIGGER THAN THE HOMES OF SOME WORLD FIGURES."
"YES, IT WAS A NETWORK OF ROOMS WITH A LARGE ENTRY HALL, A SPIRAL STAIRCASE AND TWELVE ROOMS FOR HIS CLOSE CONFIDANTS."
"PLUS, A KITCHEN, A DOCTOR'S OFFICE, ROOMS FOR ORDERLIES AND THEN HIS OWN PRIVATE QUARTERS."
"BUT IT WASN'T ENOUGH TO SAVE HIM..."
DOESN'T THE BIBLE SAY IT IS APPOINTED TO MAN ONCE TO DIE AND AFTER THAT FACE THE JUDGMENT?
WITH CERTAINTY
"THEN WITH ONE SELF-INFLICTED GUNSHOT WOUND HE MOVED FROM SECRECY TO A UNIVERSAL COURT-ROOM WHERE NOTHING IS HIDDEN."
"FACE TO FACE WITH THE REAL GOD."

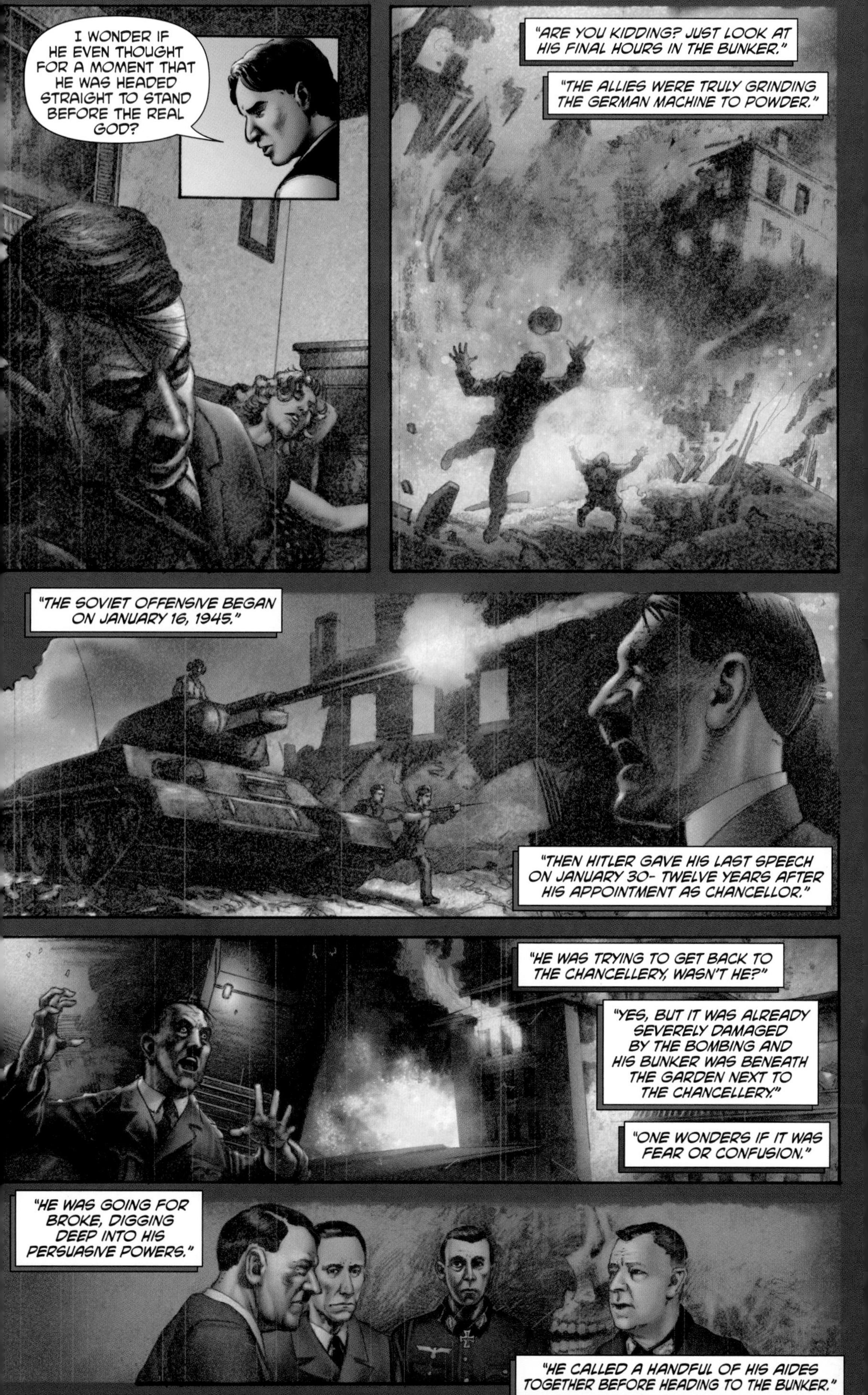
I WONDER IF HE EVEN THOUGHT FOR A MOMENT THAT HE WAS HEADED STRAIGHT TO STAND BEFORE THE REAL GOD?
"ARE YOU KIDDING? JUST LOOK AT HIS FINAL HOURS IN THE BUNKER."
"THE ALLIES WERE TRULY GRINDING THE GERMAN MACHINE TO POWDER."
"THE SOVIET OFFENSIVE BEGAN ON JANUARY 16, 1945."
"THEN HITLER GAVE HIS LAST SPEECH ON JANUARY 30- TWELVE YEARS AFTER HIS APPOINTMENT AS CHANCELLOR."
"HE WAS TRYING TO GET BACK TO THE CHANCELLERY, WASN'T HE?"
"YES, BUT IT WAS ALREADY SEVERELY DAMAGED BY THE BOMBING AND HIS BUNKER WAS BENEATH THE GARDEN NEXT TO THE CHANCELLERY."
"ONE WONDERS IF IT WAS FEAR OR CONFUSION."
"HE WAS GOING FOR BROKE, DIGGING DEEP INTO HIS PERSUASIVE POWERS."
"HE CALLED A HANDFUL OF HIS AIDES TOGETHER BEFORE HEADING TO THE BUNKER."

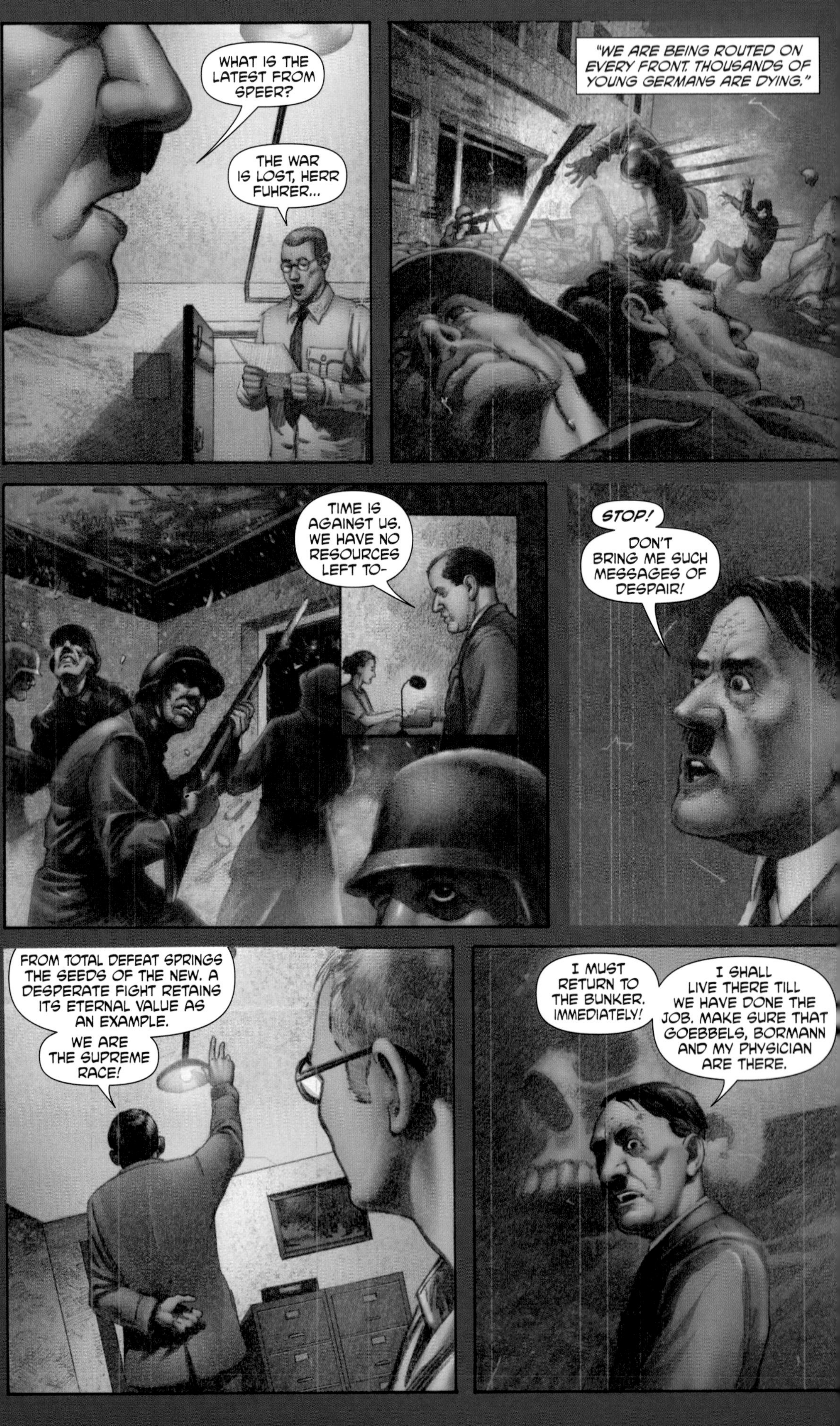
WHAT IS THE LATEST FROM SPEER?
THE WAR IS LOST, HERR FUHRER...
"WE ARE BEING ROUTED ON EVERY FRONT. THOUSANDS OF YOUNG GERMANS ARE DYING."
TIME IS AGAINST US. WE HAVE NO RESOURCES LEFT TO-
STOP!
DON'T BRING ME SUCH MESSAGES OF DESPAIR!
FROM TOTAL DEFEAT SPRINGS THE SEEDS OF THE NEW. A DESPERATE FIGHT RETAINS ITS ETERNAL VALUE AS AN EXAMPLE.
WE ARE THE SUPREME RACE!
I MUST RETURN TO THE BUNKER. IMMEDIATELY!
I SHALL LIVE THERE TILL WE HAVE DONE THE JOB. MAKE SURE THAT GOEBBELS, BORMANN AND MY PHYSICIAN ARE THERE.

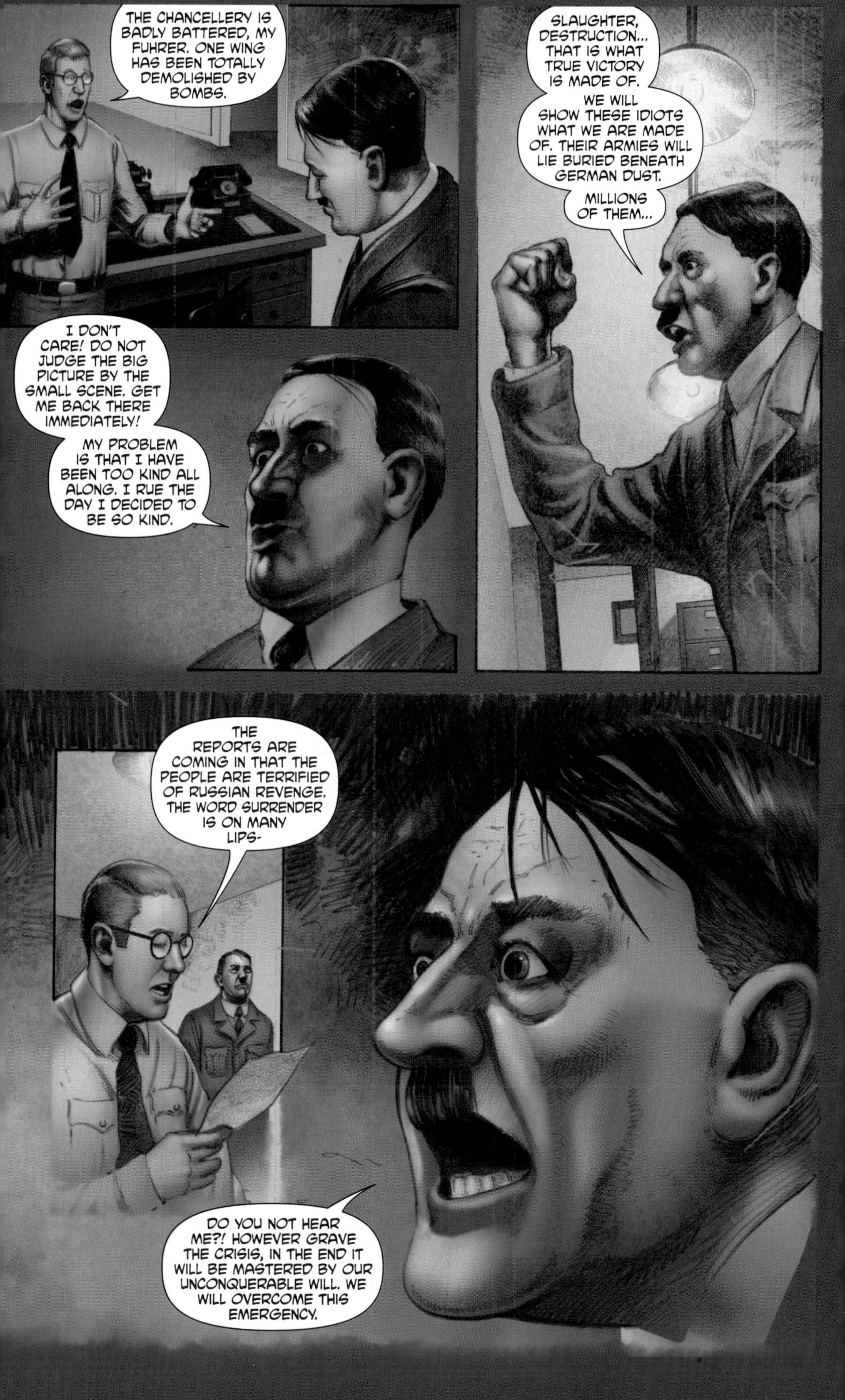
THE CHANCELLERY IS BADLY BATTERED, MY FUHRER. ONE WING HAS BEEN TOTALLY DEMOLISHED BY BOMBS.
I DON'T CARE! DO NOT JUDGE THE BIG PICTURE BY THE SMALL SCENE. GET ME BACK THERE IMMEDIATELY!
MY PROBLEM IS THAT I HAVE BEEN TOO KIND ALL ALONG. I RUE THE DAY I DECIDED TO BE SO KIND.
SLAUGHTER, DESTRUCTION... THAT IS WHAT TRUE VICTORY IS MADE OF.
WE WILL SHOW THESE IDIOTS WHAT WE ARE MADE OF. THEIR ARMIES WILL LIE BURIED BENEATH GERMAN DUST.
MILLIONS OF THEM...
THE REPORTS ARE COMING IN THAT THE PEOPLE ARE TERRIFIED OF RUSSIAN REVENGE. THE WORD SURRENDER IS ON MANY LIPS-
DO YOU NOT HEAR ME?! HOWEVER GRAVE THE CRISIS, IN THE END IT WILL BE MASTERED BY OUR UNCONQUERABLE WILL. WE WILL OVERCOME THIS EMERGENCY.

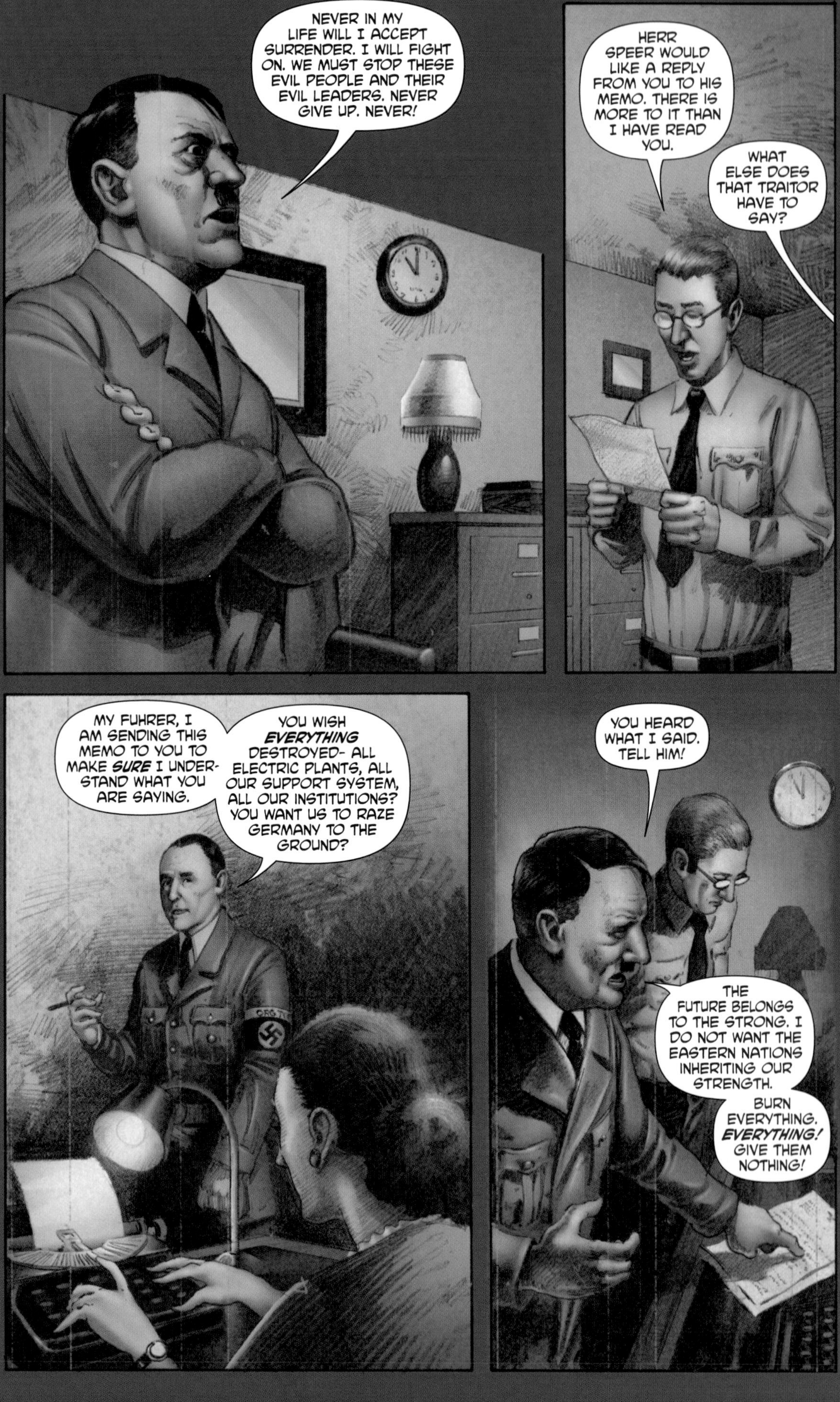

NEVER IN MY LIFE WILL I ACCEPT SURRENDER. I WILL FIGHT ON. WE MUST STOP THESE EVIL PEOPLE AND THEIR EVIL LEADERS. NEVER GIVE UP. NEVER!
HERR SPEER WOULD LIKE A REPLY FROM YOU TO HIS MEMO. THERE IS MORE TO IT THAN I HAVE READ YOU.
WHAT ELSE DOES THAT TRAITOR HAVE TO SAY?
MY FUHRER, I AM SENDING THIS MEMO TO YOU TO MAKE *SURE* I UNDERSTAND WHAT YOU ARE SAYING.
YOU WISH ***EVERYTHING*** DESTROYED- ALL ELECTRIC PLANTS, ALL OUR SUPPORT SYSTEM, ALL OUR INSTITUTIONS? YOU WANT US TO RAZE GERMANY TO THE GROUND?
YOU HEARD WHAT I SAID. TELL HIM!
THE FUTURE BELONGS TO THE STRONG. I DO NOT WANT THE EASTERN NATIONS INHERITING OUR STRENGTH.
BURN EVERYTHING. ***EVERYTHING!*** GIVE THEM NOTHING!

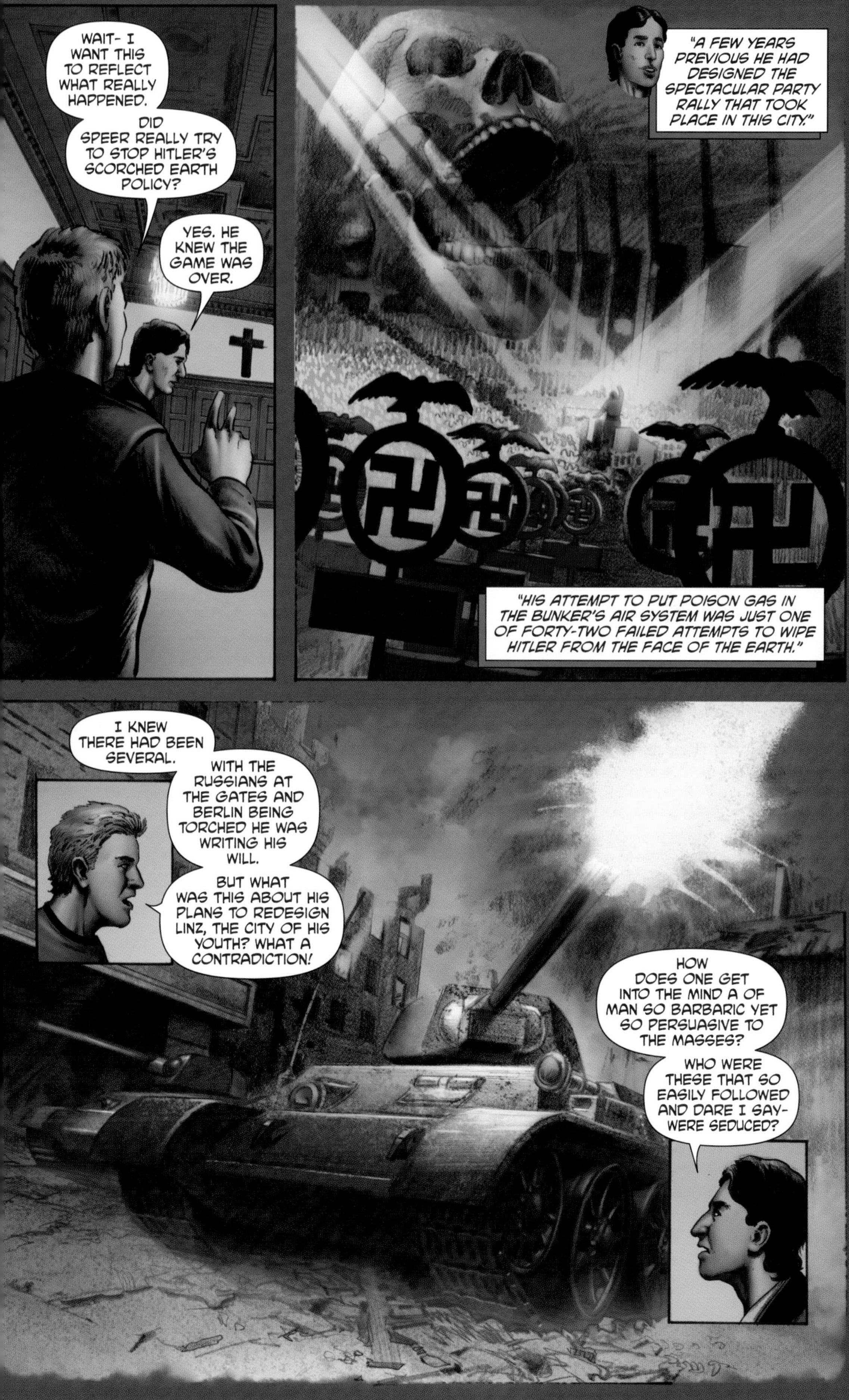
WAIT- I WANT THIS TO REFLECT WHAT REALLY HAPPENED.
DID SPEER REALLY TRY TO STOP HITLER'S SCORCHED EARTH POLICY?
YES. HE KNEW THE GAME WAS OVER.
"A FEW YEARS PREVIOUS HE HAD DESIGNED THE SPECTACULAR PARTY RALLY THAT TOOK PLACE IN THIS CITY."
"HIS ATTEMPT TO PUT POISON GAS IN THE BUNKER'S AIR SYSTEM WAS JUST ONE OF FORTY-TWO FAILED ATTEMPTS TO WIPE HITLER FROM THE FACE OF THE EARTH."
I KNEW THERE HAD BEEN SEVERAL.
WITH THE RUSSIANS AT THE GATES AND BERLIN BEING TORCHED HE WAS WRITING HIS WILL.
BUT WHAT WAS THIS ABOUT HIS PLANS TO REDESIGN LINZ, THE CITY OF HIS YOUTH? WHAT A CONTRADICTION!
HOW DOES ONE GET INTO THE MIND A OF MAN SO BARBARIC YET SO PERSUASIVE TO THE MASSES?
WHO WERE THESE THAT SO EASILY FOLLOWED AND DARE I SAY- WERE SEDUCED?

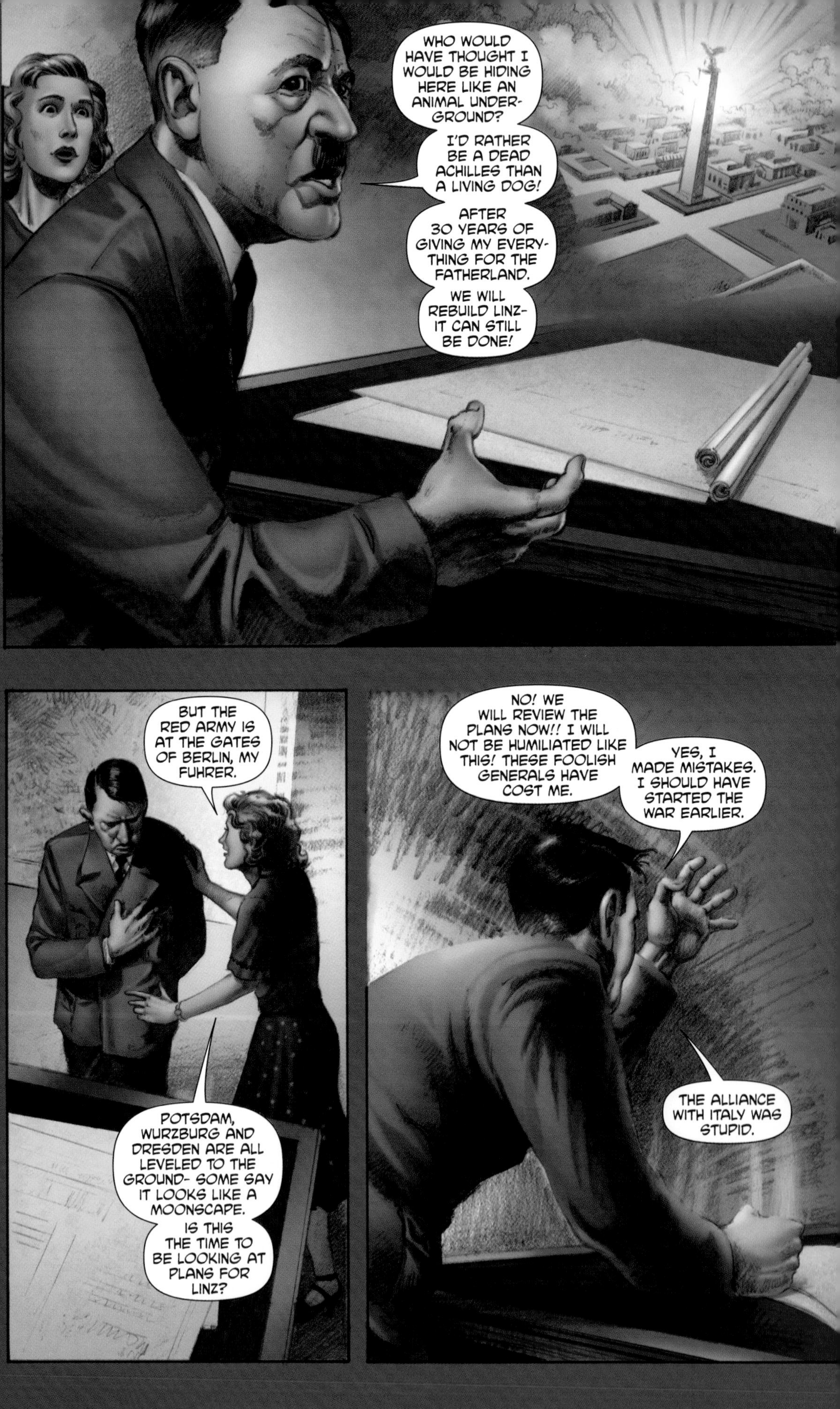
WHO WOULD HAVE THOUGHT I WOULD BE HIDING HERE LIKE AN ANIMAL UNDER-GROUND?
I'D RATHER BE A DEAD ACHILLES THAN A LIVING DOG!
AFTER 30 YEARS OF GIVING MY EVERY-THING FOR THE FATHERLAND.
WE WILL REBUILD LINZ- IT CAN STILL BE DONE!
BUT THE RED ARMY IS AT THE GATES OF BERLIN, MY FUHRER.
POTSDAM, WURZBURG AND DRESDEN ARE ALL LEVELED TO THE GROUND- SOME SAY IT LOOKS LIKE A MOONSCAPE.
IS THIS THE TIME TO BE LOOKING AT PLANS FOR LINZ?
NO! WE WILL REVIEW THE PLANS NOW!! I WILL NOT BE HUMILIATED LIKE THIS! THESE FOOLISH GENERALS HAVE COST ME.
YES, I MADE MISTAKES. I SHOULD HAVE STARTED THE WAR EARLIER.
THE ALLIANCE WITH ITALY WAS STUPID.

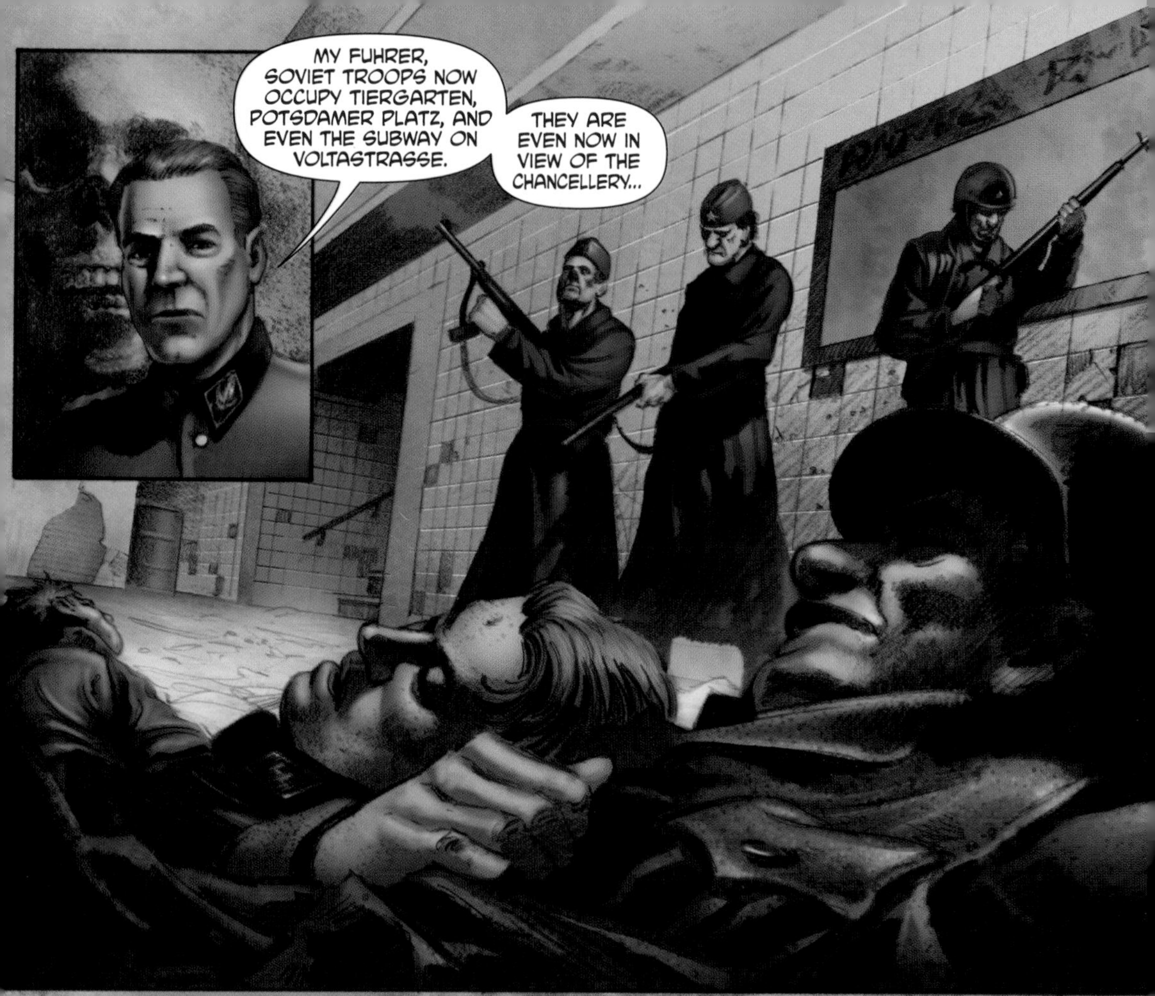
MY FUHRER, SOVIET TROOPS NOW OCCUPY TIERGARTEN, POTSDAMER PLATZ, AND EVEN THE SUBWAY ON VOLTASTRASSE.
THEY ARE EVEN NOW IN VIEW OF THE CHANCELLERY...

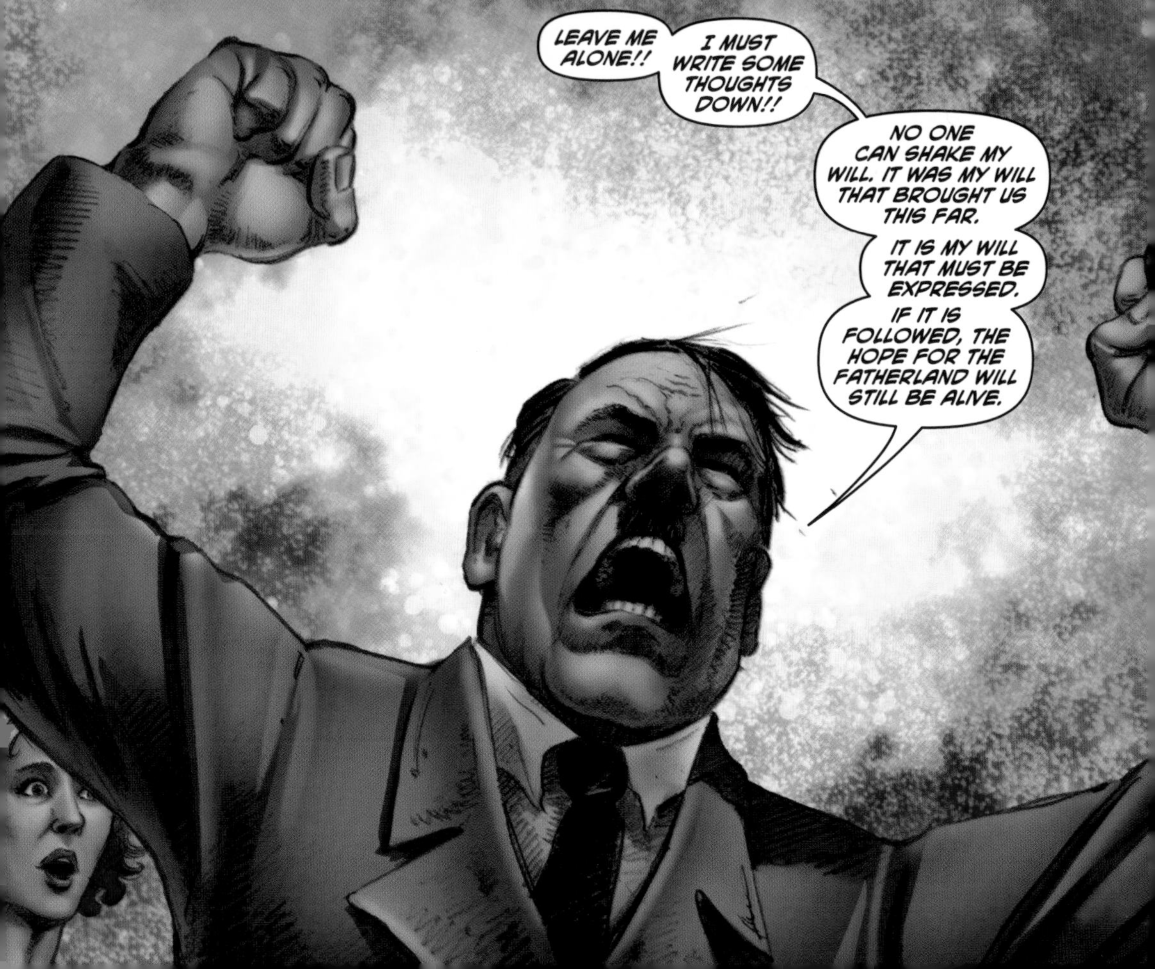
LEAVE ME ALONE!!
I MUST WRITE SOME THOUGHTS DOWN!!
NO ONE CAN SHAKE MY WILL. IT WAS MY WILL THAT BROUGHT US THIS FAR.
IT IS MY WILL THAT MUST BE EXPRESSED.
IF IT IS FOLLOWED, THE HOPE FOR THE FATHERLAND WILL STILL BE ALIVE.

THE LAST WILL AND TESTAMENT OF ADOLF HITLER

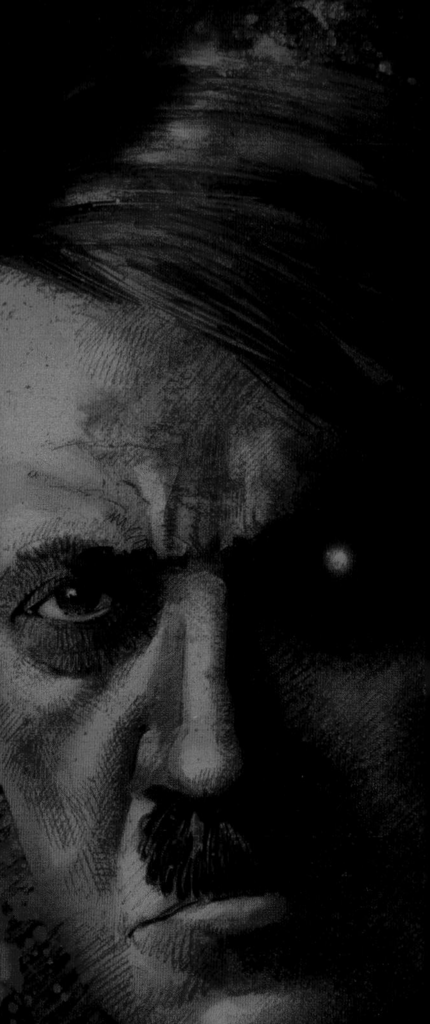

Since 1914 when, as a volunteer, I made my modest contribution in the World War which was forced upon the Reich, over thirty years have passed.

In these three decades, only love for my people and loyalty to my people have guided me in all my thoughts, actions, and life. They gave me strength to make the most difficult decisions, such as no mortal has yet had to face. I have exhausted my time, my working energy, and my health in these three decades.

It is untrue that I or anybody else in Germany wanted war in 1939. It was desired and instigated exclusively by those international statesmen who were either of Jewish origin or working for Jewish interests...Centuries may pass, but out of the ruins of our cities and monuments of art there will arise anew the hatred for the people who alone are ultimately responsible: International Jewry and its helpers!...

But I left no doubt about the fact that if the peoples of Europe were again only regarded as so many packages of stock shares by these international money and finance conspirators, then that race, too, which is the truly guilty party in this murderous struggle would also have to be held to account: the Jews! I further left no doubt that this time we would not permit millions of European children of Aryan descent to die of hunger, nor millions of grown-up men to suffer death, nor hundreds of thousands of women and children to be burned and bombed to death in their cities, without the truly guilty party having to atone for its guilt, even if through more humane means.

After six years of struggle, which in spite of all reverses will go down in history as the most glorious and most courageous manifestation of a people's will to live, I cannot separate myself from the city which is the capital of this Reich. Because our forces are too few to permit any further resistance against the enemy's assaults, and because individual resistance is rendered valueless by blinded and characterless scoundrels, I desire to share the fate that millions of others have taken upon themselves, in that I shall remain in this city. Furthermore, I do not want to fall into the hands of enemies who for the delectation of the hate-riddled masses require a new spectacle promoted by the Jews.

I have therefore resolved to remain in Berlin and there to choose death of my own will at the very moment when, as I believe, the seat of the Führer and Chancellor can no longer be defended.

I die with a joyful heart in the awareness of the immeasureable deeds and achievements of our soldiers at the front, of our women at home, the achievements of our peasants and workers, and the contribution, unique in history, of our youth, which bears my name...

Many very brave men and women have resolved to link their lives to mine to the very end. I have requested them, and finally ordered them, not to do so, but instead to take part in the continuing struggle of the nation. I ask the commanders of the army, navy, and air force to strengthen by all possible means the spirit of resistance of our soldiers in the spirit of National Socialism, emphasizing especially that I too, as founder and creator of this movement, have preferred death to cowardly flight or even capitulation.

May it be one day part of the code of honor, as it is already in the navy, that surrender of an area or of a town is impossible, and above all in this respect the leaders should give a shining example of faithful devotion to duty unto death.

Before my death I expel the former Reichsmarschall Hermann Göring and deprive him of all the rights he may enjoy by virtue of the decree of June 29, 1941, and also by virtue of my statement in the Reichstag on September 1, 1939. I appoint in his place Grossadmiral Doenitz as President of the Reich and Supreme Commander of the Armed Forces...

Göring and Himmler, by their secret negotiations with the enemy, without my knowledge or approval, and by their illegal attempts to seize power in the state, quite apart from their treachery to my person, have brought irreparable shame to the country and the whole people...

Several men such as Martin Bormann, Dr. Goebbels, etc., together with their wives, have joined me by their own free will and do not wish to leave the capital of the Reich under any circumstances, but on the contrary are willing to perish with me here. Yet I must ask them to obey my request, and in this instance place the interests of the nation above their own feelings.

Through their work and loyalty they will remain just as close to me as companions after my death, just as I hope that my spirit will remain amongst them and will always accompany them...I demand of all Germans, all National Socialists, men and women and all soldiers of the Armed Forces, that they remain faithful and obedient to the new government and to their President unto death.

Above all, I charge the leadership of the nation and their followers with the strict observance of the racial laws and with merciless resistance against the universal poisoners of all peoples, international Jewry.

As witnesses:

Given at Berlin, 29 April 1945, 4:00 A.M.

Adolf Hitler

Dr. Joseph Goebbels
Wilhelm Burgdorf
Martin Bormann
Hans Krebs

"THAT'S JUST PART OF IT, ISN'T IT?"

"YES, THEN SOMETHING VERY INTERESTING HAPPENED."

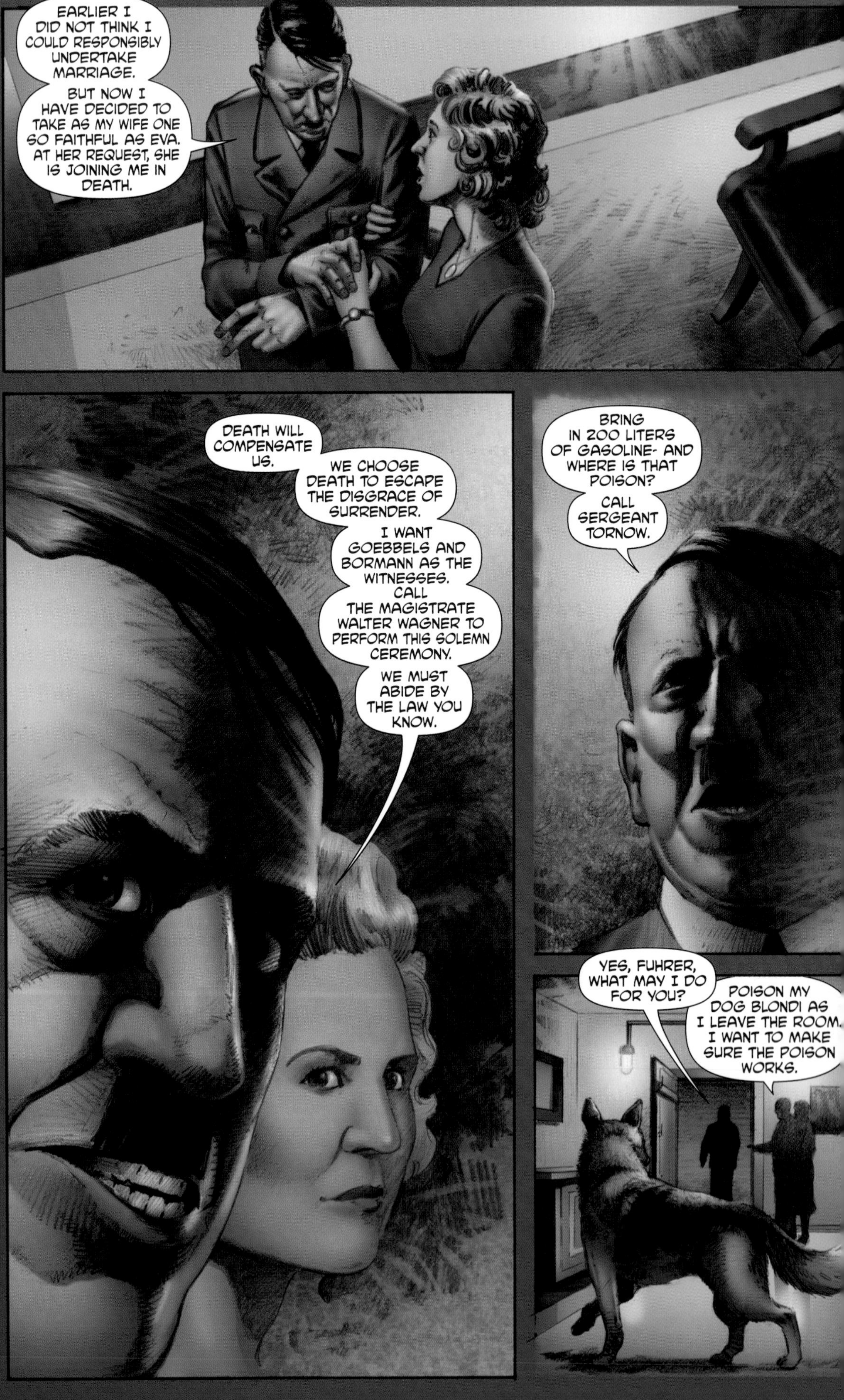
EARLIER I DID NOT THINK I COULD RESPONSIBLY UNDERTAKE MARRIAGE.
BUT NOW I HAVE DECIDED TO TAKE AS MY WIFE ONE SO FAITHFUL AS EVA. AT HER REQUEST, SHE IS JOINING ME IN DEATH.
DEATH WILL COMPENSATE US.
WE CHOOSE DEATH TO ESCAPE THE DISGRACE OF SURRENDER.
I WANT GOEBBELS AND BORMANN AS THE WITNESSES.
CALL THE MAGISTRATE WALTER WAGNER TO PERFORM THIS SOLEMN CEREMONY.
WE MUST ABIDE BY THE LAW YOU KNOW.
BRING IN 200 LITERS OF GASOLINE- AND WHERE IS THAT POISON?
CALL SERGEANT TORNOW.
YES, FUHRER, WHAT MAY I DO FOR YOU?
POISON MY DOG BLONDI AS I LEAVE THE ROOM. I WANT TO MAKE SURE THE POISON WORKS.

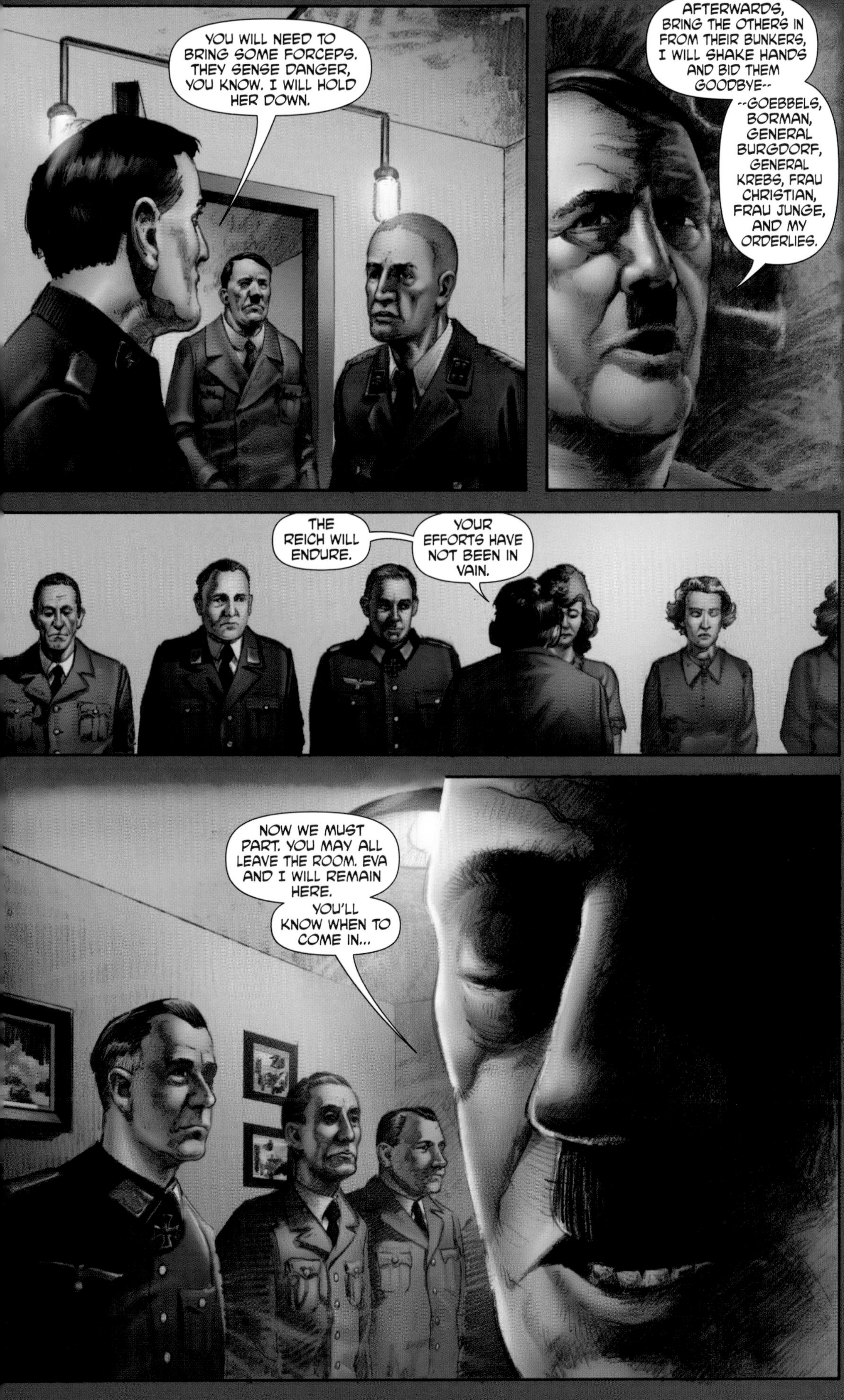
YOU WILL NEED TO BRING SOME FORCEPS. THEY SENSE DANGER, YOU KNOW. I WILL HOLD HER DOWN.
AFTERWARDS, BRING THE OTHERS IN FROM THEIR BUNKERS, I WILL SHAKE HANDS AND BID THEM GOODBYE--
--GOEBBELS, BORMAN, GENERAL BURGDORF, GENERAL KREBS, FRAU CHRISTIAN, FRAU JUNGE, AND MY ORDERLIES.
THE REICH WILL ENDURE.
YOUR EFFORTS HAVE NOT BEEN IN VAIN.
NOW WE MUST PART. YOU MAY ALL LEAVE THE ROOM. EVA AND I WILL REMAIN HERE.
YOU'LL KNOW WHEN TO COME IN...

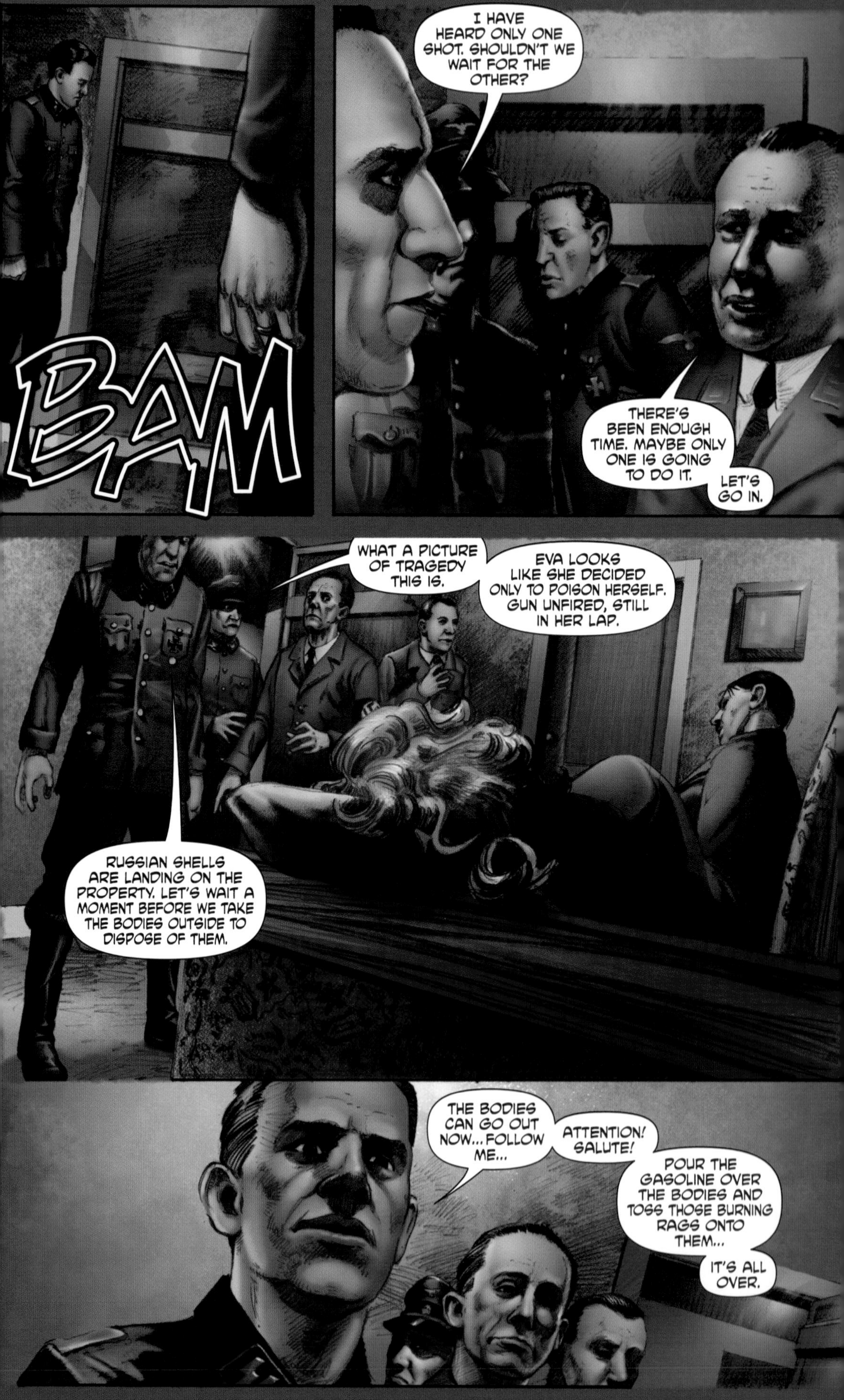
BAM
I HAVE HEARD ONLY ONE SHOT. SHOULDN'T WE WAIT FOR THE OTHER?
THERE'S BEEN ENOUGH TIME. MAYBE ONLY ONE IS GOING TO DO IT.
LET'S GO IN.
WHAT A PICTURE OF TRAGEDY THIS IS.
EVA LOOKS LIKE SHE DECIDED ONLY TO POISON HERSELF. GUN UNFIRED, STILL IN HER LAP.
RUSSIAN SHELLS ARE LANDING ON THE PROPERTY. LET'S WAIT A MOMENT BEFORE WE TAKE THE BODIES OUTSIDE TO DISPOSE OF THEM.
THE BODIES CAN GO OUT NOW... FOLLOW ME...
ATTENTION! SALUTE!
POUR THE GASOLINE OVER THE BODIES AND TOSS THOSE BURNING RAGS ONTO THEM...
IT'S ALL OVER.

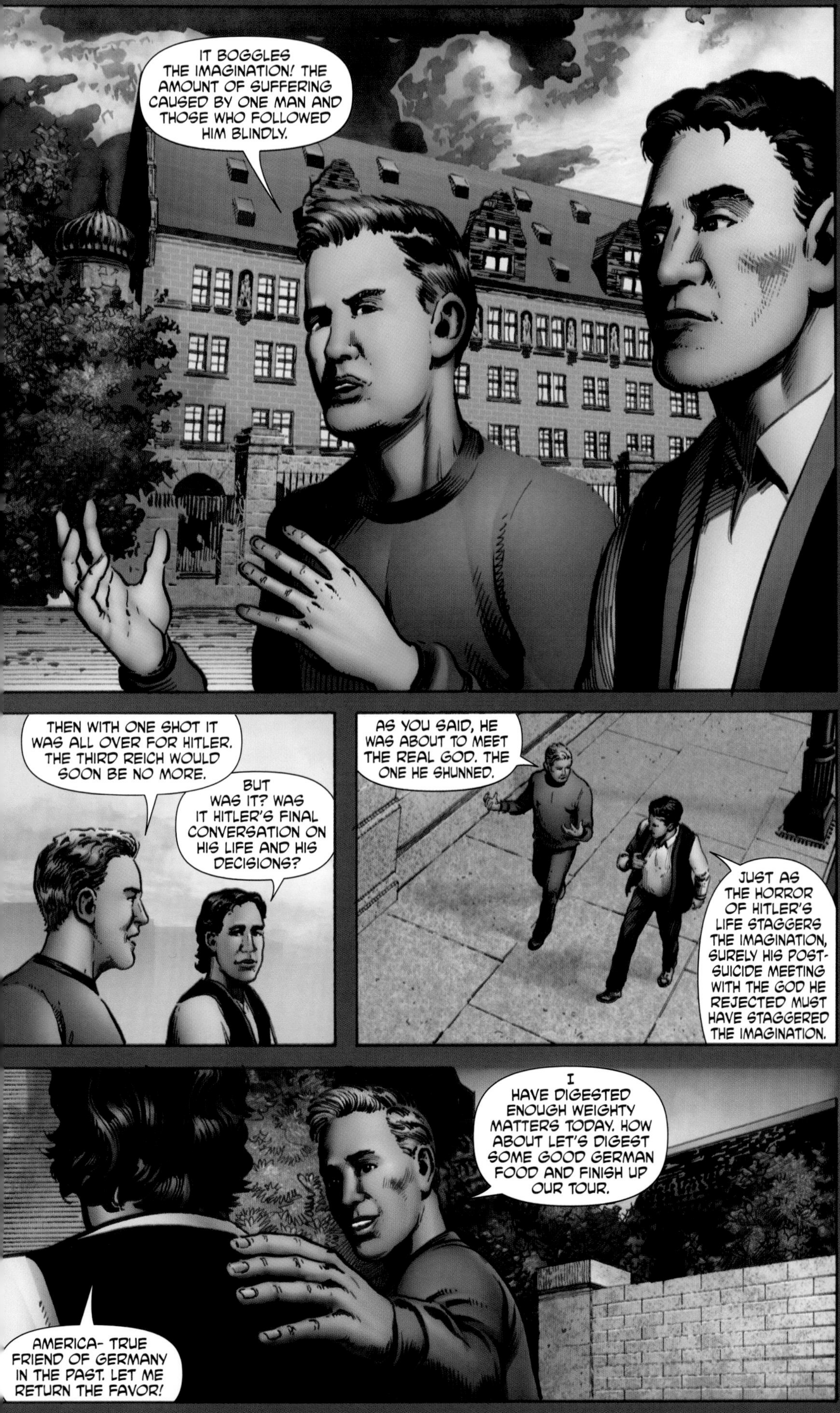
IT BOGGLES THE IMAGINATION! THE AMOUNT OF SUFFERING CAUSED BY ONE MAN AND THOSE WHO FOLLOWED HIM BLINDLY.
THEN WITH ONE SHOT IT WAS ALL OVER FOR HITLER. THE THIRD REICH WOULD SOON BE NO MORE.
BUT WAS IT? WAS IT HITLER'S FINAL CONVERSATION ON HIS LIFE AND HIS DECISIONS?
AS YOU SAID, HE WAS ABOUT TO MEET THE REAL GOD. THE ONE HE SHUNNED.
JUST AS THE HORROR OF HITLER'S LIFE STAGGERS THE IMAGINATION, SURELY HIS POST-SUICIDE MEETING WITH THE GOD HE REJECTED MUST HAVE STAGGERED THE IMAGINATION.
I HAVE DIGESTED ENOUGH WEIGHTY MATTERS TODAY. HOW ABOUT LET'S DIGEST SOME GOOD GERMAN FOOD AND FINISH UP OUR TOUR.
AMERICA- TRUE FRIEND OF GERMANY IN THE PAST. LET ME RETURN THE FAVOR!

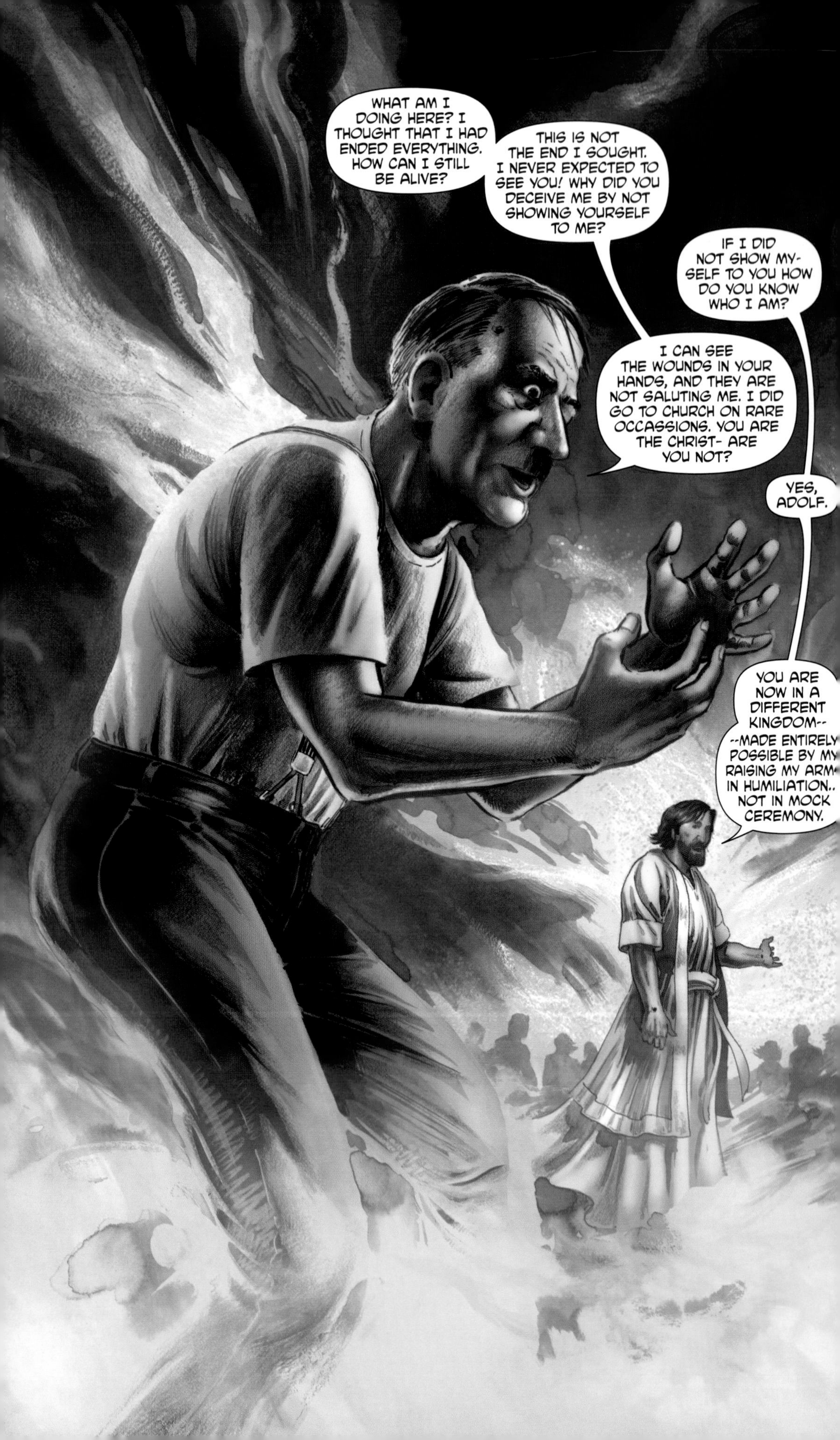
WHAT AM I DOING HERE? I THOUGHT THAT I HAD ENDED EVERYTHING. HOW CAN I STILL BE ALIVE?
THIS IS NOT THE END I SOUGHT. I NEVER EXPECTED TO SEE YOU! WHY DID YOU DECEIVE ME BY NOT SHOWING YOURSELF TO ME?
IF I DID NOT SHOW MY-SELF TO YOU HOW DO YOU KNOW WHO I AM?
I CAN SEE THE WOUNDS IN YOUR HANDS, AND THEY ARE NOT SALUTING ME. I DID GO TO CHURCH ON RARE OCCASSIONS. YOU ARE THE CHRIST- ARE YOU NOT?
YES, ADOLF.
YOU ARE NOW IN A DIFFERENT KINGDOM--
--MADE ENTIRELY POSSIBLE BY MY RAISING MY ARM IN HUMILIATION.. NOT IN MOCK CEREMONY.

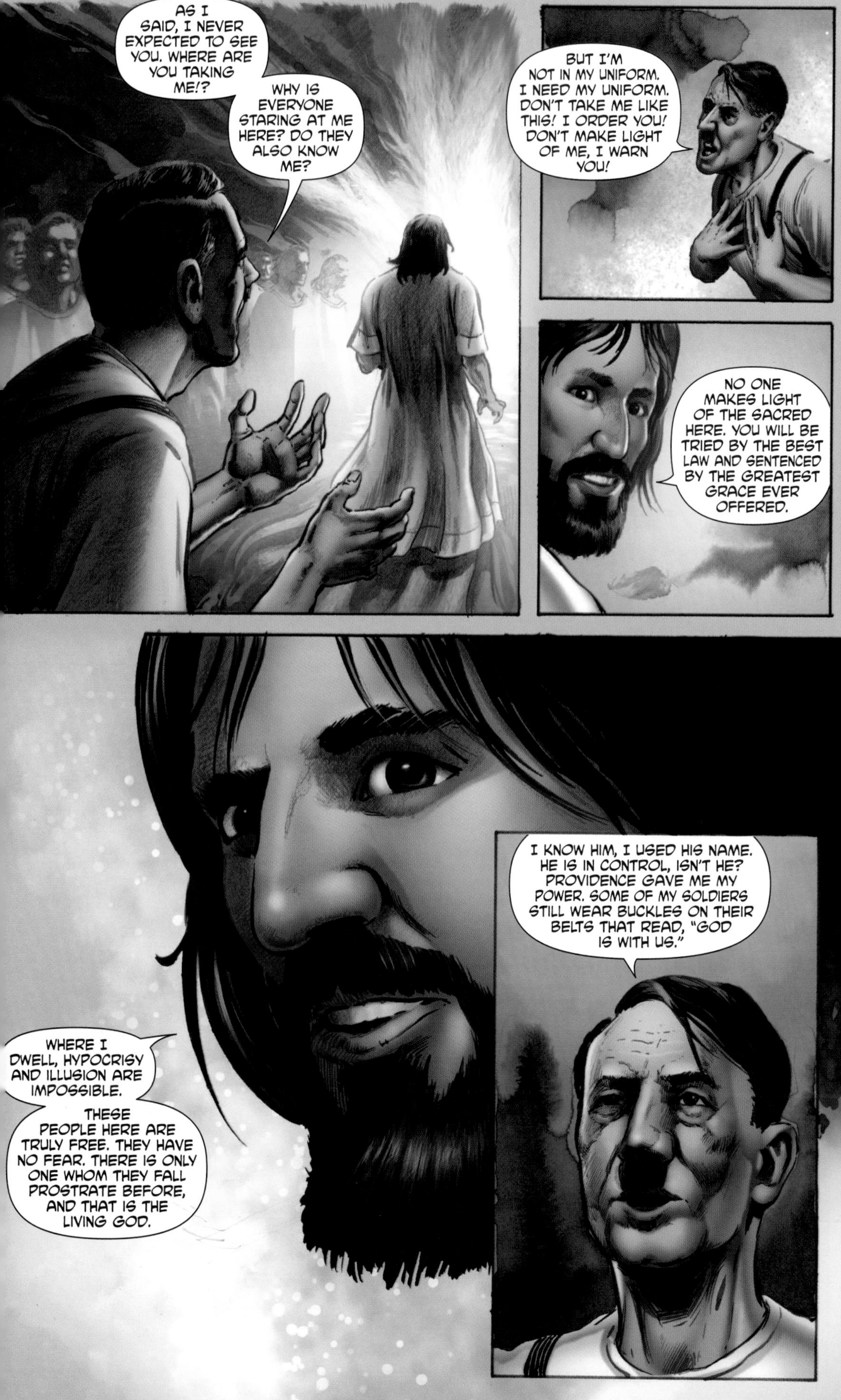
AS I SAID, I NEVER EXPECTED TO SEE YOU. WHERE ARE YOU TAKING ME!?
WHY IS EVERYONE STARING AT ME HERE? DO THEY ALSO KNOW ME?
BUT I'M NOT IN MY UNIFORM. I NEED MY UNIFORM. DON'T TAKE ME LIKE THIS! I ORDER YOU! DON'T MAKE LIGHT OF ME, I WARN YOU!
NO ONE MAKES LIGHT OF THE SACRED HERE. YOU WILL BE TRIED BY THE BEST LAW AND SENTENCED BY THE GREATEST GRACE EVER OFFERED.
I KNOW HIM, I USED HIS NAME. HE IS IN CONTROL, ISN'T HE? PROVIDENCE GAVE ME MY POWER. SOME OF MY SOLDIERS STILL WEAR BUCKLES ON THEIR BELTS THAT READ, "GOD IS WITH US."
WHERE I DWELL, HYPOCRISY AND ILLUSION ARE IMPOSSIBLE.
THESE PEOPLE HERE ARE TRULY FREE. THEY HAVE NO FEAR. THERE IS ONLY ONE WHOM THEY FALL PROSTRATE BEFORE, AND THAT IS THE LIVING GOD.

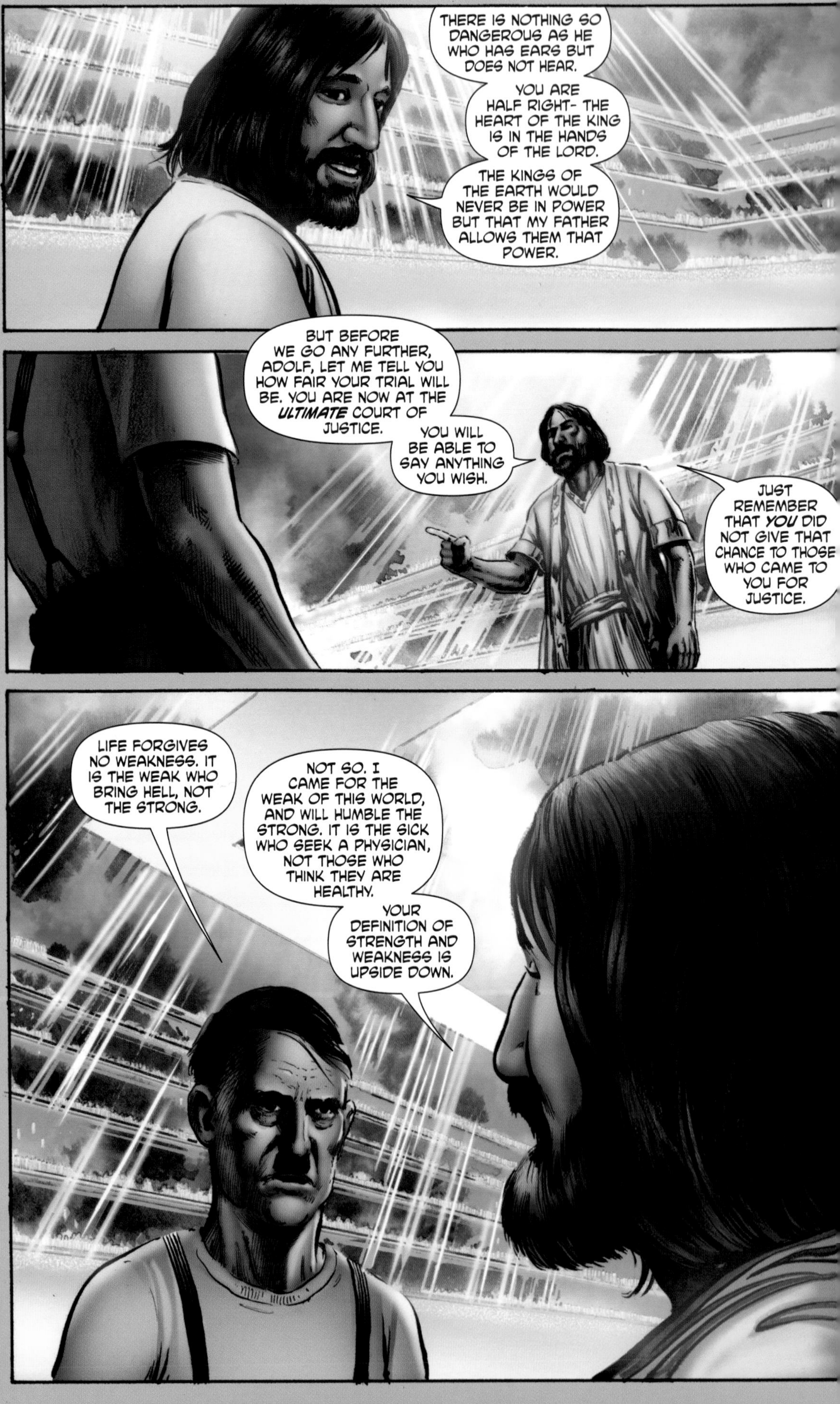
THERE IS NOTHING SO DANGEROUS AS HE WHO HAS EARS BUT DOES NOT HEAR.
YOU ARE HALF RIGHT- THE HEART OF THE KING IS IN THE HANDS OF THE LORD.
THE KINGS OF THE EARTH WOULD NEVER BE IN POWER BUT THAT MY FATHER ALLOWS THEM THAT POWER.
BUT BEFORE WE GO ANY FURTHER, ADOLF, LET ME TELL YOU HOW FAIR YOUR TRIAL WILL BE. YOU ARE NOW AT THE ***ULTIMATE*** COURT OF JUSTICE.
YOU WILL BE ABLE TO SAY ANYTHING YOU WISH.
JUST REMEMBER THAT ***YOU*** DID NOT GIVE THAT CHANCE TO THOSE WHO CAME TO YOU FOR JUSTICE.
LIFE FORGIVES NO WEAKNESS. IT IS THE WEAK WHO BRING HELL, NOT THE STRONG.
NOT SO. I CAME FOR THE WEAK OF THIS WORLD, AND WILL HUMBLE THE STRONG. IT IS THE SICK WHO SEEK A PHYSICIAN, NOT THOSE WHO THINK THEY ARE HEALTHY.
YOUR DEFINITION OF STRENGTH AND WEAKNESS IS UPSIDE DOWN.

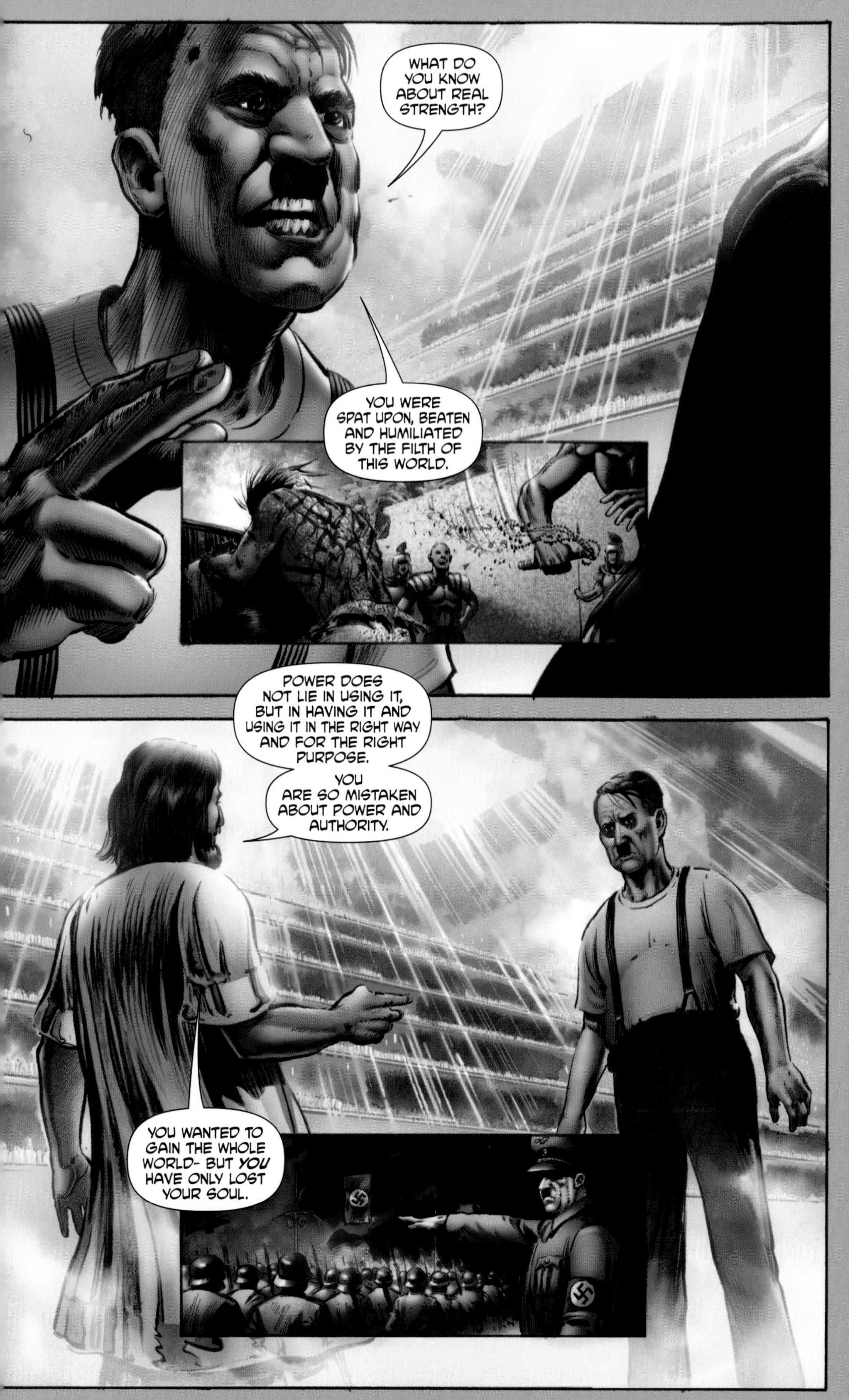
WHAT DO YOU KNOW ABOUT REAL STRENGTH?
YOU WERE SPAT UPON, BEATEN AND HUMILIATED BY THE FILTH OF THIS WORLD.
POWER DOES NOT LIE IN USING IT, BUT IN HAVING IT AND USING IT IN THE RIGHT WAY AND FOR THE RIGHT PURPOSE.
YOU ARE SO MISTAKEN ABOUT POWER AND AUTHORITY.
YOU WANTED TO GAIN THE WHOLE WORLD- BUT *YOU* HAVE ONLY LOST YOUR SOUL.

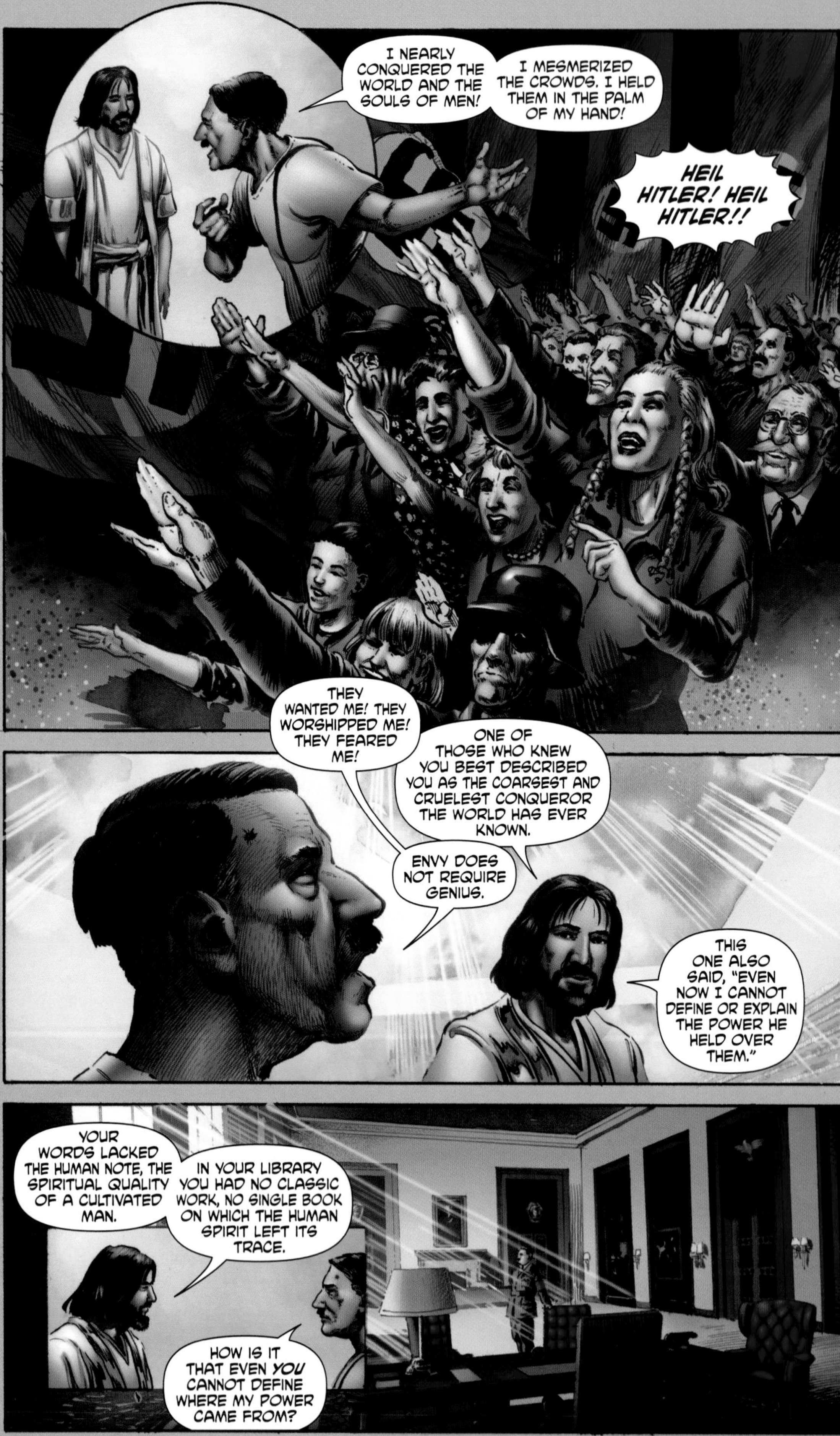
I NEARLY CONQUERED THE WORLD AND THE SOULS OF MEN!
I MESMERIZED THE CROWDS. I HELD THEM IN THE PALM OF MY HAND!
HEIL HITLER! HEIL HITLER!!
THEY WANTED ME! THEY WORSHIPPED ME! THEY FEARED ME!
ONE OF THOSE WHO KNEW YOU BEST DESCRIBED YOU AS THE COARSEST AND CRUELEST CONQUEROR THE WORLD HAS EVER KNOWN.
ENVY DOES NOT REQUIRE GENIUS.
THIS ONE ALSO SAID, "EVEN NOW I CANNOT DEFINE OR EXPLAIN THE POWER HE HELD OVER THEM."
YOUR WORDS LACKED THE HUMAN NOTE, THE SPIRITUAL QUALITY OF A CULTIVATED MAN.
IN YOUR LIBRARY YOU HAD NO CLASSIC WORK, NO SINGLE BOOK ON WHICH THE HUMAN SPIRIT LEFT ITS TRACE.
HOW IS IT THAT EVEN *YOU* CANNOT DEFINE WHERE MY POWER CAME FROM?

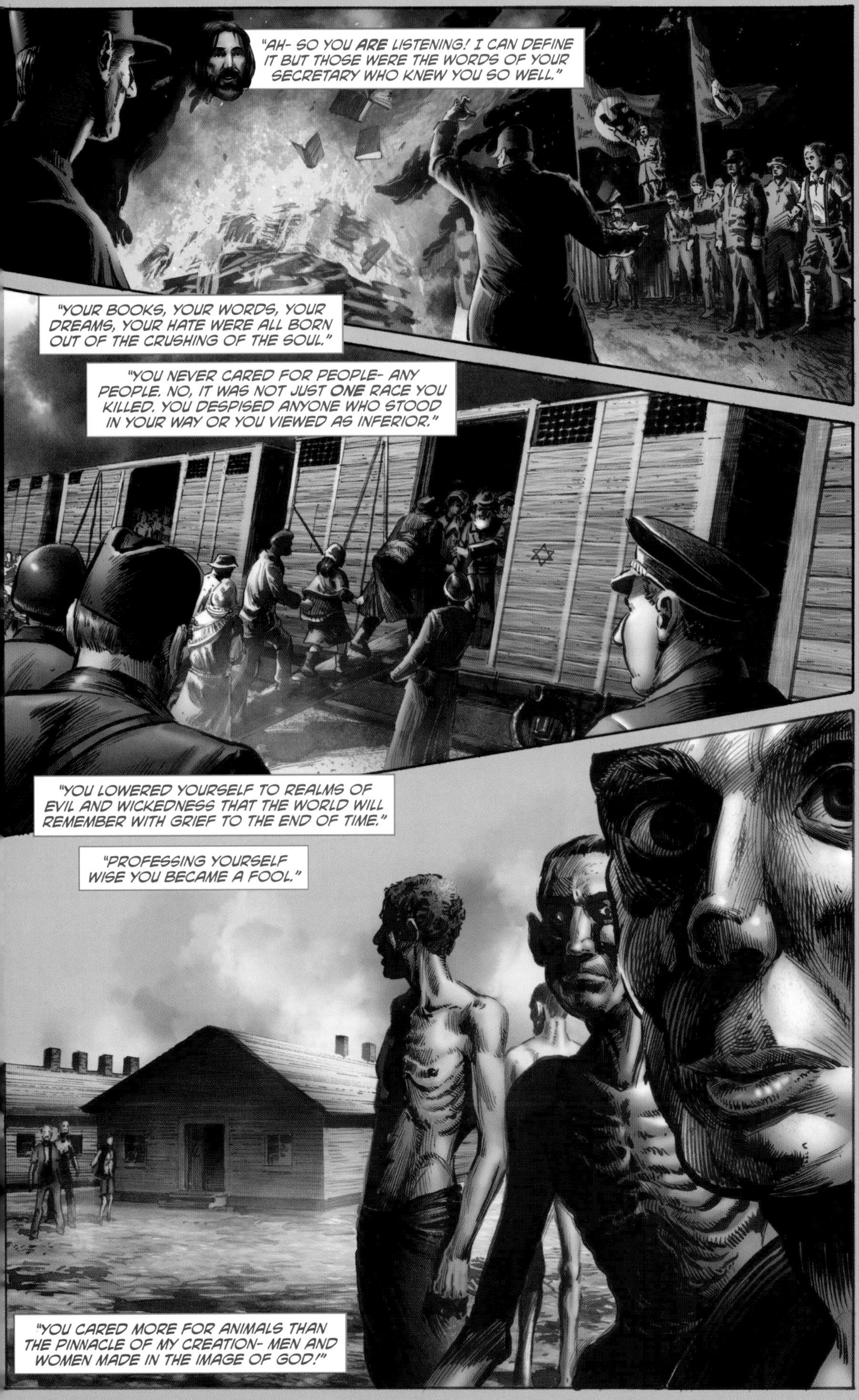
"AH- SO YOU ARE LISTENING! I CAN DEFINE IT BUT THOSE WERE THE WORDS OF YOUR SECRETARY WHO KNEW YOU SO WELL."
"YOUR BOOKS, YOUR WORDS, YOUR DREAMS, YOUR HATE WERE ALL BORN OUT OF THE CRUSHING OF THE SOUL."
"YOU NEVER CARED FOR PEOPLE- ANY PEOPLE. NO, IT WAS NOT JUST ONE RACE YOU KILLED. YOU DESPISED ANYONE WHO STOOD IN YOUR WAY OR YOU VIEWED AS INFERIOR."
"YOU LOWERED YOURSELF TO REALMS OF EVIL AND WICKEDNESS THAT THE WORLD WILL REMEMBER WITH GRIEF TO THE END OF TIME."
"PROFESSING YOURSELF WISE YOU BECAME A FOOL."
"YOU CARED MORE FOR ANIMALS THAN THE PINNACLE OF MY CREATION- MEN AND WOMEN MADE IN THE IMAGE OF GOD!"

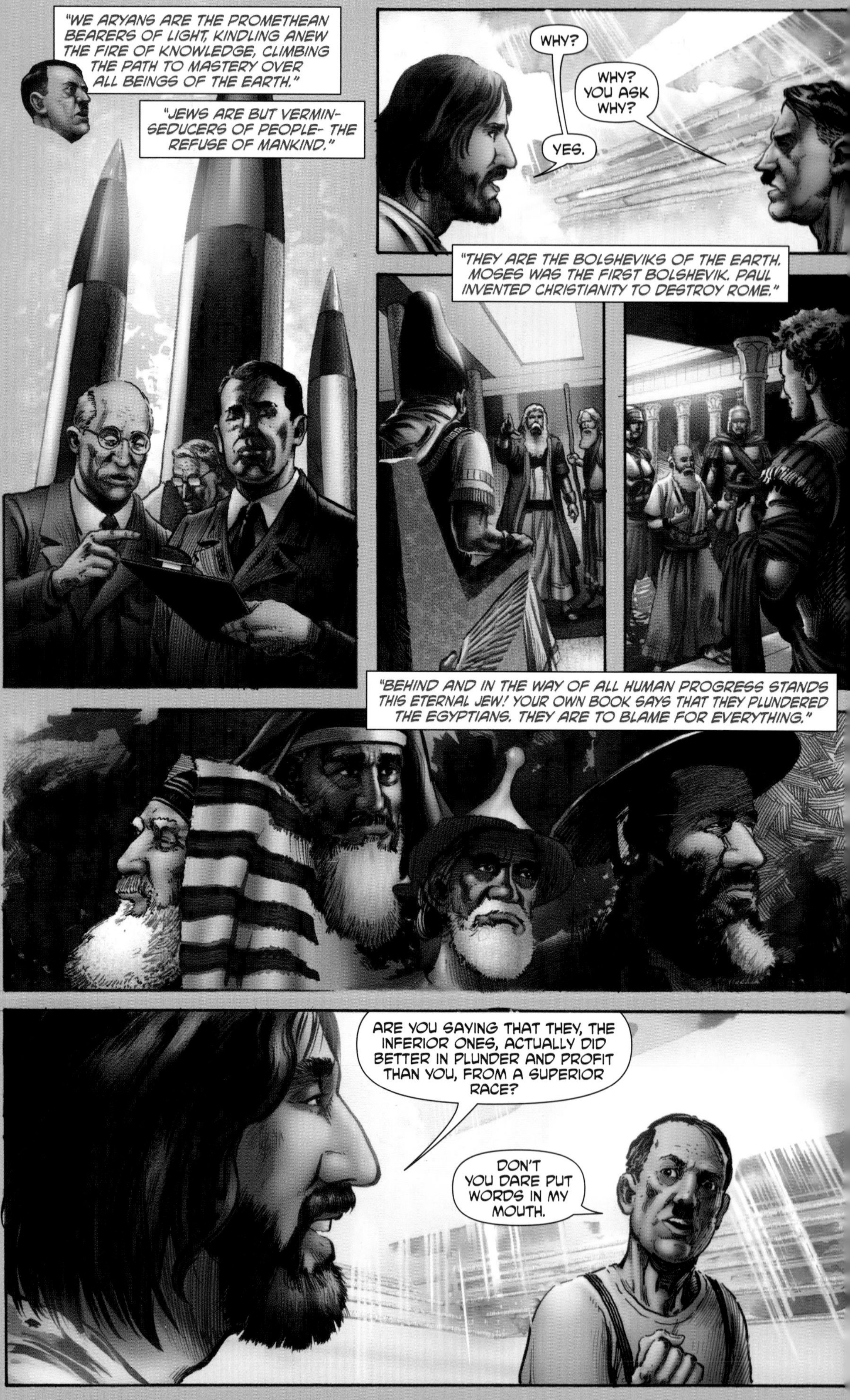
"WE ARYANS ARE THE PROMETHEAN BEARERS OF LIGHT, KINDLING ANEW THE FIRE OF KNOWLEDGE, CLIMBING THE PATH TO MASTERY OVER ALL BEINGS OF THE EARTH."
"JEWS ARE BUT VERMIN-SEDUCERS OF PEOPLE- THE REFUSE OF MANKIND."
WHY?
WHY? YOU ASK WHY?
YES.
"THEY ARE THE BOLSHEVIKS OF THE EARTH. MOSES WAS THE FIRST BOLSHEVIK. PAUL INVENTED CHRISTIANITY TO DESTROY ROME."
"BEHIND AND IN THE WAY OF ALL HUMAN PROGRESS STANDS THIS ETERNAL JEW! YOUR OWN BOOK SAYS THAT THEY PLUNDERED THE EGYPTIANS. THEY ARE TO BLAME FOR EVERYTHING."
ARE YOU SAYING THAT THEY, THE INFERIOR ONES, ACTUALLY DID BETTER IN PLUNDER AND PROFIT THAN YOU, FROM A SUPERIOR RACE?
DON'T YOU DARE PUT WORDS IN MY MOUTH.

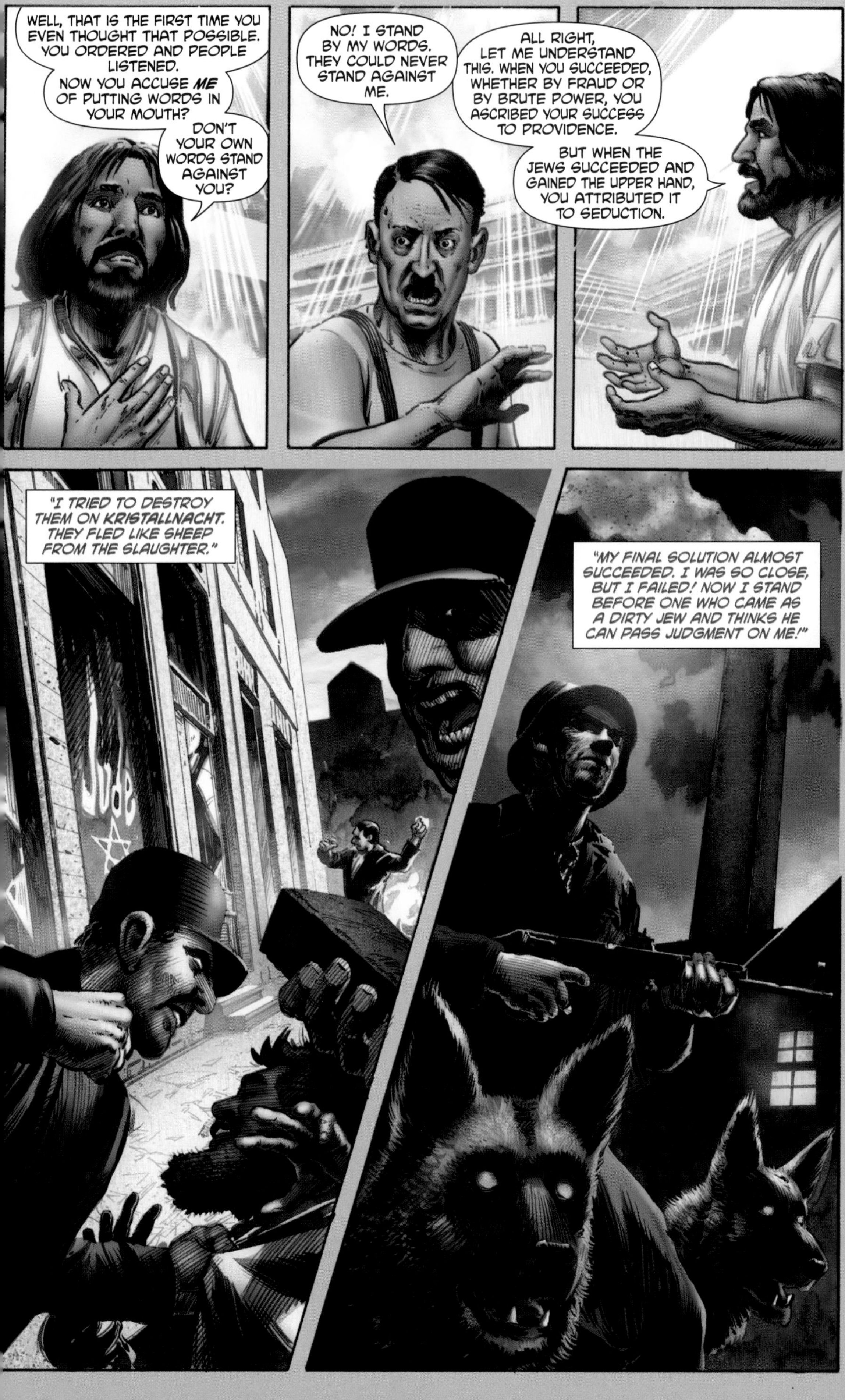
WELL, THAT IS THE FIRST TIME YOU EVEN THOUGHT THAT POSSIBLE. YOU ORDERED AND PEOPLE LISTENED.
NOW YOU ACCUSE *ME* OF PUTTING WORDS IN YOUR MOUTH?
DON'T YOUR OWN WORDS STAND AGAINST YOU?
NO! I STAND BY MY WORDS. THEY COULD NEVER STAND AGAINST ME.
ALL RIGHT, LET ME UNDERSTAND THIS. WHEN YOU SUCCEEDED, WHETHER BY FRAUD OR BY BRUTE POWER, YOU ASCRIBED YOUR SUCCESS TO PROVIDENCE.
BUT WHEN THE JEWS SUCCEEDED AND GAINED THE UPPER HAND, YOU ATTRIBUTED IT TO SEDUCTION.
"I TRIED TO DESTROY THEM ON *KRISTALLNACHT*. THEY FLED LIKE SHEEP FROM THE SLAUGHTER."
"MY FINAL SOLUTION ALMOST SUCCEEDED. I WAS SO CLOSE, BUT I FAILED! NOW I STAND BEFORE ONE WHO CAME AS A DIRTY JEW AND THINKS HE CAN PASS JUDGMENT ON ME!"

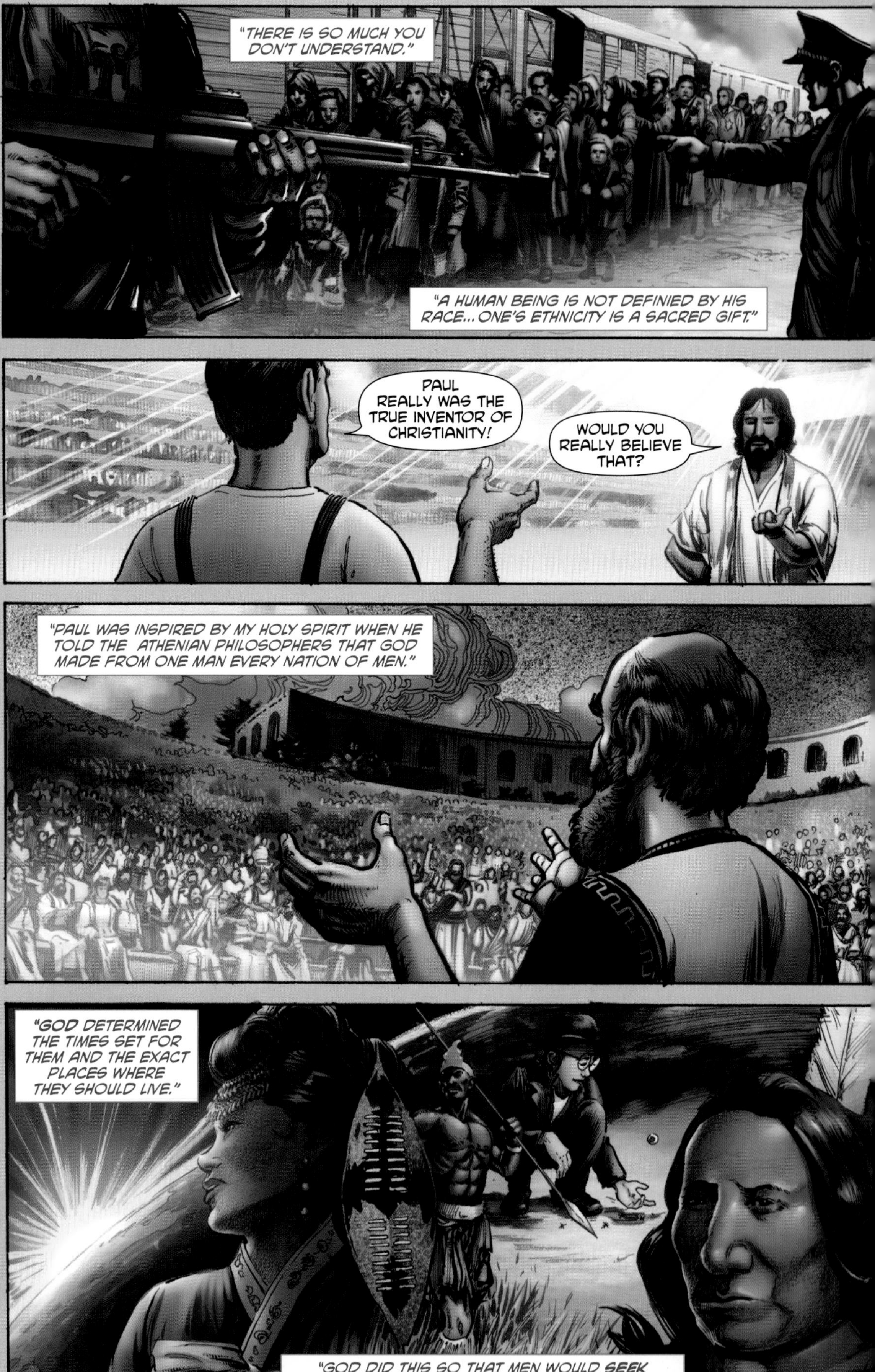
"THERE IS SO MUCH YOU DON'T UNDERSTAND."
"A HUMAN BEING IS NOT DEFINIED BY HIS RACE... ONE'S ETHNICITY IS A SACRED GIFT."
PAUL REALLY WAS THE TRUE INVENTOR OF CHRISTIANITY!
WOULD YOU REALLY BELIEVE THAT?
"PAUL WAS INSPIRED BY MY HOLY SPIRIT WHEN HE TOLD THE ATHENIAN PHILOSOPHERS THAT GOD MADE FROM ONE MAN EVERY NATION OF MEN."
"GOD DETERMINED THE TIMES SET FOR THEM AND THE EXACT PLACES WHERE THEY SHOULD LIVE."
"GOD DID THIS SO THAT MEN WOULD SEEK HIM AND PERHAPS REACH OUT FOR HIM AND FIND HIM... THOUGH HE IS NOT FAR FROM EACH ONE."

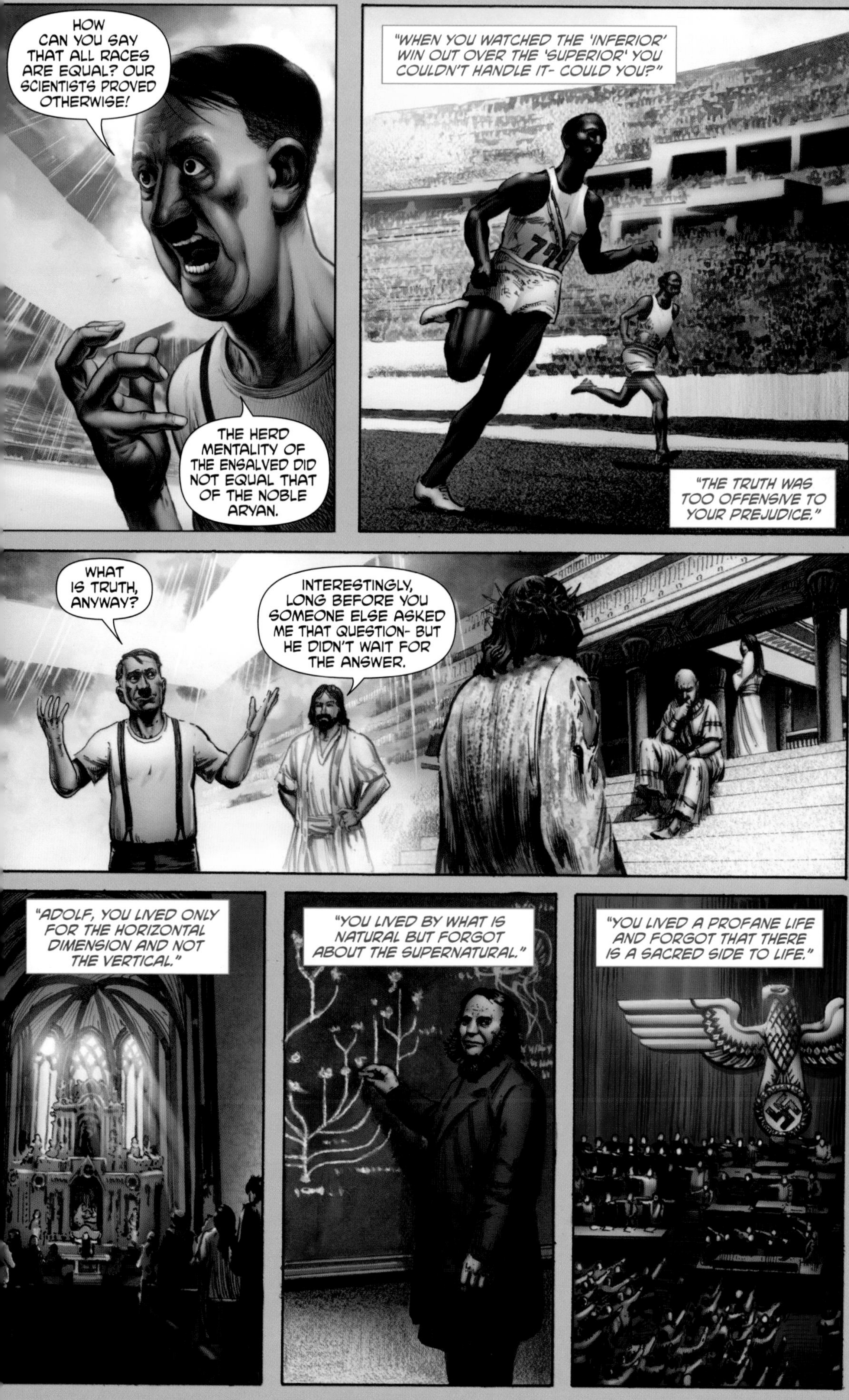
HOW CAN YOU SAY THAT ALL RACES ARE EQUAL? OUR SCIENTISTS PROVED OTHERWISE!
THE HERD MENTALITY OF THE ENSALVED DID NOT EQUAL THAT OF THE NOBLE ARYAN.
"WHEN YOU WATCHED THE 'INFERIOR' WIN OUT OVER THE 'SUPERIOR' YOU COULDN'T HANDLE IT- COULD YOU?"
"THE TRUTH WAS TOO OFFENSIVE TO YOUR PREJUDICE."
WHAT IS TRUTH, ANYWAY?
INTERESTINGLY, LONG BEFORE YOU SOMEONE ELSE ASKED ME THAT QUESTION- BUT HE DIDN'T WAIT FOR THE ANSWER.
"ADOLF, YOU LIVED ONLY FOR THE HORIZONTAL DIMENSION AND NOT THE VERTICAL."
"YOU LIVED BY WHAT IS NATURAL BUT FORGOT ABOUT THE SUPERNATURAL."
"YOU LIVED A PROFANE LIFE AND FORGOT THAT THERE IS A SACRED SIDE TO LIFE."

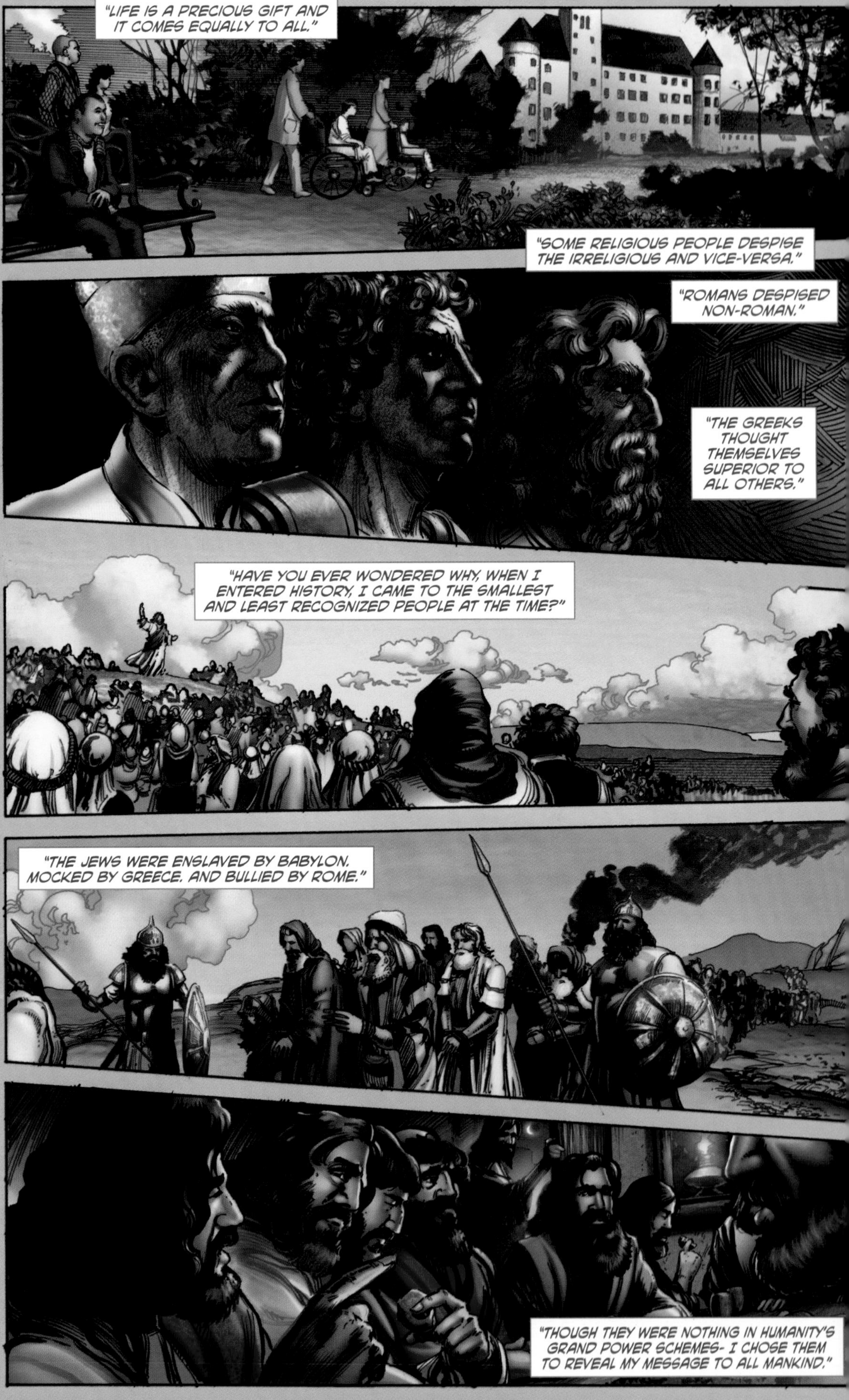
"LIFE IS A PRECIOUS GIFT AND IT COMES EQUALLY TO ALL."
"SOME RELIGIOUS PEOPLE DESPISE THE IRRELIGIOUS AND VICE-VERSA."
"ROMANS DESPISED NON-ROMAN."
"THE GREEKS THOUGHT THEMSELVES SUPERIOR TO ALL OTHERS."
"HAVE YOU EVER WONDERED WHY, WHEN I ENTERED HISTORY, I CAME TO THE SMALLEST AND LEAST RECOGNIZED PEOPLE AT THE TIME?"
"THE JEWS WERE ENSLAVED BY BABYLON. MOCKED BY GREECE. AND BULLIED BY ROME."
"THOUGH THEY WERE NOTHING IN HUMANITY'S GRAND POWER SCHEMES- I CHOSE THEM TO REVEAL MY MESSAGE TO ALL MANKIND."

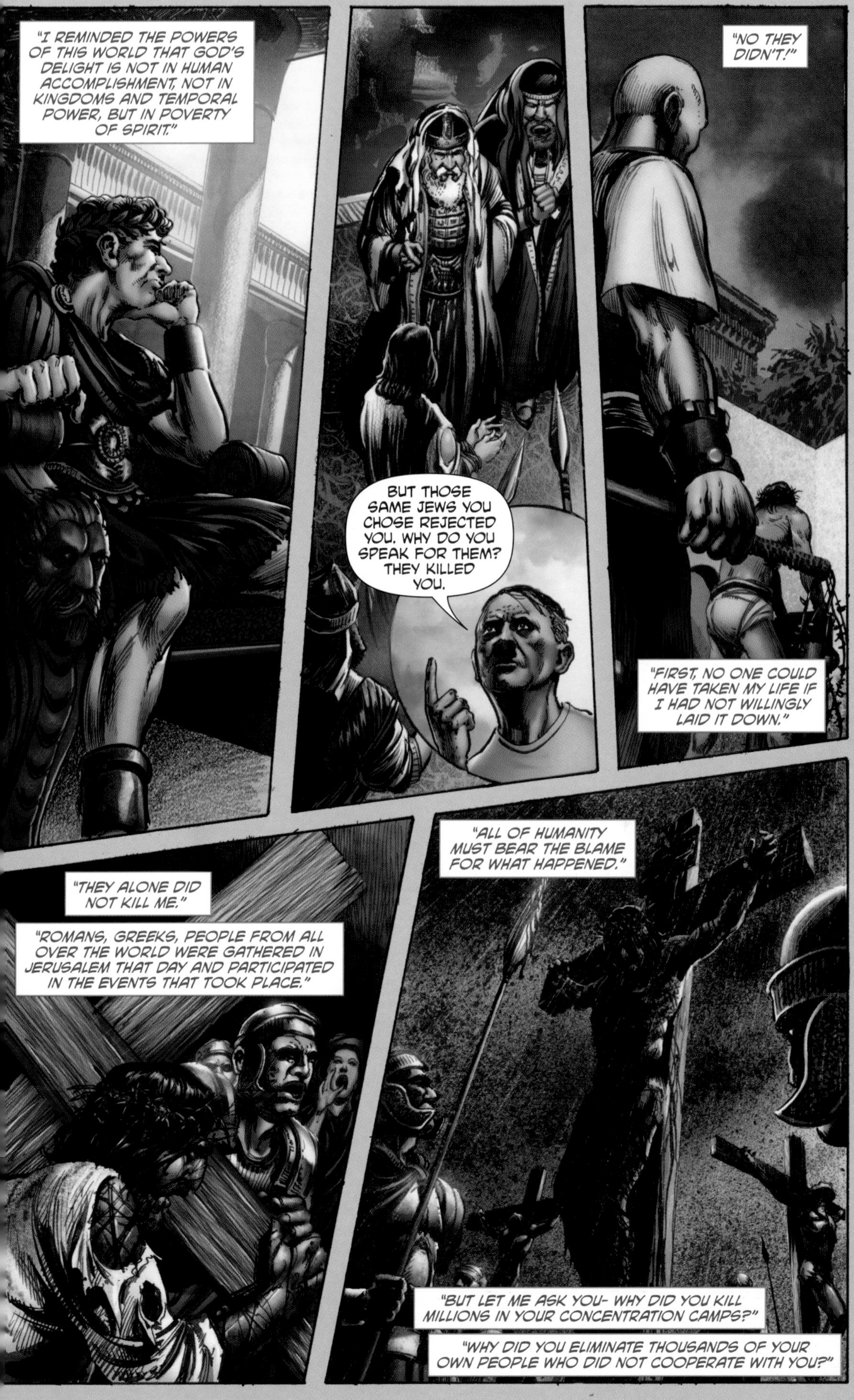
"I REMINDED THE POWERS OF THIS WORLD THAT GOD'S DELIGHT IS NOT IN HUMAN ACCOMPLISHMENT, NOT IN KINGDOMS AND TEMPORAL POWER, BUT IN POVERTY OF SPIRIT."
BUT THOSE SAME JEWS YOU CHOSE REJECTED YOU. WHY DO YOU SPEAK FOR THEM? THEY KILLED YOU.
"NO THEY DIDN'T!"
"FIRST, NO ONE COULD HAVE TAKEN MY LIFE IF I HAD NOT WILLINGLY LAID IT DOWN."
"THEY ALONE DID NOT KILL ME."
"ROMANS, GREEKS, PEOPLE FROM ALL OVER THE WORLD WERE GATHERED IN JERUSALEM THAT DAY AND PARTICIPATED IN THE EVENTS THAT TOOK PLACE."
"ALL OF HUMANITY MUST BEAR THE BLAME FOR WHAT HAPPENED."
"BUT LET ME ASK YOU- WHY DID YOU KILL MILLIONS IN YOUR CONCENTRATION CAMPS?"
"WHY DID YOU ELIMINATE THOUSANDS OF YOUR OWN PEOPLE WHO DID NOT COOPERATE WITH YOU?"

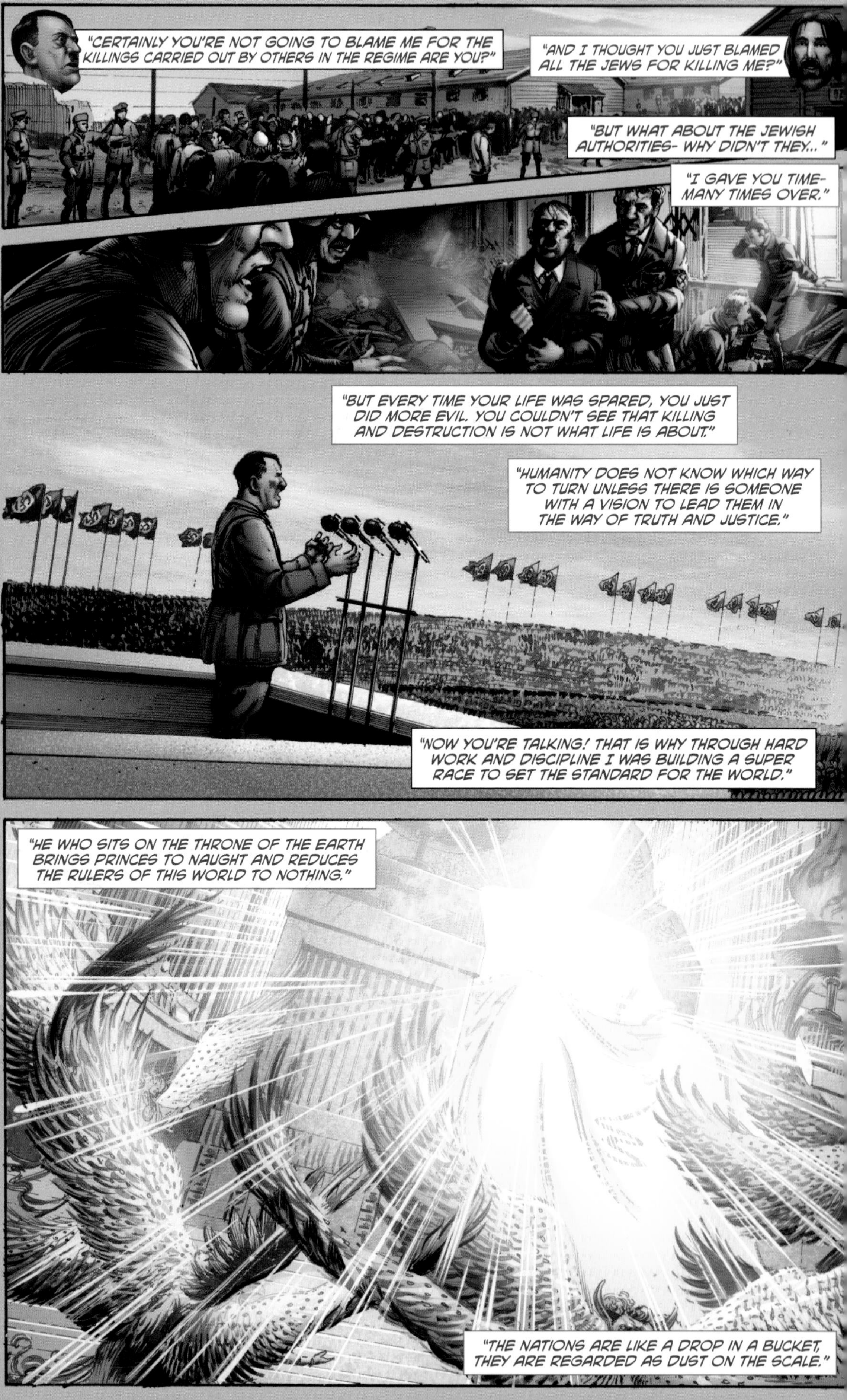
"CERTAINLY YOU'RE NOT GOING TO BLAME ME FOR THE KILLINGS CARRIED OUT BY OTHERS IN THE REGIME ARE YOU?"
"AND I THOUGHT YOU JUST BLAMED ALL THE JEWS FOR KILLING ME?"
"BUT WHAT ABOUT THE JEWISH AUTHORITIES- WHY DIDN'T THEY..."
"I GAVE YOU TIME- MANY TIMES OVER."
"BUT EVERY TIME YOUR LIFE WAS SPARED, YOU JUST DID MORE EVIL. YOU COULDN'T SEE THAT KILLING AND DESTRUCTION IS NOT WHAT LIFE IS ABOUT."
"HUMANITY DOES NOT KNOW WHICH WAY TO TURN UNLESS THERE IS SOMEONE WITH A VISION TO LEAD THEM IN THE WAY OF TRUTH AND JUSTICE."
"NOW YOU'RE TALKING! THAT IS WHY THROUGH HARD WORK AND DISCIPLINE I WAS BUILDING A SUPER RACE TO SET THE STANDARD FOR THE WORLD."
"HE WHO SITS ON THE THRONE OF THE EARTH BRINGS PRINCES TO NAUGHT AND REDUCES THE RULERS OF THIS WORLD TO NOTHING."
"THE NATIONS ARE LIKE A DROP IN A BUCKET, THEY ARE REGARDED AS DUST ON THE SCALE."

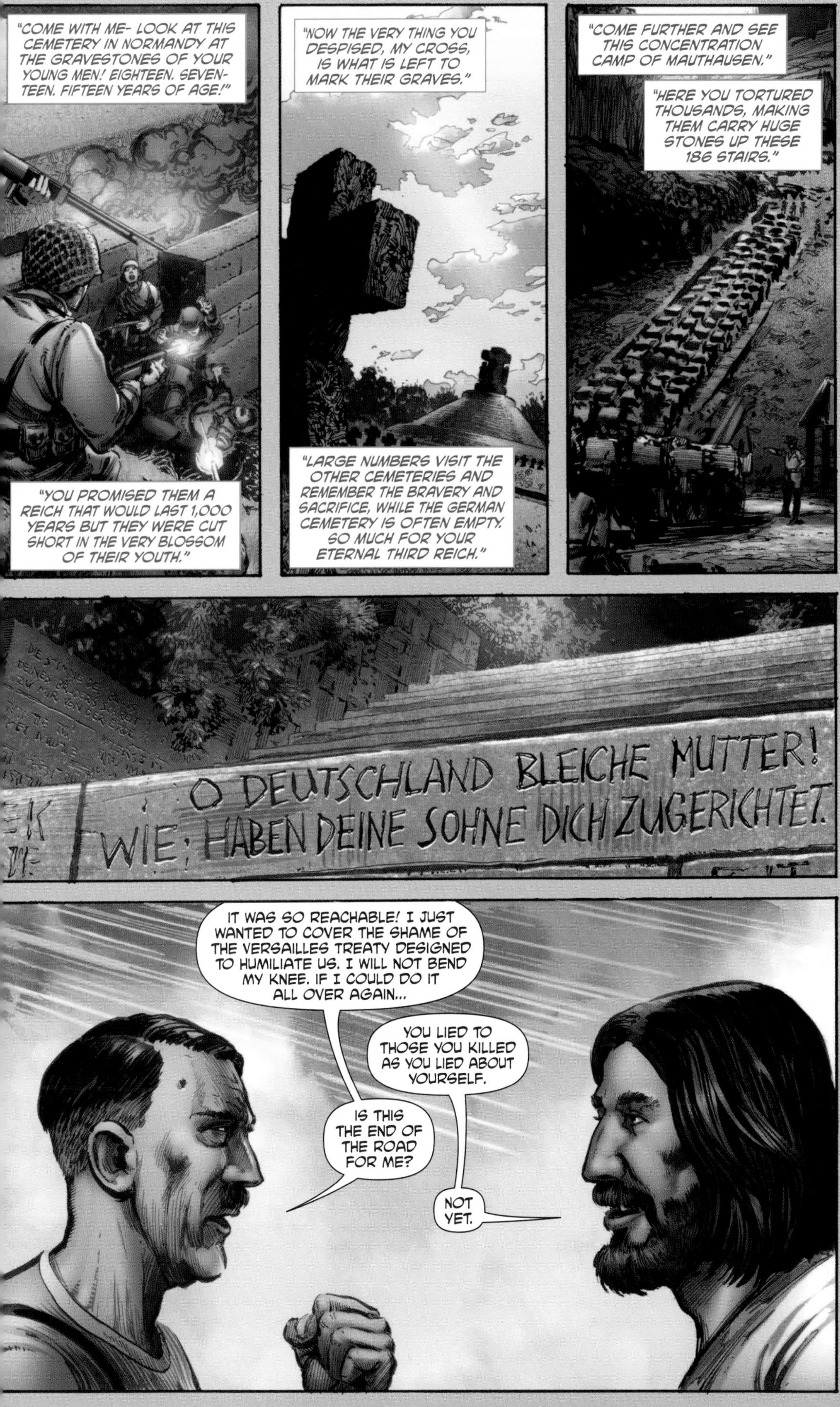
"COME WITH ME- LOOK AT THIS CEMETERY IN NORMANDY AT THE GRAVESTONES OF YOUR YOUNG MEN! EIGHTEEN. SEVEN-TEEN. FIFTEEN YEARS OF AGE!"
"YOU PROMISED THEM A REICH THAT WOULD LAST 1,000 YEARS BUT THEY WERE CUT SHORT IN THE VERY BLOSSOM OF THEIR YOUTH."
"NOW THE VERY THING YOU DESPISED, MY CROSS, IS WHAT IS LEFT TO MARK THEIR GRAVES."
"LARGE NUMBERS VISIT THE OTHER CEMETERIES AND REMEMBER THE BRAVERY AND SACRIFICE, WHILE THE GERMAN CEMETERY IS OFTEN EMPTY. SO MUCH FOR YOUR ETERNAL THIRD REICH."
"COME FURTHER AND SEE THIS CONCENTRATION CAMP OF MAUTHAUSEN."
"HERE YOU TORTURED THOUSANDS, MAKING THEM CARRY HUGE STONES UP THESE 186 STAIRS."
O DEUTSCHLAND BLEICHE MUTTER!
WIE; HABEN DEINE SOHNE DICH ZUGERICHTET.
IT WAS SO REACHABLE! I JUST WANTED TO COVER THE SHAME OF THE VERSAILLES TREATY DESIGNED TO HUMILIATE US. I WILL NOT BEND MY KNEE. IF I COULD DO IT ALL OVER AGAIN...
YOU LIED TO THOSE YOU KILLED AS YOU LIED ABOUT YOURSELF.
IS THIS THE END OF THE ROAD FOR ME?
NOT YET.

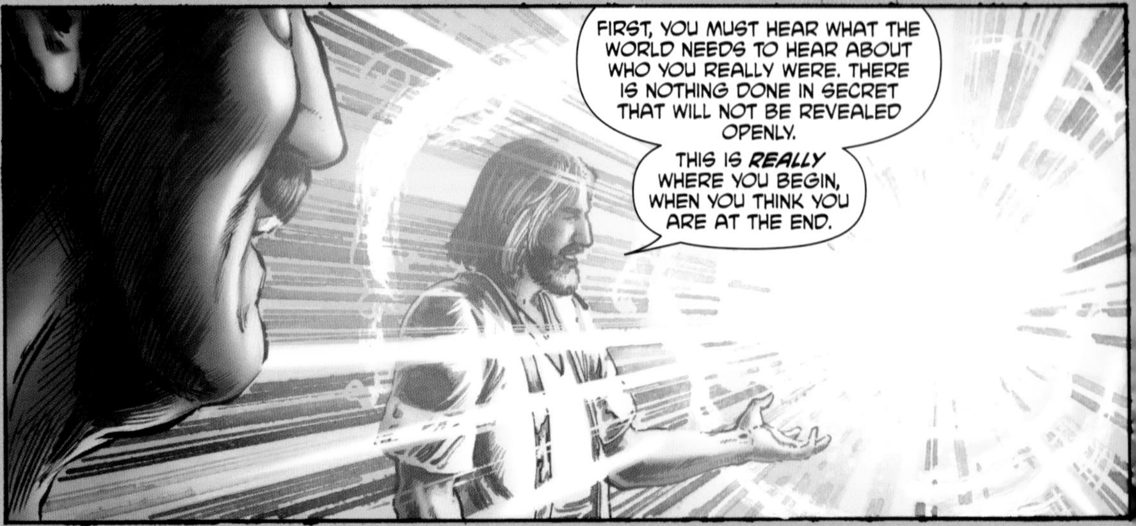
FIRST, YOU MUST HEAR WHAT THE WORLD NEEDS TO HEAR ABOUT WHO YOU REALLY WERE. THERE IS NOTHING DONE IN SECRET THAT WILL NOT BE REVEALED OPENLY.
THIS IS *REALLY* WHERE YOU BEGIN, WHEN YOU THINK YOU ARE AT THE END.

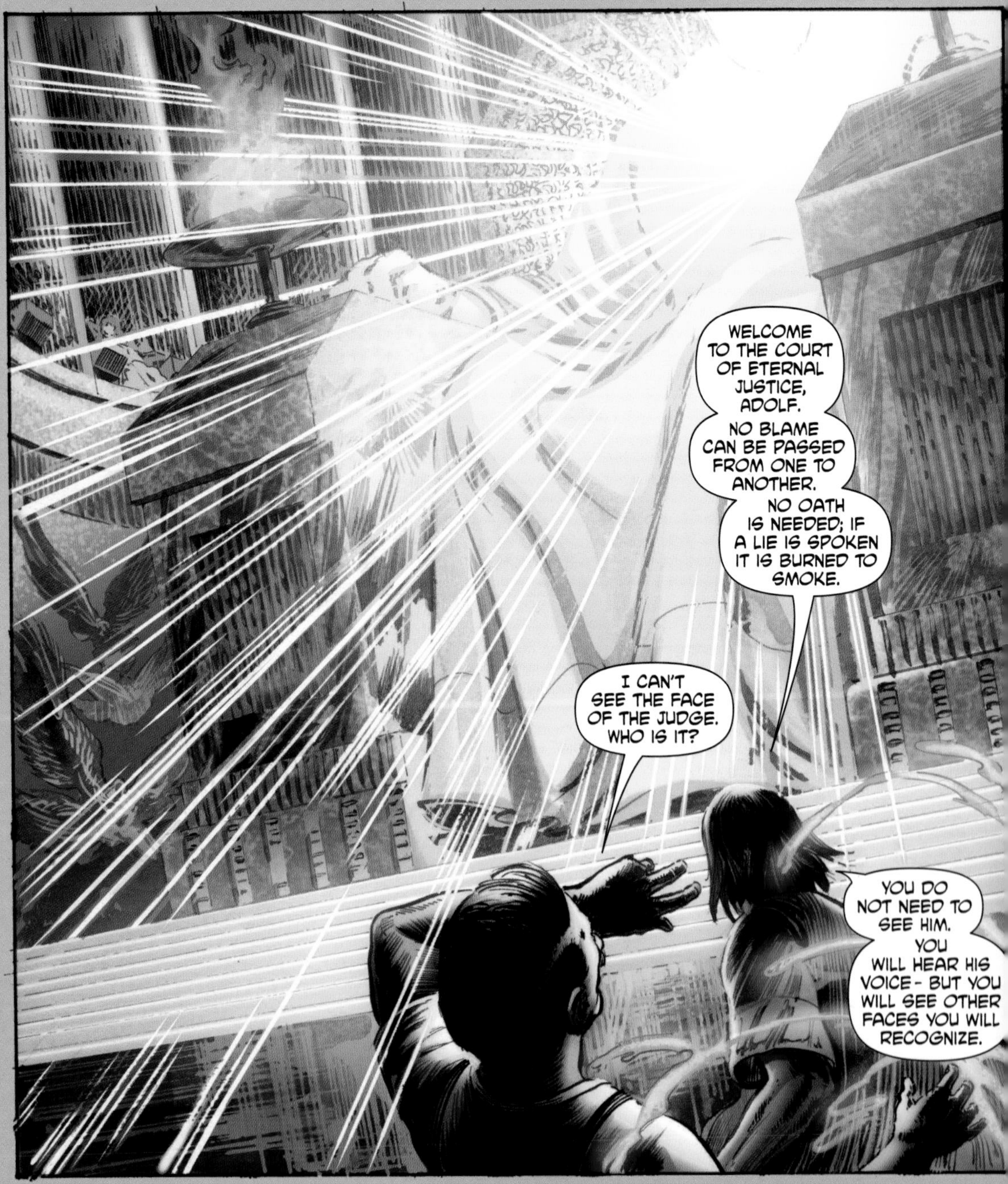
WELCOME TO THE COURT OF ETERNAL JUSTICE, ADOLF.
NO BLAME CAN BE PASSED FROM ONE TO ANOTHER.
NO OATH IS NEEDED; IF A LIE IS SPOKEN IT IS BURNED TO SMOKE.
I CAN'T SEE THE FACE OF THE JUDGE. WHO IS IT?
YOU DO NOT NEED TO SEE HIM.
YOU WILL HEAR HIS VOICE - BUT YOU WILL SEE OTHER FACES YOU WILL RECOGNIZE.

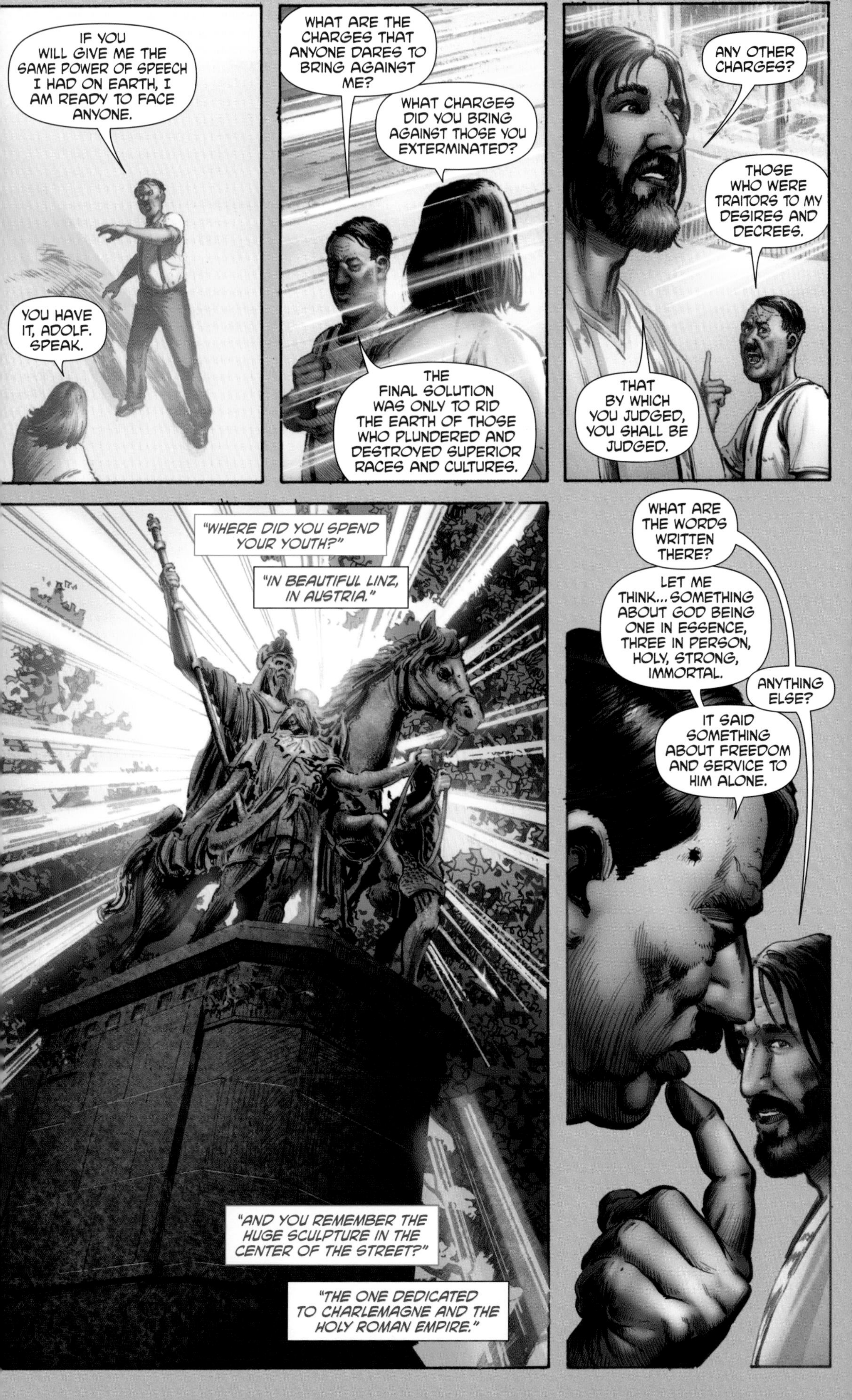
IF YOU WILL GIVE ME THE SAME POWER OF SPEECH I HAD ON EARTH, I AM READY TO FACE ANYONE.
YOU HAVE IT, ADOLF. SPEAK.
WHAT ARE THE CHARGES THAT ANYONE DARES TO BRING AGAINST ME?
WHAT CHARGES DID YOU BRING AGAINST THOSE YOU EXTERMINATED?
THE FINAL SOLUTION WAS ONLY TO RID THE EARTH OF THOSE WHO PLUNDERED AND DESTROYED SUPERIOR RACES AND CULTURES.
ANY OTHER CHARGES?
THOSE WHO WERE TRAITORS TO MY DESIRES AND DECREES.
THAT BY WHICH YOU JUDGED, YOU SHALL BE JUDGED.
"WHERE DID YOU SPEND YOUR YOUTH?"
"IN BEAUTIFUL LINZ, IN AUSTRIA."
"AND YOU REMEMBER THE HUGE SCULPTURE IN THE CENTER OF THE STREET?"
"THE ONE DEDICATED TO CHARLEMAGNE AND THE HOLY ROMAN EMPIRE."
WHAT ARE THE WORDS WRITTEN THERE?
LET ME THINK... SOMETHING ABOUT GOD BEING ONE IN ESSENCE, THREE IN PERSON, HOLY, STRONG, IMMORTAL.
ANYTHING ELSE?
IT SAID SOMETHING ABOUT FREEDOM AND SERVICE TO HIM ALONE.

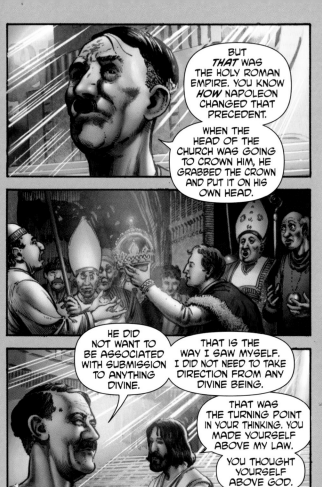

BUT *THAT* WAS THE HOLY ROMAN EMPIRE. YOU KNOW *HOW* NAPOLEON CHANGED THAT PRECEDENT.

WHEN THE HEAD OF THE CHURCH WAS GOING TO CROWN HIM, HE GRABBED THE CROWN AND PUT IT ON HIS OWN HEAD.

HE DID NOT WANT TO BE ASSOCIATED WITH SUBMISSION TO ANYTHING DIVINE.

THAT IS THE WAY I SAW MYSELF. I DID NOT NEED TO TAKE DIRECTION FROM ANY DIVINE BEING.

THAT WAS THE TURNING POINT IN YOUR THINKING. YOU MADE YOURSELF ABOVE MY LAW.

YOU THOUGHT YOURSELF ABOVE GOD.

"I WAS *NOT* GOING TO ALLOW THE CHURCH TO INFLUENCE MY PEOPLE!"

"I NEVER COMMISSIONED THE CHURCH TO RULE OVER GOVERNMENT."

ON TWO OCCASIONS MY DISCIPLES TRIED TO CROWN ME KING BUT I CLEARLY TOLD THEM MY KINGDOM WAS NOT OF THIS WORLD.

YOU DO NOT UNDERSTAND HOW TO RULE PEOPLE. YOU WILL NEVER WIN A PERSON'S HEART WITH A SWORD.

WHAT IS *HE* DOING HERE?!

HE IS THE FIRST WITNESS TO SPEAK TO YOUR SELF-GLORY.

BUT THIS IS SPEER! WHY, YOU TRAITOR...

NO NEED TO FILL THE ROOM WITH SMOKE ADOLF— LET HIM SPEAK.

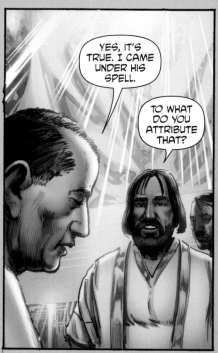

YES, IT'S TRUE. I CAME UNDER HIS SPELL.

TO WHAT DO YOU ATTRIBUTE THAT?

"AT FIRST I WAS JUST AN ARCHITECT WITH PLANS AND AMBITION FOR MY CAREER. AND HE WAS AN ADMIRER OF MY SKILL. THEN IT MOVED TO ME ADMIRING HIM."

"KEEP TALKING AND YOUR OWN MOUTH WILL CONVICT YOU."

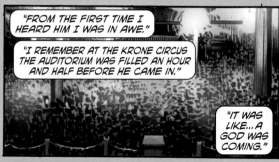

"FROM THE FIRST TIME I HEARD HIM I WAS IN AWE."

"I REMEMBER AT THE KRONE CIRCUS THE AUDITORIUM WAS FILLED AN HOUR AND HALF BEFORE HE CAME IN."

"IT WAS LIKE...A GOD WAS COMING."

"AND THE SONG..."

♪ THE STORM TROOPS STAND AT READY THE RACIAL FIGHT TO LEAD UNTIL THE JEWS ARE BLEEDING WE KNOW WE ARE NOT FREED. ♪

NOW AS I LOOK BACK... AT HOW THE CROWDS—

HOW THE CROWDS WHAT?

LET HIM FINISH.

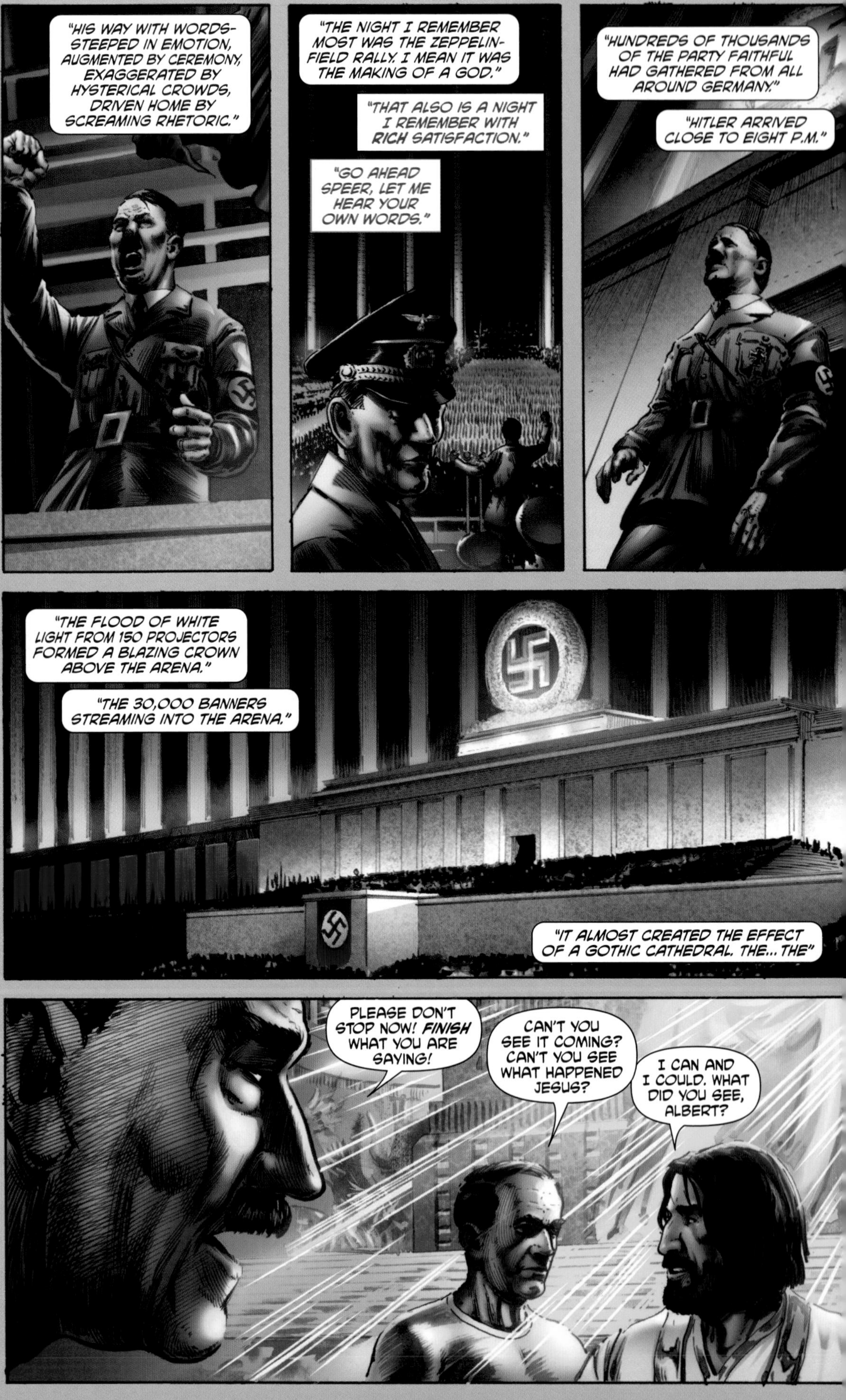
"HIS WAY WITH WORDS- STEEPED IN EMOTION, AUGMENTED BY CEREMONY, EXAGGERATED BY HYSTERICAL CROWDS, DRIVEN HOME BY SCREAMING RHETORIC."
"THE NIGHT I REMEMBER MOST WAS THE ZEPPELIN-FIELD RALLY. I MEAN IT WAS THE MAKING OF A GOD."
"THAT ALSO IS A NIGHT I REMEMBER WITH RICH SATISFACTION."
"GO AHEAD SPEER, LET ME HEAR YOUR OWN WORDS."
"HUNDREDS OF THOUSANDS OF THE PARTY FAITHFUL HAD GATHERED FROM ALL AROUND GERMANY."
"HITLER ARRIVED CLOSE TO EIGHT P.M."
"THE FLOOD OF WHITE LIGHT FROM 150 PROJECTORS FORMED A BLAZING CROWN ABOVE THE ARENA."
"THE 30,000 BANNERS STREAMING INTO THE ARENA."
"IT ALMOST CREATED THE EFFECT OF A GOTHIC CATHEDRAL. THE... THE"
PLEASE DON'T STOP NOW! FINISH WHAT YOU ARE SAYING!
CAN'T YOU SEE IT COMING? CAN'T YOU SEE WHAT HAPPENED JESUS?
I CAN AND I COULD. WHAT DID YOU SEE, ALBERT?

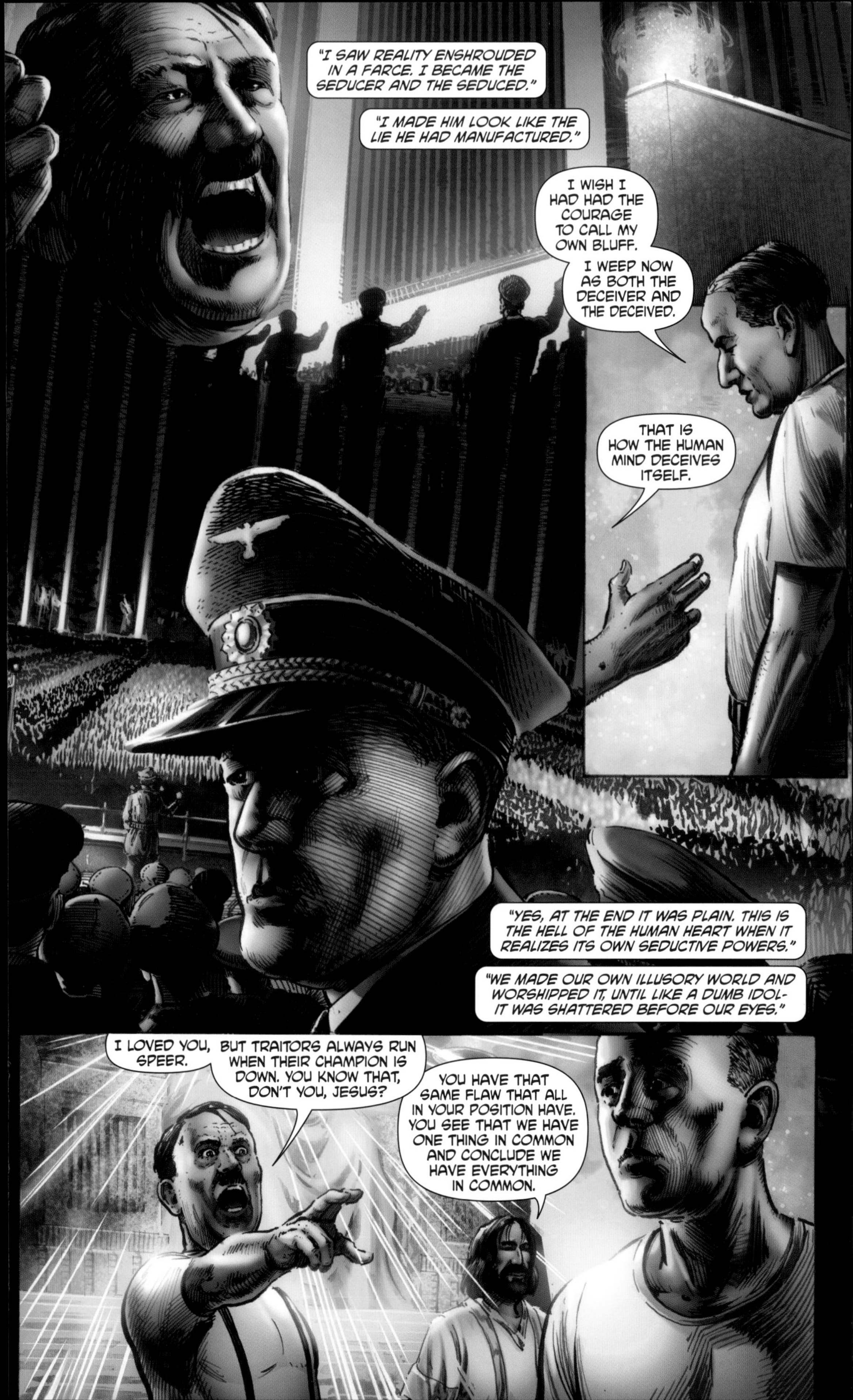
"I SAW REALITY ENSHROUDED IN A FARCE. I BECAME THE SEDUCER AND THE SEDUCED."
"I MADE HIM LOOK LIKE THE LIE HE HAD MANUFACTURED."
I WISH I HAD HAD THE COURAGE TO CALL MY OWN BLUFF.
I WEEP NOW AS BOTH THE DECEIVER AND THE DECEIVED.
THAT IS HOW THE HUMAN MIND DECEIVES ITSELF.
"YES, AT THE END IT WAS PLAIN. THIS IS THE HELL OF THE HUMAN HEART WHEN IT REALIZES ITS OWN SEDUCTIVE POWERS."
"WE MADE OUR OWN ILLUSORY WORLD AND WORSHIPPED IT, UNTIL LIKE A DUMB IDOL- IT WAS SHATTERED BEFORE OUR EYES."
I LOVED YOU, SPEER.
BUT TRAITORS ALWAYS RUN WHEN THEIR CHAMPION IS DOWN. YOU KNOW THAT, DON'T YOU, JESUS?
YOU HAVE THAT SAME FLAW THAT ALL IN YOUR POSITION HAVE. YOU SEE THAT WE HAVE ONE THING IN COMMON AND CONCLUDE WE HAVE EVERYTHING IN COMMON.

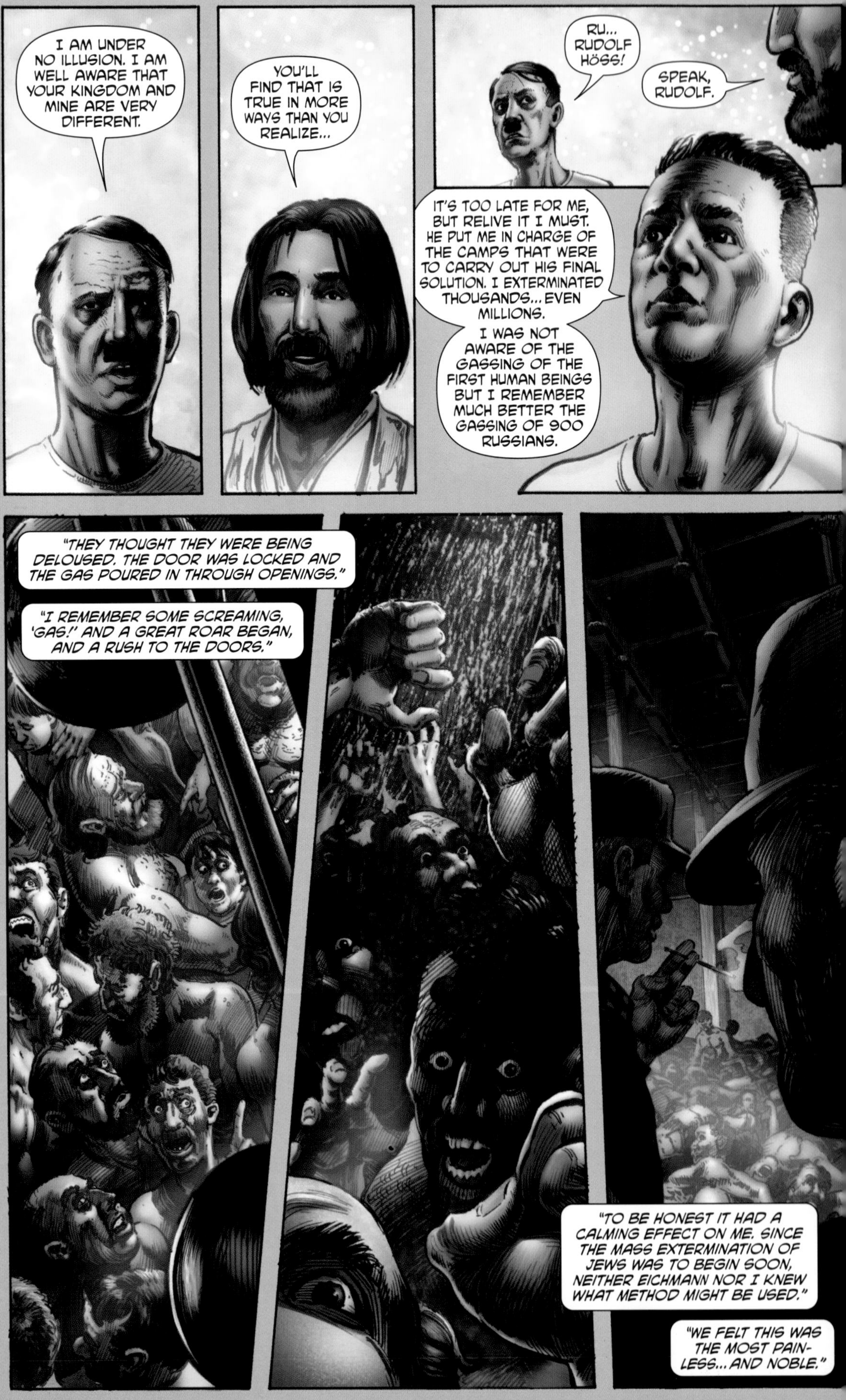
I AM UNDER NO ILLUSION. I AM WELL AWARE THAT YOUR KINGDOM AND MINE ARE VERY DIFFERENT.
YOU'LL FIND THAT IS TRUE IN MORE WAYS THAN YOU REALIZE...
RU... RUDOLF HÖSS!
SPEAK, RUDOLF.
IT'S TOO LATE FOR ME, BUT RELIVE IT I MUST. HE PUT ME IN CHARGE OF THE CAMPS THAT WERE TO CARRY OUT HIS FINAL SOLUTION. I EXTERMINATED THOUSANDS... EVEN MILLIONS.
I WAS NOT AWARE OF THE GASSING OF THE FIRST HUMAN BEINGS BUT I REMEMBER MUCH BETTER THE GASSING OF 900 RUSSIANS.
"THEY THOUGHT THEY WERE BEING DELOUSED. THE DOOR WAS LOCKED AND THE GAS POURED IN THROUGH OPENINGS."
"I REMEMBER SOME SCREAMING, 'GAS!' AND A GREAT ROAR BEGAN, AND A RUSH TO THE DOORS."
"TO BE HONEST IT HAD A CALMING EFFECT ON ME. SINCE THE MASS EXTERMINATION OF JEWS WAS TO BEGIN SOON, NEITHER EICHMANN NOR I KNEW WHAT METHOD MIGHT BE USED."
"WE FELT THIS WAS THE MOST PAIN-LESS... AND NOBLE."

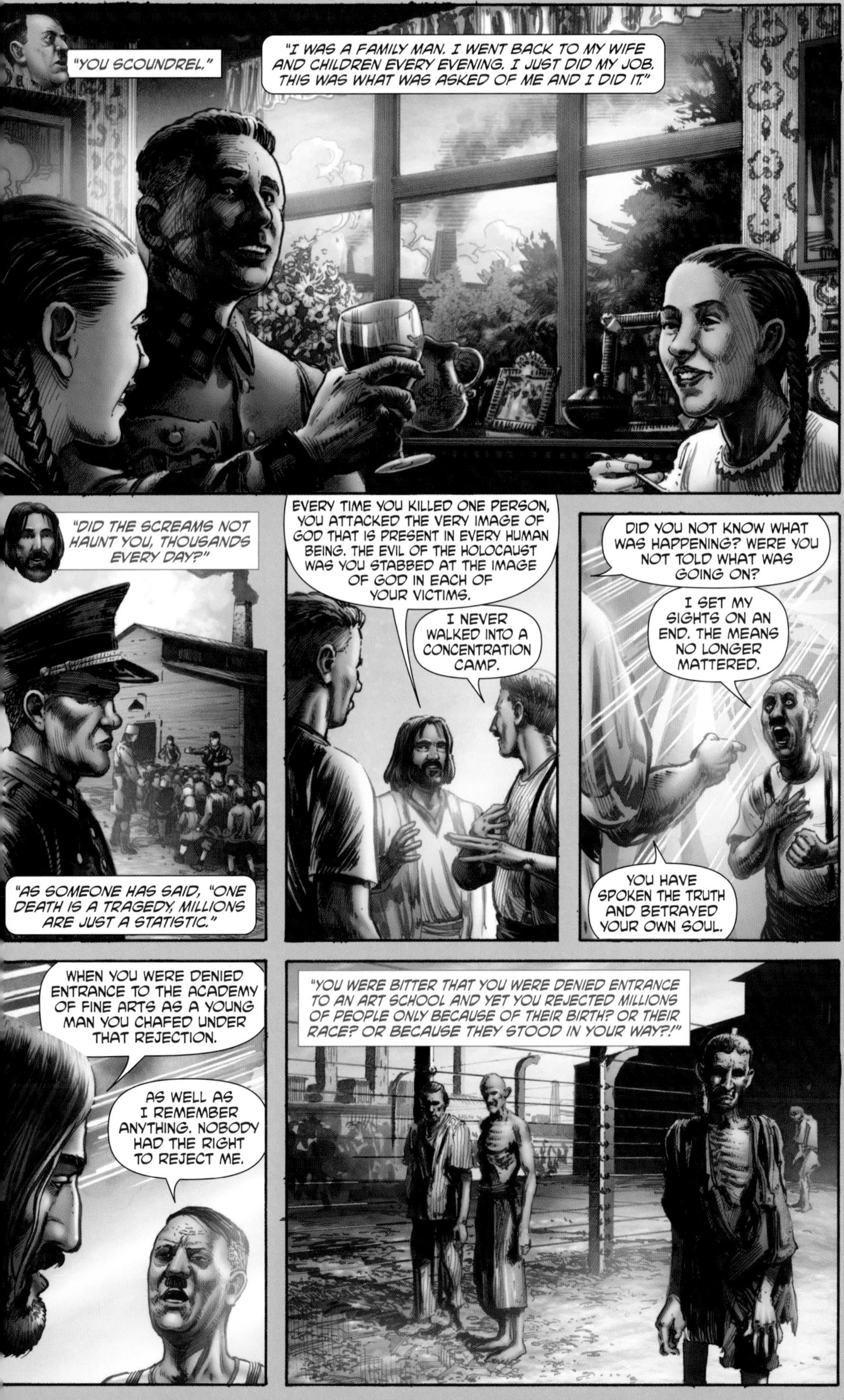
"YOU SCOUNDREL."
"I WAS A FAMILY MAN. I WENT BACK TO MY WIFE AND CHILDREN EVERY EVENING. I JUST DID MY JOB. THIS WAS WHAT WAS ASKED OF ME AND I DID IT."
"DID THE SCREAMS NOT HAUNT YOU, THOUSANDS EVERY DAY?"
"AS SOMEONE HAS SAID, "ONE DEATH IS A TRAGEDY, MILLIONS ARE JUST A STATISTIC."
EVERY TIME YOU KILLED ONE PERSON, YOU ATTACKED THE VERY IMAGE OF GOD THAT IS PRESENT IN EVERY HUMAN BEING. THE EVIL OF THE HOLOCAUST WAS YOU STABBED AT THE IMAGE OF GOD IN EACH OF YOUR VICTIMS.
I NEVER WALKED INTO A CONCENTRATION CAMP.
DID YOU NOT KNOW WHAT WAS HAPPENING? WERE YOU NOT TOLD WHAT WAS GOING ON?
I SET MY SIGHTS ON AN END. THE MEANS NO LONGER MATTERED.
YOU HAVE SPOKEN THE TRUTH AND BETRAYED YOUR OWN SOUL.
WHEN YOU WERE DENIED ENTRANCE TO THE ACADEMY OF FINE ARTS AS A YOUNG MAN YOU CHAFED UNDER THAT REJECTION.
AS WELL AS I REMEMBER ANYTHING. NOBODY HAD THE RIGHT TO REJECT ME.
"YOU WERE BITTER THAT YOU WERE DENIED ENTRANCE TO AN ART SCHOOL AND YET YOU REJECTED MILLIONS OF PEOPLE ONLY BECAUSE OF THEIR BIRTH? OR THEIR RACE? OR BECAUSE THEY STOOD IN YOUR WAY?!"

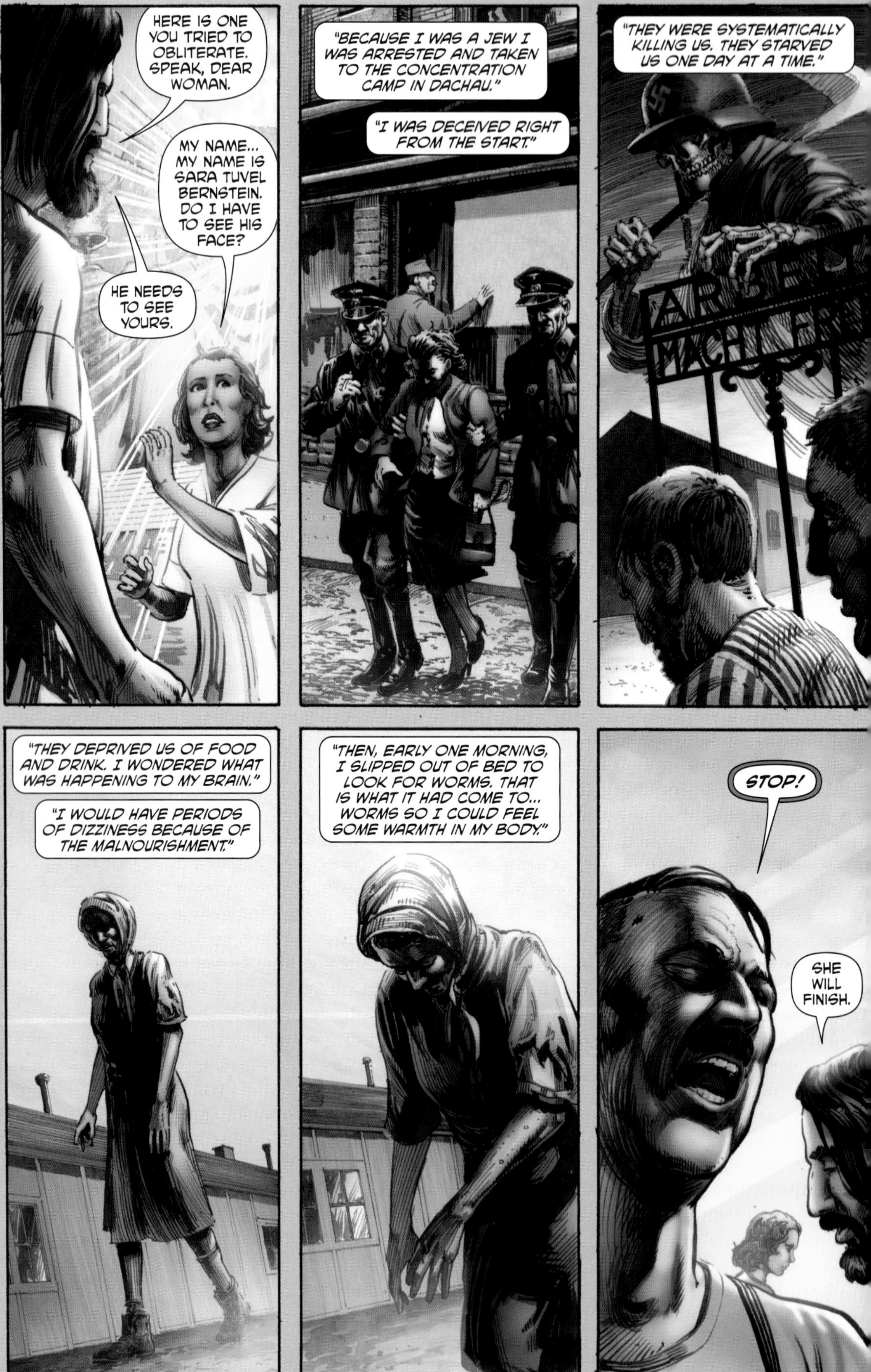
HERE IS ONE YOU TRIED TO OBLITERATE. SPEAK, DEAR WOMAN.
MY NAME... MY NAME IS SARA TUVEL BERNSTEIN. DO I HAVE TO SEE HIS FACE?
HE NEEDS TO SEE YOURS.
"BECAUSE I WAS A JEW I WAS ARRESTED AND TAKEN TO THE CONCENTRATION CAMP IN DACHAU."
"I WAS DECEIVED RIGHT FROM THE START."
"THEY WERE SYSTEMATICALLY KILLING US. THEY STARVED US ONE DAY AT A TIME."
"THEY DEPRIVED US OF FOOD AND DRINK. I WONDERED WHAT WAS HAPPENING TO MY BRAIN."
"I WOULD HAVE PERIODS OF DIZZINESS BECAUSE OF THE MALNOURISHMENT."
"THEN, EARLY ONE MORNING, I SLIPPED OUT OF BED TO LOOK FOR WORMS. THAT IS WHAT IT HAD COME TO... WORMS SO I COULD FEEL SOME WARMTH IN MY BODY."
STOP!
SHE WILL FINISH.

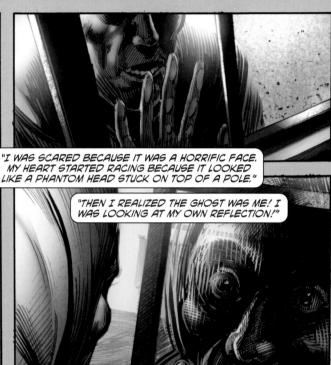

"I WAS BENT DOWN, PORING OVER THE GRASS WHEN SUDDENLY I FELT EYES STARING BACK AT ME FROM THE OTHER SIDE OF THE WINDOW."

"I WAS SCARED BECAUSE IT WAS A HORRIFIC FACE. MY HEART STARTED RACING BECAUSE IT LOOKED LIKE A PHANTOM HEAD STUCK ON TOP OF A POLE."

"THEN I REALIZED THE GHOST WAS ME! I WAS LOOKING AT MY OWN REFLECTION!"

DON'T TRY TO AROUSE MY PITY. SHE WOULD HAVE BEEN BETTER OFF GASSED INSTEAD OF PROLONGING HER SUFFERING.

BECAUSE SHE WAS JEWISH, IS THAT RIGHT?

HOW OFTEN DO YOU WANT ME TO SAY IT? YES!

"ANOTHER. MEET THIS MAN, ADOLF."

"HE'S NOT JEWISH, HE'S ONE OF YOUR OWN."

"I WAS ON THE ROAD TO BERLIN, WE WERE HOURS AWAY FROM BEING CRUSHED BY THE RUSSIAN ARMY."

"ON THE DESOLATE STREET I SEE TWO STORM TROOPERS STANDING BESIDE A LAMPPOST."

"THEN I MAKE OUT WHAT IT IS..."

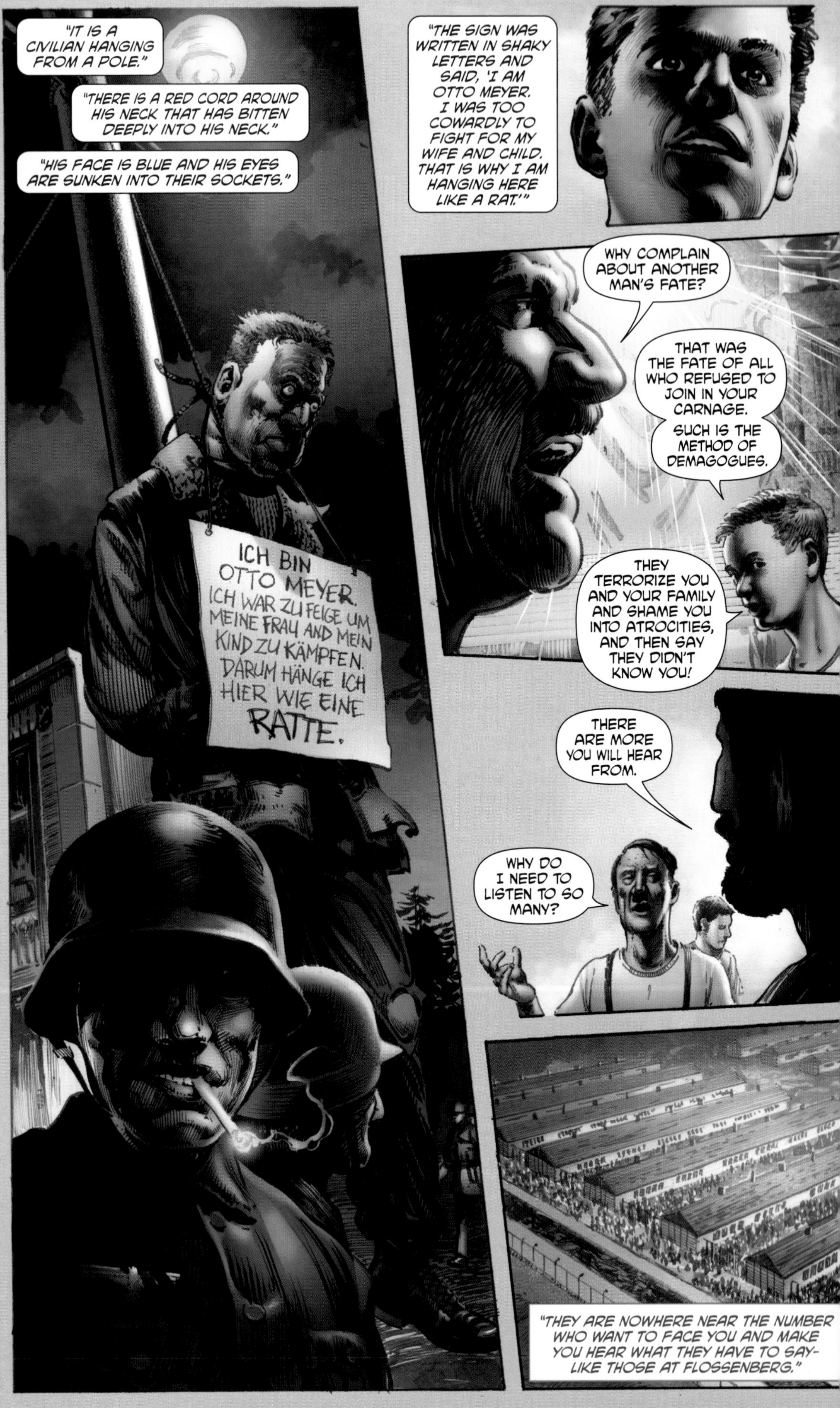
"IT IS A CIVILIAN HANGING FROM A POLE."
"THERE IS A RED CORD AROUND HIS NECK THAT HAS BITTEN DEEPLY INTO HIS NECK."
"HIS FACE IS BLUE AND HIS EYES ARE SUNKEN INTO THEIR SOCKETS."
ICH BIN OTTO MEYER. ICH WAR ZU FEIGE UM MEINE FRAU AND MEIN KIND ZU KÄMPFEN. DARUM HÄNGE ICH HIER WIE EINE RATTE.
"THE SIGN WAS WRITTEN IN SHAKY LETTERS AND SAID, 'I AM OTTO MEYER. I WAS TOO COWARDLY TO FIGHT FOR MY WIFE AND CHILD. THAT IS WHY I AM HANGING HERE LIKE A RAT.'"
WHY COMPLAIN ABOUT ANOTHER MAN'S FATE?
THAT WAS THE FATE OF ALL WHO REFUSED TO JOIN IN YOUR CARNAGE.
SUCH IS THE METHOD OF DEMAGOGUES.
THEY TERRORIZE YOU AND YOUR FAMILY AND SHAME YOU INTO ATROCITIES, AND THEN SAY THEY DIDN'T KNOW YOU!
THERE ARE MORE YOU WILL HEAR FROM.
WHY DO I NEED TO LISTEN TO SO MANY?
"THEY ARE NOWHERE NEAR THE NUMBER WHO WANT TO FACE YOU AND MAKE YOU HEAR WHAT THEY HAVE TO SAY-LIKE THOSE AT FLOSSENBERG."

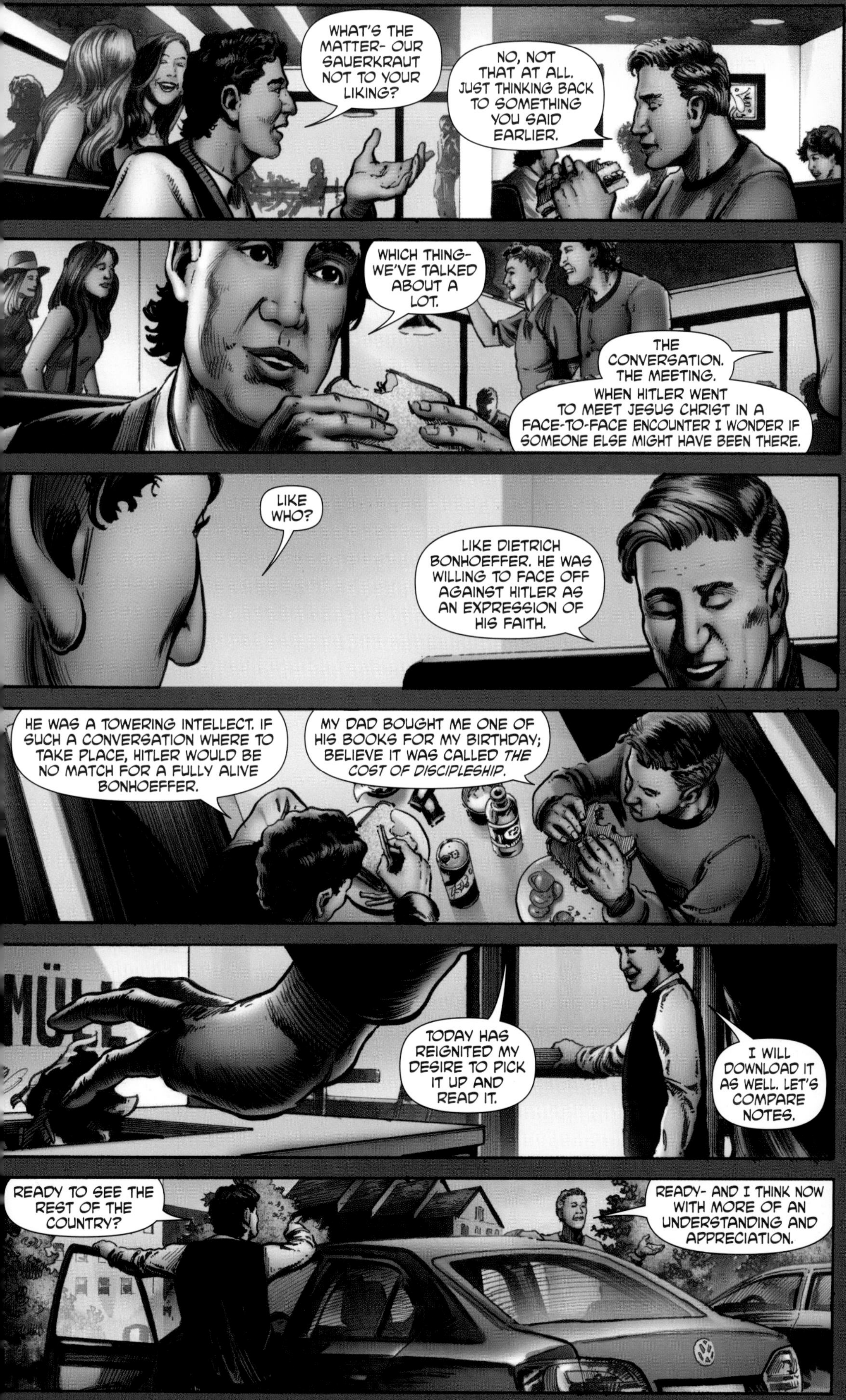

WHAT'S THE MATTER- OUR SAUERKRAUT NOT TO YOUR LIKING?
NO, NOT THAT AT ALL. JUST THINKING BACK TO SOMETHING YOU SAID EARLIER.
WHICH THING- WE'VE TALKED ABOUT A LOT.
THE CONVERSATION. THE MEETING. WHEN HITLER WENT TO MEET JESUS CHRIST IN A FACE-TO-FACE ENCOUNTER I WONDER IF SOMEONE ELSE MIGHT HAVE BEEN THERE.
LIKE WHO?
LIKE DIETRICH BONHOEFFER. HE WAS WILLING TO FACE OFF AGAINST HITLER AS AN EXPRESSION OF HIS FAITH.
HE WAS A TOWERING INTELLECT. IF SUCH A CONVERSATION WHERE TO TAKE PLACE, HITLER WOULD BE NO MATCH FOR A FULLY ALIVE BONHOEFFER.
MY DAD BOUGHT ME ONE OF HIS BOOKS FOR MY BIRTHDAY; BELIEVE IT WAS CALLED *THE COST OF DISCIPLESHIP*.
TODAY HAS REIGNITED MY DESIRE TO PICK IT UP AND READ IT.
I WILL DOWNLOAD IT AS WELL. LET'S COMPARE NOTES.
READY TO SEE THE REST OF THE COUNTRY?
READY- AND I THINK NOW WITH MORE OF AN UNDERSTANDING AND APPRECIATION.

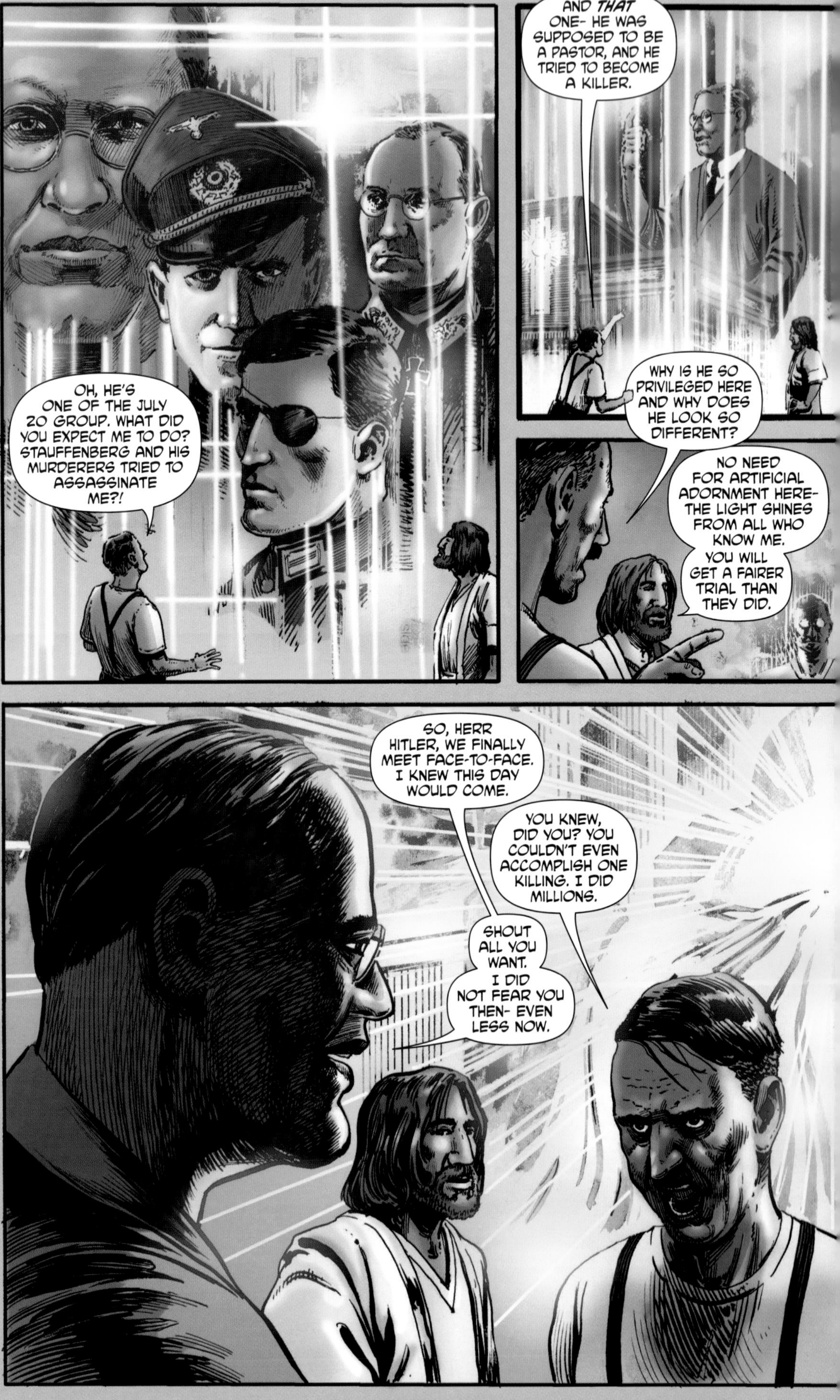
OH, HE'S ONE OF THE JULY 20 GROUP. WHAT DID YOU EXPECT ME TO DO? STAUFFENBERG AND HIS MURDERERS TRIED TO ASSASSINATE ME?!
AND *THAT* ONE- HE WAS SUPPOSED TO BE A PASTOR, AND HE TRIED TO BECOME A KILLER.
WHY IS HE SO PRIVILEGED HERE AND WHY DOES HE LOOK SO DIFFERENT?
NO NEED FOR ARTIFICIAL ADORNMENT HERE- THE LIGHT SHINES FROM ALL WHO KNOW ME.
YOU WILL GET A FAIRER TRIAL THAN THEY DID.
SO, HERR HITLER, WE FINALLY MEET FACE-TO-FACE. I KNEW THIS DAY WOULD COME.
YOU KNEW, DID YOU? YOU COULDN'T EVEN ACCOMPLISH ONE KILLING. I DID MILLIONS.
SHOUT ALL YOU WANT. I DID NOT FEAR YOU THEN- EVEN LESS NOW.

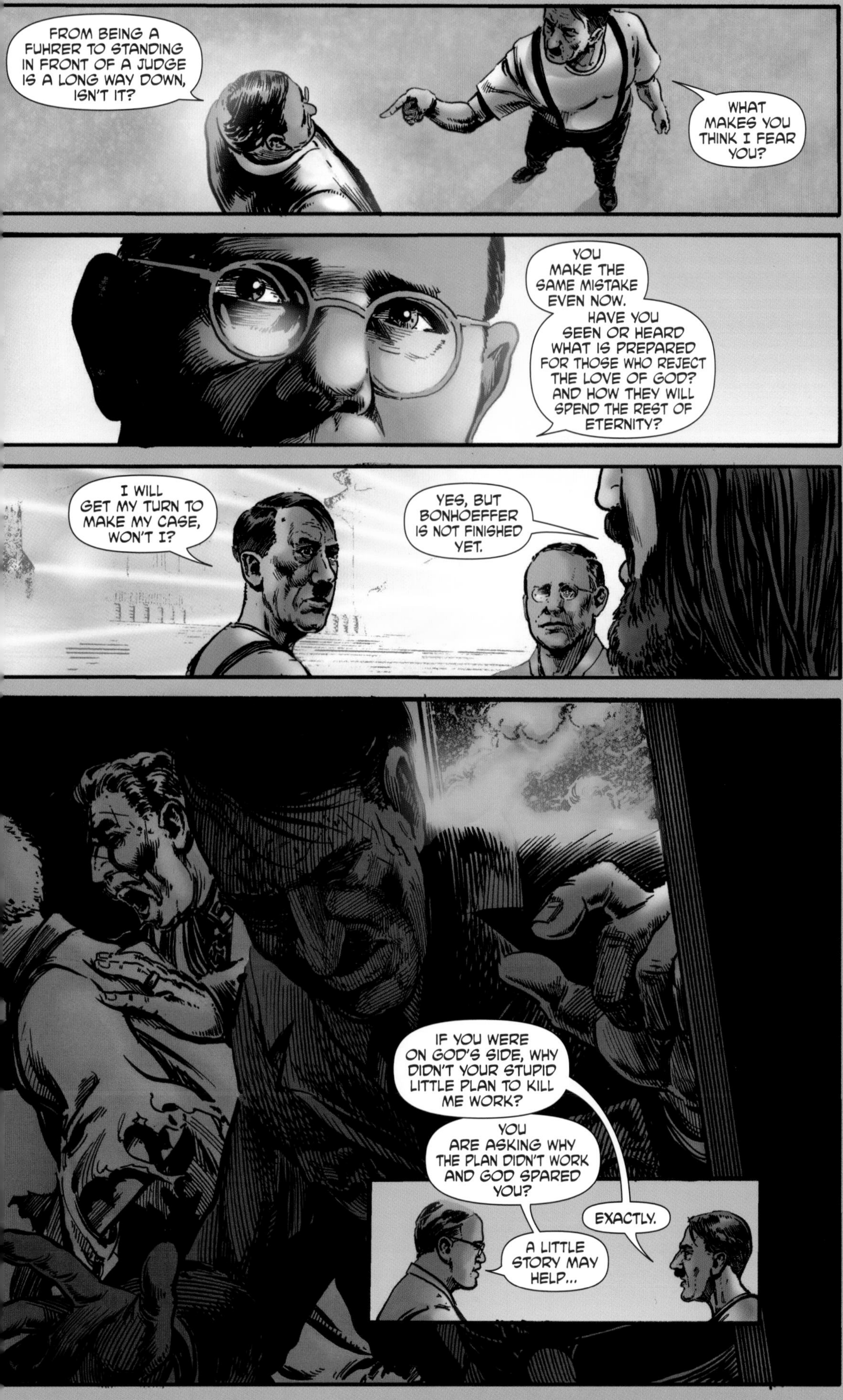
FROM BEING A FUHRER TO STANDING IN FRONT OF A JUDGE IS A LONG WAY DOWN, ISN'T IT?
WHAT MAKES YOU THINK I FEAR YOU?
YOU MAKE THE SAME MISTAKE EVEN NOW.
HAVE YOU SEEN OR HEARD WHAT IS PREPARED FOR THOSE WHO REJECT THE LOVE OF GOD? AND HOW THEY WILL SPEND THE REST OF ETERNITY?
I WILL GET MY TURN TO MAKE MY CASE, WON'T I?
YES, BUT BONHOEFFER IS NOT FINISHED YET.
IF YOU WERE ON GOD'S SIDE, WHY DIDN'T YOUR STUPID LITTLE PLAN TO KILL ME WORK?
YOU ARE ASKING WHY THE PLAN DIDN'T WORK AND GOD SPARED YOU?
EXACTLY.
A LITTLE STORY MAY HELP...

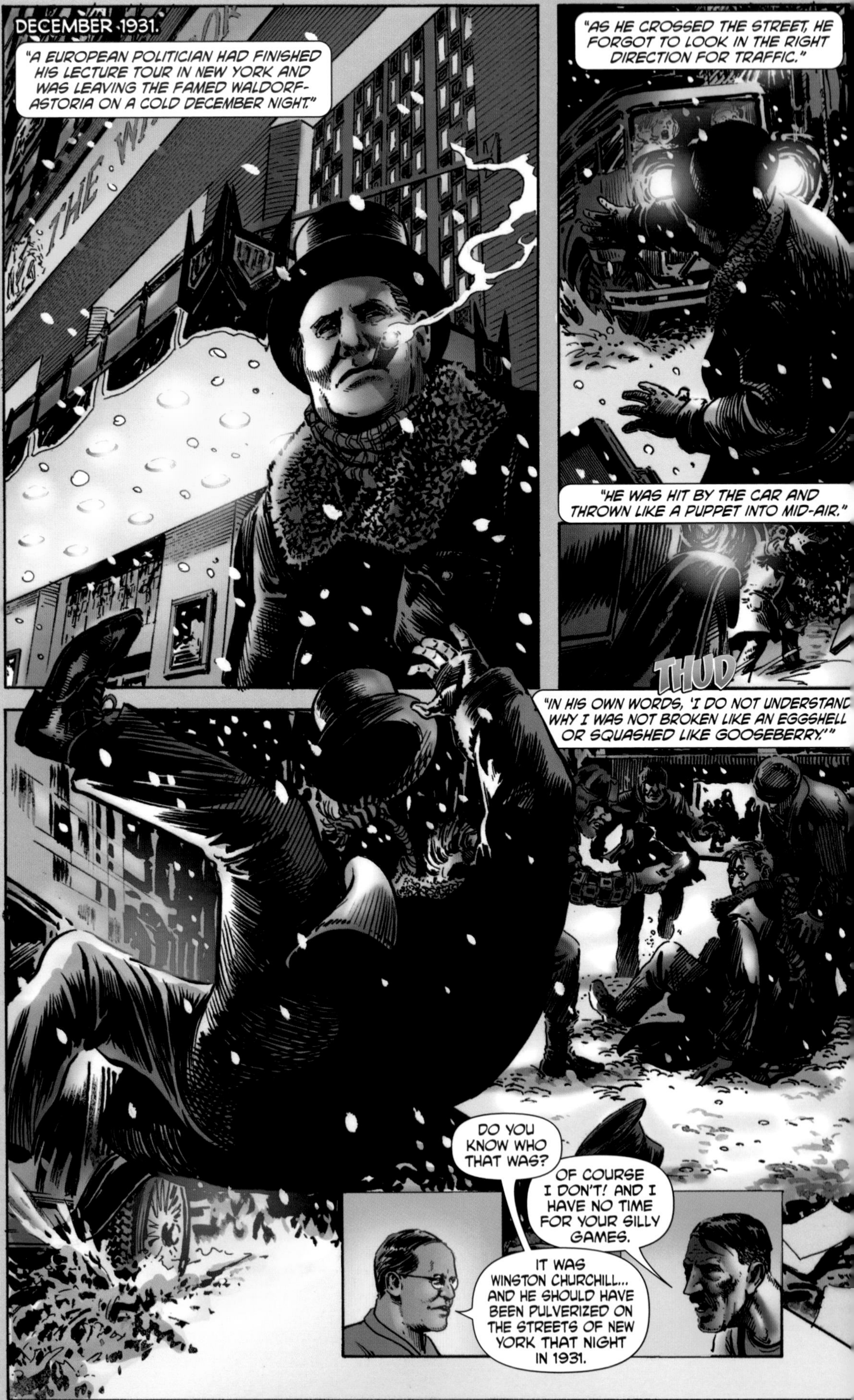
DECEMBER 1931.
"A EUROPEAN POLITICIAN HAD FINISHED HIS LECTURE TOUR IN NEW YORK AND WAS LEAVING THE FAMED WALDORF-ASTORIA ON A COLD DECEMBER NIGHT."
"AS HE CROSSED THE STREET, HE FORGOT TO LOOK IN THE RIGHT DIRECTION FOR TRAFFIC."
"HE WAS HIT BY THE CAR AND THROWN LIKE A PUPPET INTO MID-AIR."
THUD
"IN HIS OWN WORDS, 'I DO NOT UNDERSTAND WHY I WAS NOT BROKEN LIKE AN EGGSHELL OR SQUASHED LIKE GOOSEBERRY.'"
DO YOU KNOW WHO THAT WAS?
OF COURSE I DON'T! AND I HAVE NO TIME FOR YOUR SILLY GAMES.
IT WAS WINSTON CHURCHILL... AND HE SHOULD HAVE BEEN PULVERIZED ON THE STREETS OF NEW YORK THAT NIGHT IN 1931.

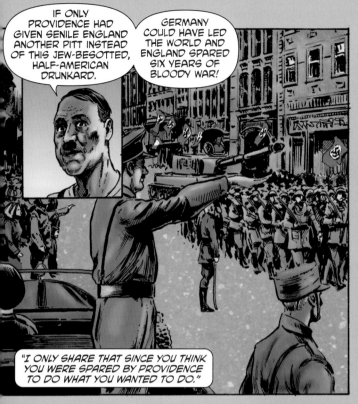

IF ONLY PROVIDENCE HAD GIVEN SENILE ENGLAND ANOTHER PITT INSTEAD OF THIS JEW-BESOTTED, HALF-AMERICAN DRUNKARD.

GERMANY COULD HAVE LED THE WORLD AND ENGLAND SPARED SIX YEARS OF BLOODY WAR!

"I ONLY SHARE THAT SINCE YOU THINK YOU WERE SPARED BY PROVIDENCE TO DO WHAT YOU WANTED TO DO."

"WHAT MAKES YOU THINK YOU WERE NOT ANTICIPATED AND THAT A NEMESIS WASN'T SPARED AND RAISED UP TO STOP YOU?"

"GOD DIDN'T HAVE TO STOP YOU IN *OUR* WAY. HE STOPPED YOU IN *HIS* WAY AND ALLOWED ALL TO SEE WHAT A WORLD WITHOUT GOD LOOKED LIKE."

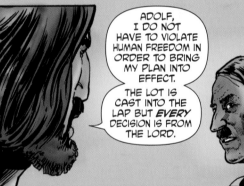

ADOLF, I DO NOT HAVE TO VIOLATE HUMAN FREEDOM IN ORDER TO BRING MY PLAN INTO EFFECT.

THE LOT IS CAST INTO THE LAP BUT *EVERY* DECISION IS FROM THE LORD.

"WITH THE RIGHTEOUS, I SHOW MYSELF RIGHTEOUS."

"WITH THE SHREWD, I SHOW MYSELF SHREWD."

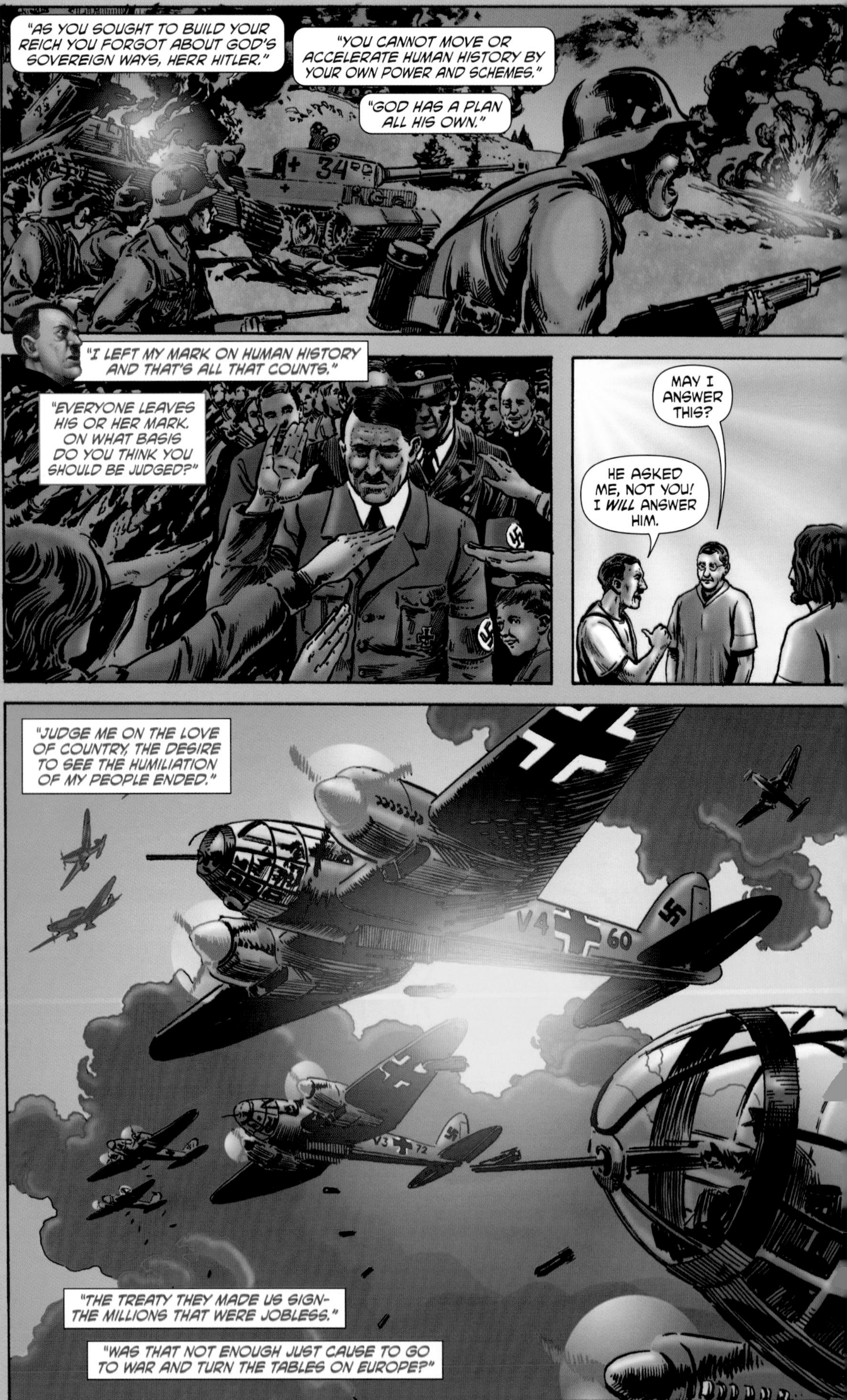
"AS YOU SOUGHT TO BUILD YOUR REICH YOU FORGOT ABOUT GOD'S SOVEREIGN WAYS, HERR HITLER."
"YOU CANNOT MOVE OR ACCELERATE HUMAN HISTORY BY YOUR OWN POWER AND SCHEMES."
"GOD HAS A PLAN ALL HIS OWN."
"I LEFT MY MARK ON HUMAN HISTORY AND THAT'S ALL THAT COUNTS."
"EVERYONE LEAVES HIS OR HER MARK. ON WHAT BASIS DO YOU THINK YOU SHOULD BE JUDGED?"
MAY I ANSWER THIS?
HE ASKED ME, NOT YOU! I WILL ANSWER HIM.
"JUDGE ME ON THE LOVE OF COUNTRY, THE DESIRE TO SEE THE HUMILIATION OF MY PEOPLE ENDED."
"THE TREATY THEY MADE US SIGN- THE MILLIONS THAT WERE JOBLESS."
"WAS THAT NOT ENOUGH JUST CAUSE TO GO TO WAR AND TURN THE TABLES ON EUROPE?"

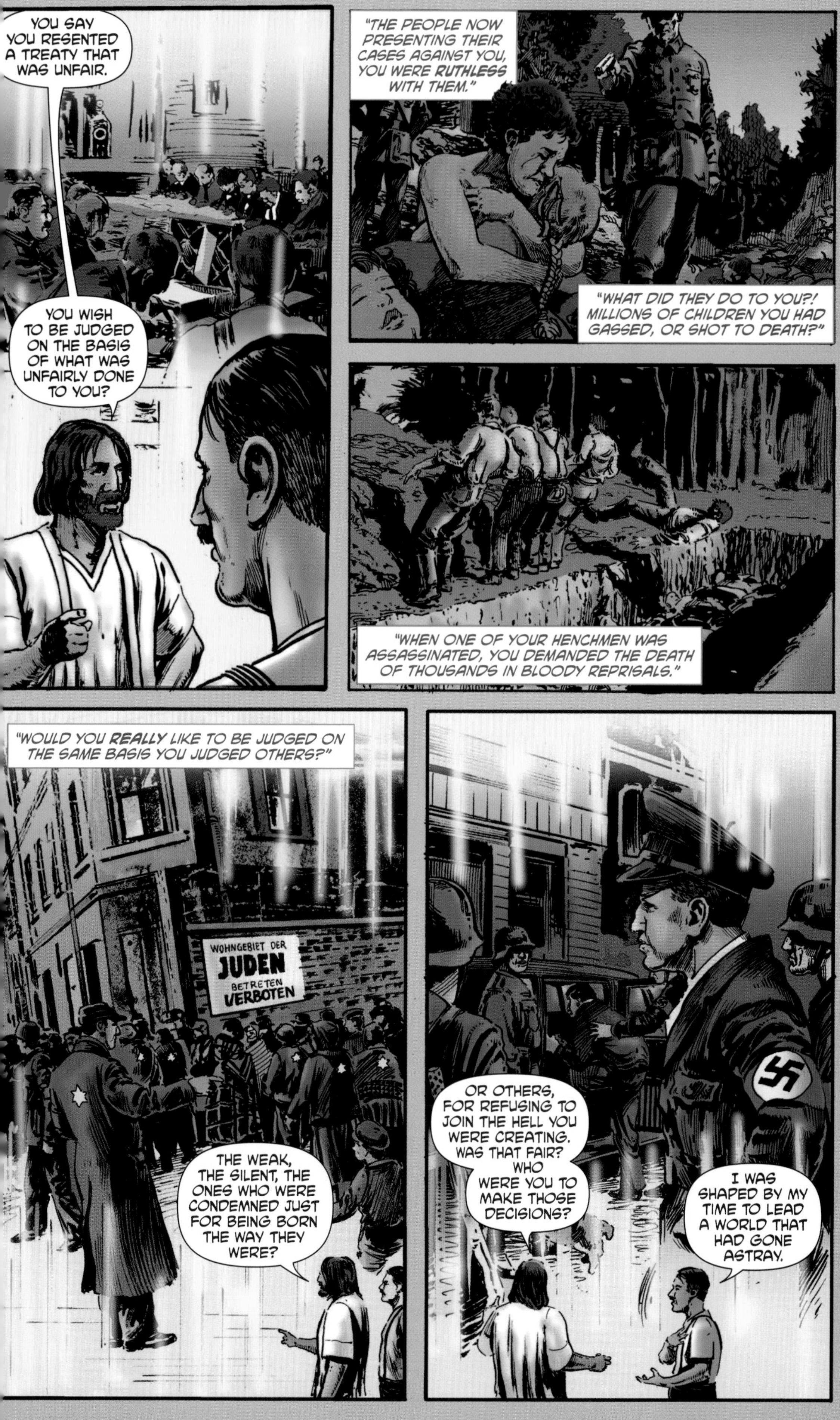
YOU SAY YOU RESENTED A TREATY THAT WAS UNFAIR.
YOU WISH TO BE JUDGED ON THE BASIS OF WHAT WAS UNFAIRLY DONE TO YOU?
"THE PEOPLE NOW PRESENTING THEIR CASES AGAINST YOU, YOU WERE RUTHLESS WITH THEM."
"WHAT DID THEY DO TO YOU?! MILLIONS OF CHILDREN YOU HAD GASSED, OR SHOT TO DEATH?"
"WHEN ONE OF YOUR HENCHMEN WAS ASSASSINATED, YOU DEMANDED THE DEATH OF THOUSANDS IN BLOODY REPRISALS."
"WOULD YOU REALLY LIKE TO BE JUDGED ON THE SAME BASIS YOU JUDGED OTHERS?"
WOHNGEBIET DER JUDEN BETRETEN VERBOTEN
THE WEAK, THE SILENT, THE ONES WHO WERE CONDEMNED JUST FOR BEING BORN THE WAY THEY WERE?
OR OTHERS, FOR REFUSING TO JOIN THE HELL YOU WERE CREATING. WAS THAT FAIR? WHO WERE YOU TO MAKE THOSE DECISIONS?
I WAS SHAPED BY MY TIME TO LEAD A WORLD THAT HAD GONE ASTRAY.

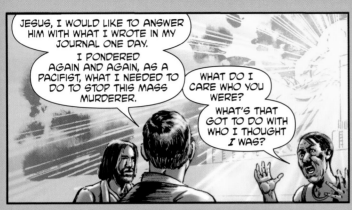

JESUS, I WOULD LIKE TO ANSWER HIM WITH WHAT I WROTE IN MY JOURNAL ONE DAY.

I PONDERED AGAIN AND AGAIN, AS A PACIFIST, WHAT I NEEDED TO DO TO STOP THIS MASS MURDERER.

WHAT DO I CARE WHO YOU WERE?

WHAT'S THAT GOT TO DO WITH WHO I THOUGHT I WAS?

Who am I?

They often tell me I could step from my cell's confinement like a country squire.

Am I really that which other men tell of?

Or am I only what I know myself, restless and longing and sick, like a bird in a cage...

EVERYTHING!! I WRESTLED WITH THE PURPOSE OF LIFE. I KEPT ASKING, "WHO AM I?"

I KNEW THAT AT THE CORE OF EVERYONE'S BEING THIS QUESTION HAS TO BE ANSWERED.

WHEN YOU IMPRISONED ME I PENNED THESE WORDS...

Yearning for colors, for flowers, for the voices of birds.

Thirsting for words of kindness and neighborliness.

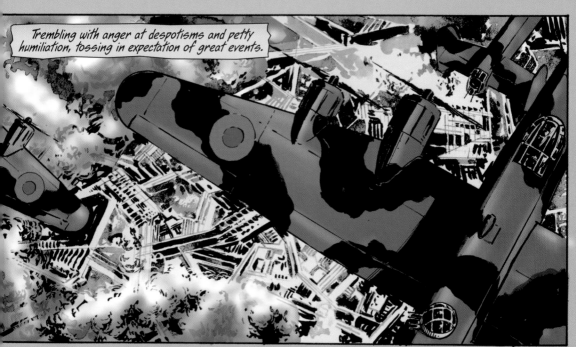

Trembling with anger at despotisms and petty humiliation, tossing in expectation of great events.

Powerlessly trembling for friends at an infinite distance,

Weary and empty, at praying, at thinking, at making,

Faint, and ready to say farewell to it all?

"WHO AM I? THEY MOCK ME, THESE LONELY QUESTIONS OF MINE."

WHOEVER I AM, THOU KNOWEST, O GOD, I AM THINE.

ONCE I ANSWERED THE QUESTION IN THOSE TERMS, LIFE TOOK ON A WHOLE *NEW* PURPOSE. I BELONGED TO THIS GOD WHO LOVED ME AND CREATED ME IN HIS LOVE AND FOR HIS LOVE.

YES, OF COURSE.

YET YOU BLAME GOD FOR HOW YOU TURNED OUT BECAUSE OF THE TWISTS OF HISTORY?

WE SHAPE OURSELVES, HERR HITLER. WE SHAPE OURSELVES...

ADOLF, IT IS NOT WHAT PEOPLE SAY, NOT THE UNIFORM YOU WEAR, OR THE ACCOLADES THAT DEFINE YOU.

IT IS HOW YOU DEFINE YOURSELF IN RELATION TO ME.

THAT... IS WHAT LIFE IS.

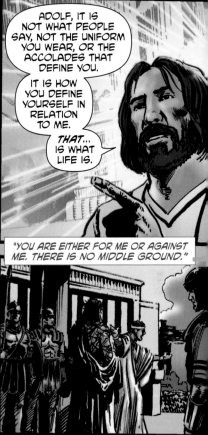

YOU SEE— EVEN THERE MY KINDNESS ALLOWED YOU TO BE ABLE TO WRITE IN PRISON AND BRING YOURSELF SOME HEALING.

HOW YOU MISS THE POINT!

SO YOU GAVE ME THE OPPORTUNITY TO SHAPE MY THOUGHTS?

"YOU ARE EITHER FOR ME OR AGAINST ME. THERE IS NO MIDDLE GROUND."

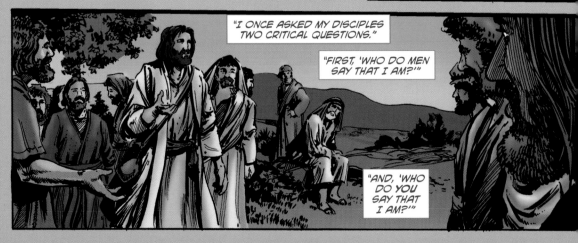

"I ONCE ASKED MY DISCIPLES TWO CRITICAL QUESTIONS."

"FIRST, 'WHO DO MEN SAY THAT I AM?'"

"AND, 'WHO DO YOU SAY THAT I AM?'"

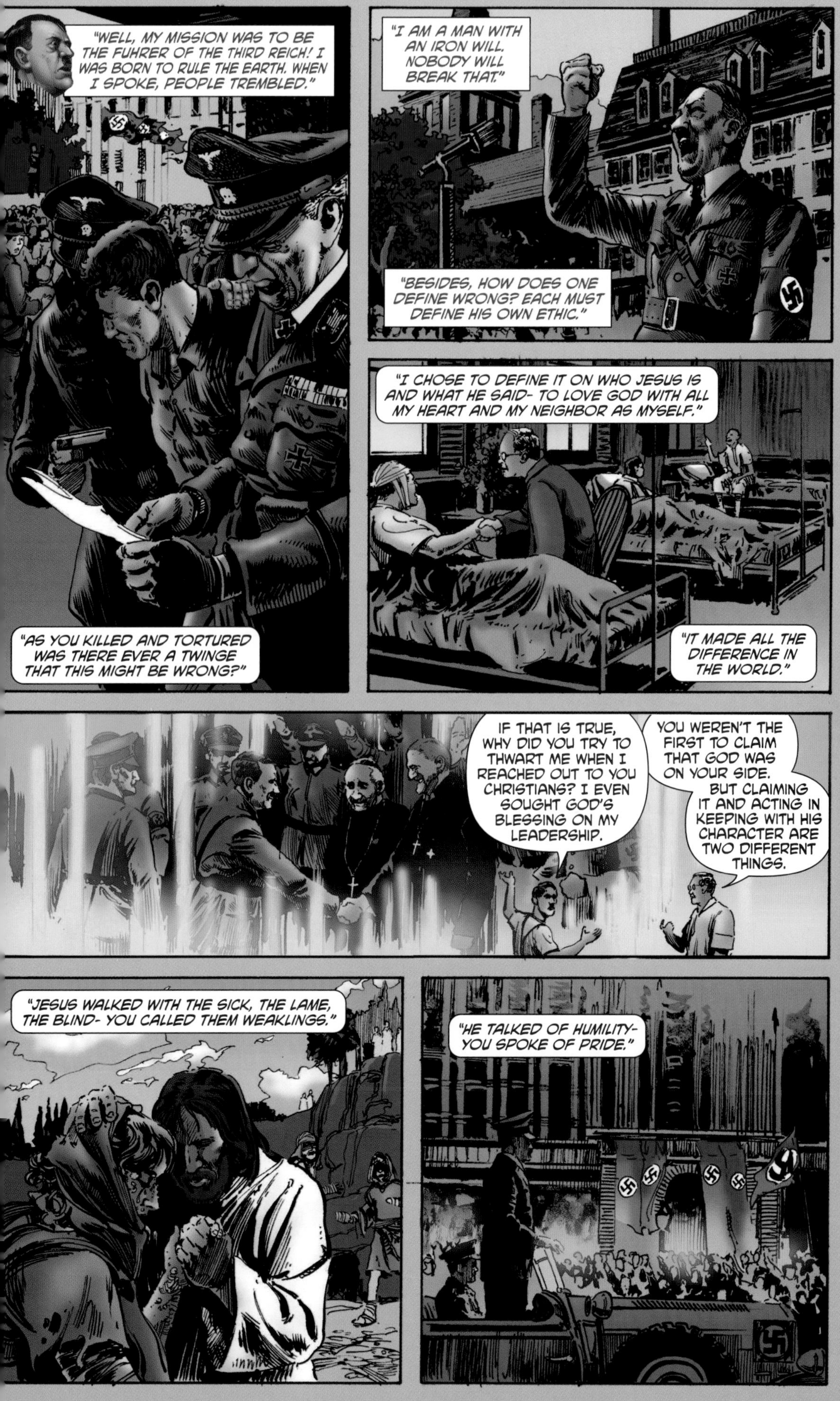
"WELL, MY MISSION WAS TO BE THE FUHRER OF THE THIRD REICH! I WAS BORN TO RULE THE EARTH. WHEN I SPOKE, PEOPLE TREMBLED."
"AS YOU KILLED AND TORTURED WAS THERE EVER A TWINGE THAT THIS MIGHT BE WRONG?"
"I AM A MAN WITH AN IRON WILL. NOBODY WILL BREAK THAT."
"BESIDES, HOW DOES ONE DEFINE WRONG? EACH MUST DEFINE HIS OWN ETHIC."
"I CHOSE TO DEFINE IT ON WHO JESUS IS AND WHAT HE SAID- TO LOVE GOD WITH ALL MY HEART AND MY NEIGHBOR AS MYSELF."
"IT MADE ALL THE DIFFERENCE IN THE WORLD."
IF THAT IS TRUE, WHY DID YOU TRY TO THWART ME WHEN I REACHED OUT TO YOU CHRISTIANS? I EVEN SOUGHT GOD'S BLESSING ON MY LEADERSHIP.
YOU WEREN'T THE FIRST TO CLAIM THAT GOD WAS ON YOUR SIDE.
BUT CLAIMING IT AND ACTING IN KEEPING WITH HIS CHARACTER ARE TWO DIFFERENT THINGS.
"JESUS WALKED WITH THE SICK, THE LAME, THE BLIND- YOU CALLED THEM WEAKLINGS."
"HE TALKED OF HUMILITY- YOU SPOKE OF PRIDE."

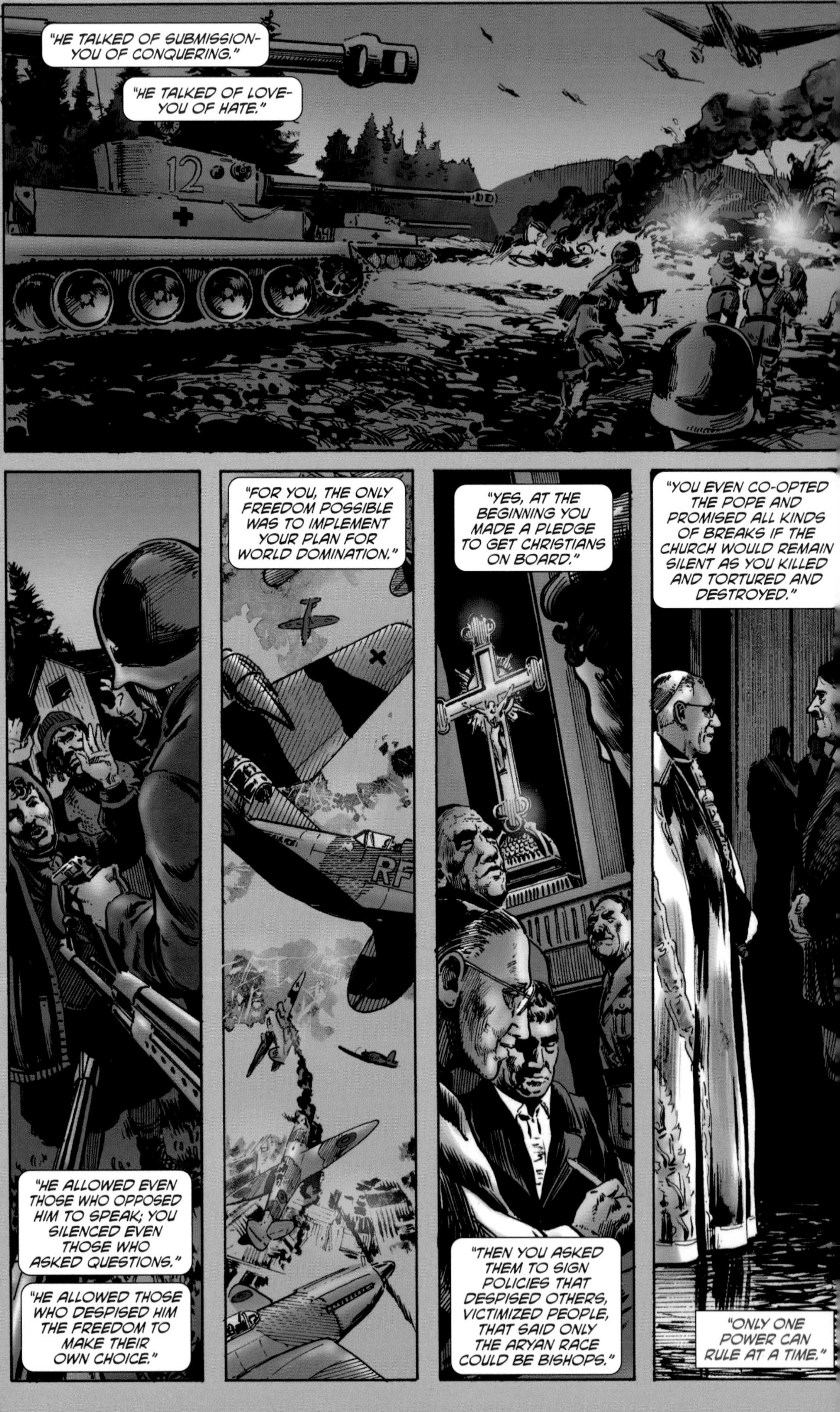
"HE TALKED OF SUBMISSION-
YOU OF CONQUERING."
"HE TALKED OF LOVE-
YOU OF HATE."
"HE ALLOWED EVEN THOSE WHO OPPOSED HIM TO SPEAK; YOU SILENCED EVEN THOSE WHO ASKED QUESTIONS."
"HE ALLOWED THOSE WHO DESPISED HIM THE FREEDOM TO MAKE THEIR OWN CHOICE."
"FOR YOU, THE ONLY FREEDOM POSSIBLE WAS TO IMPLEMENT YOUR PLAN FOR WORLD DOMINATION."
RF
"YES, AT THE BEGINNING YOU MADE A PLEDGE TO GET CHRISTIANS ON BOARD."
"THEN YOU ASKED THEM TO SIGN POLICIES THAT DESPISED OTHERS, VICTIMIZED PEOPLE, THAT SAID ONLY THE ARYAN RACE COULD BE BISHOPS."
"YOU EVEN CO-OPTED THE POPE AND PROMISED ALL KINDS OF BREAKS IF THE CHURCH WOULD REMAIN SILENT AS YOU KILLED AND TORTURED AND DESTROYED."
"ONLY ONE POWER CAN RULE AT A TIME."

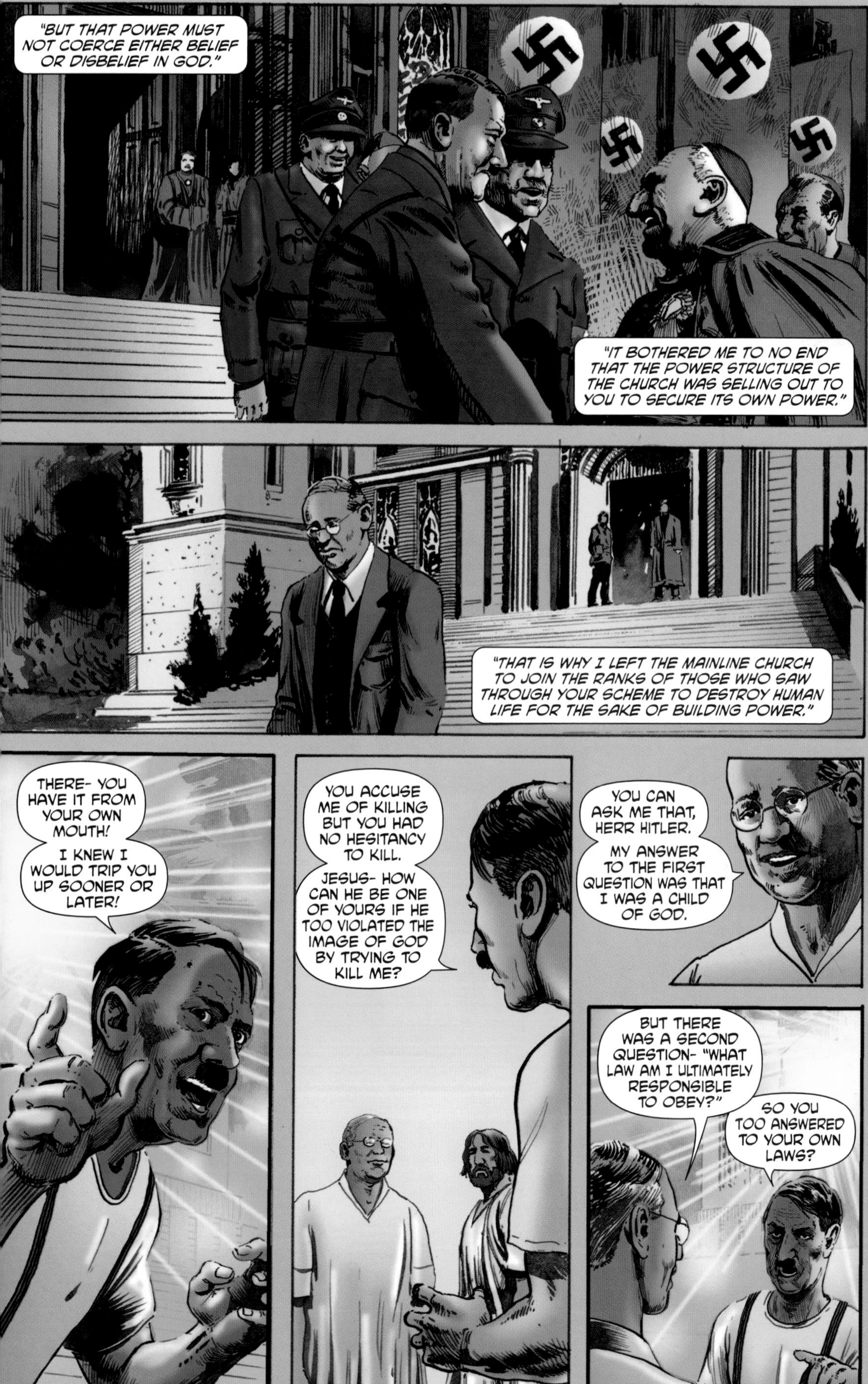
"BUT THAT POWER MUST NOT COERCE EITHER BELIEF OR DISBELIEF IN GOD."
"IT BOTHERED ME TO NO END THAT THE POWER STRUCTURE OF THE CHURCH WAS SELLING OUT TO YOU TO SECURE ITS OWN POWER."
"THAT IS WHY I LEFT THE MAINLINE CHURCH TO JOIN THE RANKS OF THOSE WHO SAW THROUGH YOUR SCHEME TO DESTROY HUMAN LIFE FOR THE SAKE OF BUILDING POWER."
THERE- YOU HAVE IT FROM YOUR OWN MOUTH!
I KNEW I WOULD TRIP YOU UP SOONER OR LATER!
YOU ACCUSE ME OF KILLING BUT YOU HAD NO HESITANCY TO KILL.
JESUS- HOW CAN HE BE ONE OF YOURS IF HE TOO VIOLATED THE IMAGE OF GOD BY TRYING TO KILL ME?
YOU CAN ASK ME THAT, HERR HITLER.
MY ANSWER TO THE FIRST QUESTION WAS THAT I WAS A CHILD OF GOD.
BUT THERE WAS A SECOND QUESTION- "WHAT LAW AM I ULTIMATELY RESPONSIBLE TO OBEY?"
SO YOU TOO ANSWERED TO YOUR OWN LAWS?

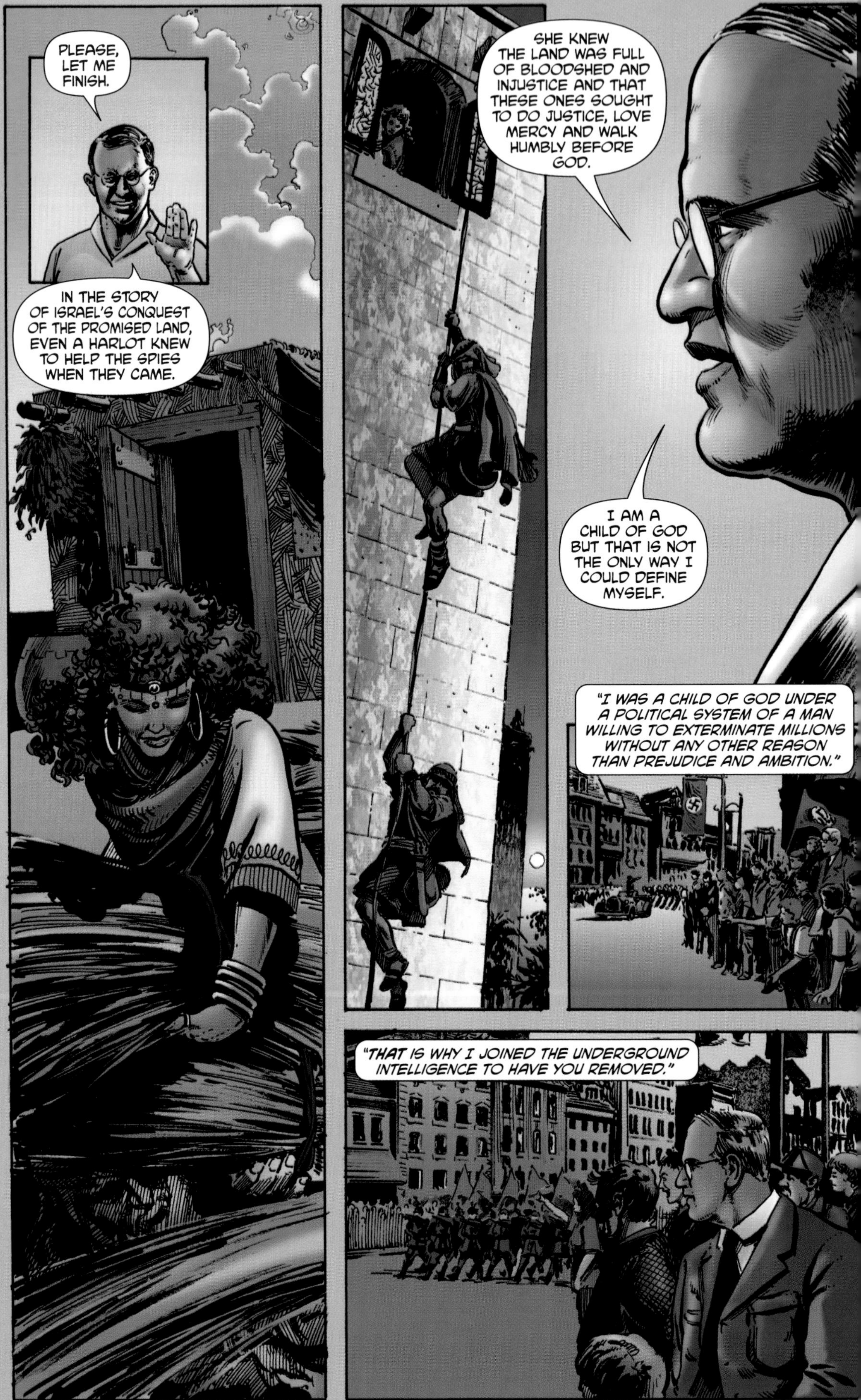
PLEASE, LET ME FINISH.
IN THE STORY OF ISRAEL'S CONQUEST OF THE PROMISED LAND, EVEN A HARLOT KNEW TO HELP THE SPIES WHEN THEY CAME.
SHE KNEW THE LAND WAS FULL OF BLOODSHED AND INJUSTICE AND THAT THESE ONES SOUGHT TO DO JUSTICE, LOVE MERCY AND WALK HUMBLY BEFORE GOD.
I AM A CHILD OF GOD BUT THAT IS NOT THE ONLY WAY I COULD DEFINE MYSELF.
"I WAS A CHILD OF GOD UNDER A POLITICAL SYSTEM OF A MAN WILLING TO EXTERMINATE MILLIONS WITHOUT ANY OTHER REASON THAN PREJUDICE AND AMBITION."
"THAT IS WHY I JOINED THE UNDERGROUND INTELLIGENCE TO HAVE YOU REMOVED."

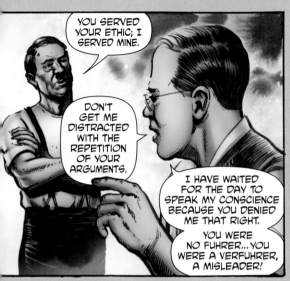

YOU SERVED YOUR ETHIC; I SERVED MINE.

DON'T GET ME DISTRACTED WITH THE REPETITION OF YOUR ARGUMENTS.

I HAVE WAITED FOR THE DAY TO SPEAK MY CONSCIENCE BECAUSE YOU DENIED ME THAT RIGHT.

YOU WERE NO FUHRER... YOU WERE A VERFUHRER, A MISLEADER!

YES, I REMEMBER HOW YOU USED THAT WORD IN ONE OF YOUR LITTLE SERMONS. I STOPPED YOU AND THAT WAS SO FUNNY TO ME.

WE PULLED THE PLUG ON YOU IN THE MIDDLE OF YOUR SERMON.

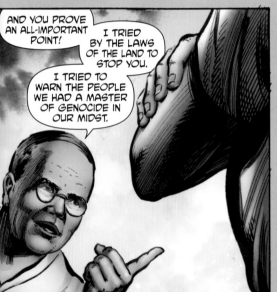

AND YOU PROVE AN ALL-IMPORTANT POINT!

I TRIED BY THE LAWS OF THE LAND TO STOP YOU.

I TRIED TO WARN THE PEOPLE WE HAD A MASTER OF GENOCIDE IN OUR MIDST.

"I REMEMBER THAT DAY MY BROTHER-IN-LAW, HANS, READ ME THE VERSE FROM MATTHEW 26 THAT 'ALL WHO DRAW THE SWORD WILL DIE BY THE SWORD.'"

"AND YOU CERTAINLY DID."

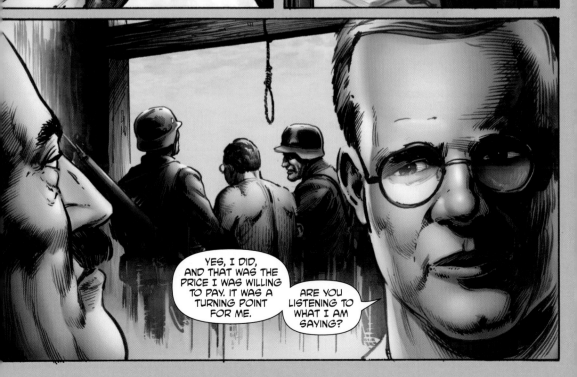

YES, I DID, AND THAT WAS THE PRICE I WAS WILLING TO PAY. IT WAS A TURNING POINT FOR ME.

ARE YOU LISTENING TO WHAT I AM SAYING?

I AM LISTENING...

BUT JESUS, IF EVERYTHING I SAY CAN BE USED AGAINST ME, CAN I BE FORGIVEN IF I CHOOSE TO REPENT?

YOU WILL HAVE YOUR ANSWER IN MOST UNCERTAIN TERMS. DIETRICH, CONTINUE...

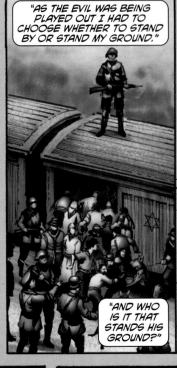

"AS THE EVIL WAS BEING PLAYED OUT I HAD TO CHOOSE WHETHER TO STAND BY OR STAND MY GROUND."

"AND WHO IS IT THAT STANDS HIS GROUND?"

"NOT THE RATIONALIST. HE THINKS A SMALL DOSE OF REASON WILL PUT THE WORLD ARIGHT. BUT SOON HE IS DISAPPOINTED BY THE IRRATIONALITY OF THE WORLD."

"NOT THE MORAL PURIST. THE POWER OF EVIL TRAPS HIM INTO NONESSENTIALS TILL EVERYTHING BECOMES DEFINED BUT WITH NO POWER TO ACT."

"NOT THE MAN OF CONSCIENCE. EVEN IN THE END HE BECOMES CONTENT WITH A SALVED CONSCIENCE RATHER THAN A CLEAR ONE AS EVIL DECEIVES HIM AS WELL."

DUTY THEN SEEMS THE OTHER OPTION. BUT DUTY FINDS CONFLICTS WITH SO MANY TO WHOM HE OWES SOME ALLEGIANCE AND ENDS UP GIVING THE DEVIL HIS DUE.

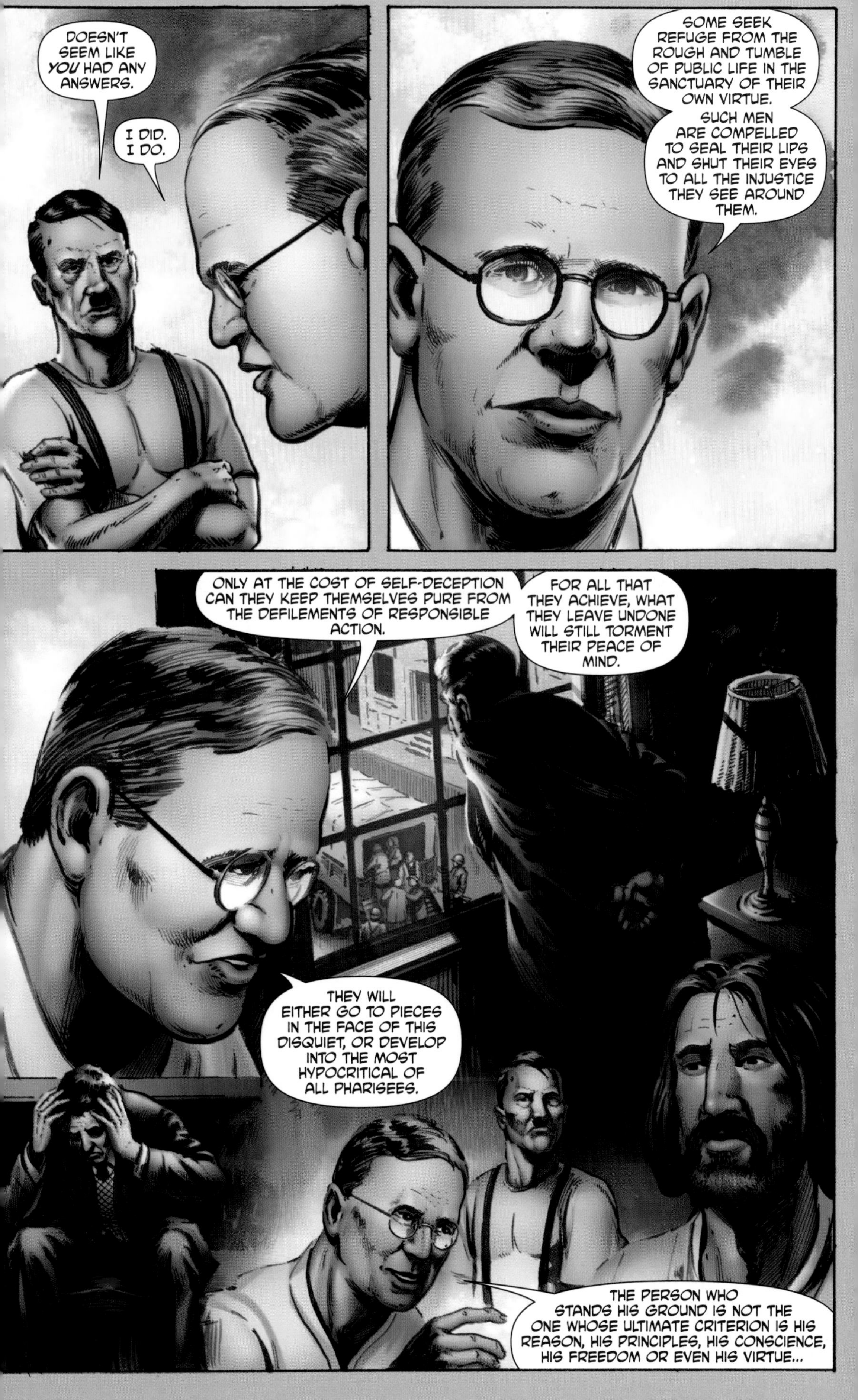
DOESN'T SEEM LIKE *YOU* HAD ANY ANSWERS.
I DID. I DO.
SOME SEEK REFUGE FROM THE ROUGH AND TUMBLE OF PUBLIC LIFE IN THE SANCTUARY OF THEIR OWN VIRTUE.
SUCH MEN ARE COMPELLED TO SEAL THEIR LIPS AND SHUT THEIR EYES TO ALL THE INJUSTICE THEY SEE AROUND THEM.
ONLY AT THE COST OF SELF-DECEPTION CAN THEY KEEP THEMSELVES PURE FROM THE DEFILEMENTS OF RESPONSIBLE ACTION.
FOR ALL THAT THEY ACHIEVE, WHAT THEY LEAVE UNDONE WILL STILL TORMENT THEIR PEACE OF MIND.
THEY WILL EITHER GO TO PIECES IN THE FACE OF THIS DISQUIET, OR DEVELOP INTO THE MOST HYPOCRITICAL OF ALL PHARISEES.
THE PERSON WHO STANDS HIS GROUND IS NOT THE ONE WHOSE ULTIMATE CRITERION IS HIS REASON, HIS PRINCIPLES, HIS CONSCIENCE, HIS FREEDOM OR EVEN HIS VIRTUE...

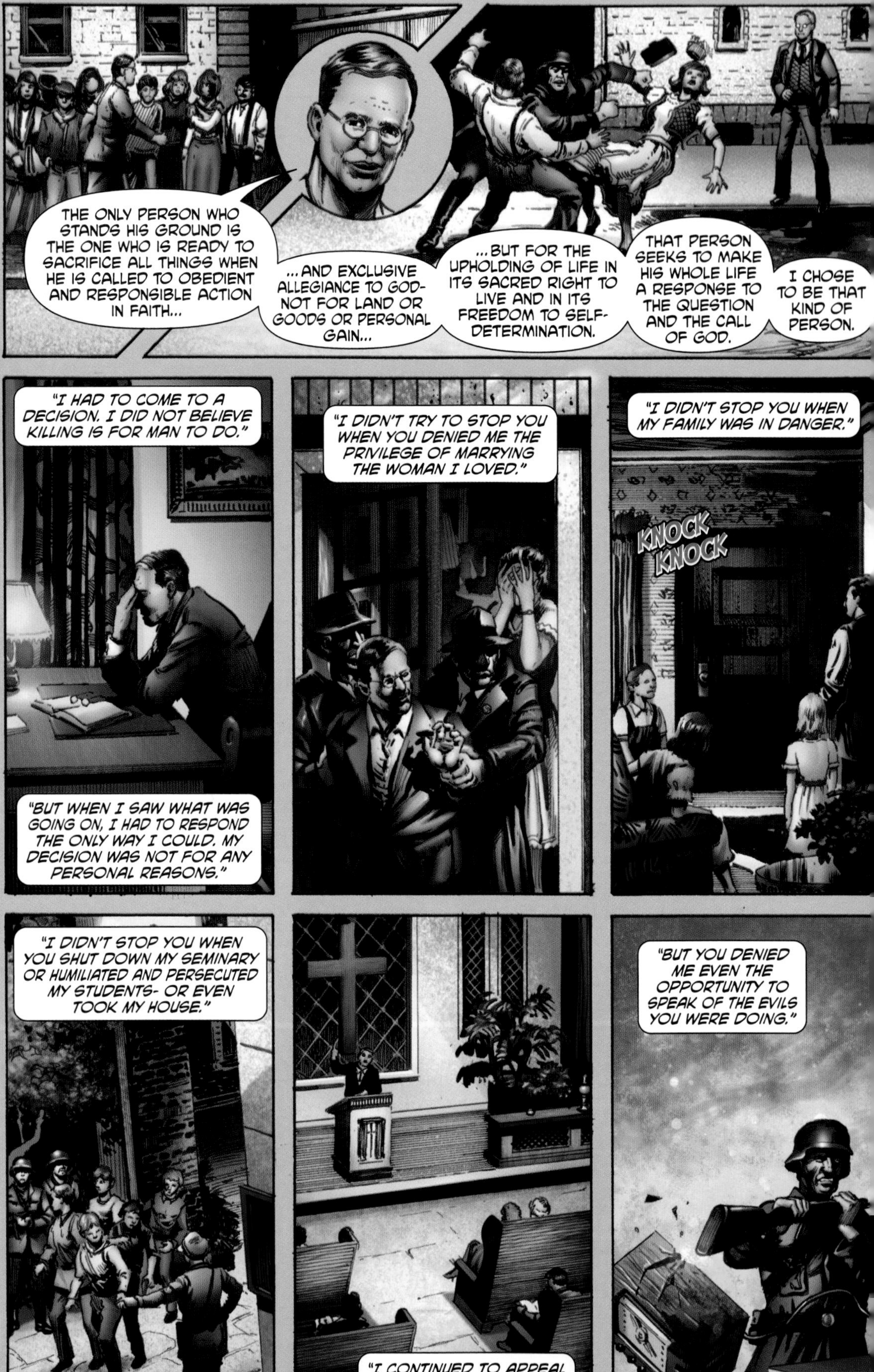

THE ONLY PERSON WHO STANDS HIS GROUND IS THE ONE WHO IS READY TO SACRIFICE ALL THINGS WHEN HE IS CALLED TO OBEDIENT AND RESPONSIBLE ACTION IN FAITH...
...AND EXCLUSIVE ALLEGIANCE TO GOD- NOT FOR LAND OR GOODS OR PERSONAL GAIN...
...BUT FOR THE UPHOLDING OF LIFE IN ITS SACRED RIGHT TO LIVE AND IN ITS FREEDOM TO SELF-DETERMINATION.
THAT PERSON SEEKS TO MAKE HIS WHOLE LIFE A RESPONSE TO THE QUESTION AND THE CALL OF GOD.
I CHOSE TO BE THAT KIND OF PERSON.
"I HAD TO COME TO A DECISION. I DID NOT BELIEVE KILLING IS FOR MAN TO DO."
"BUT WHEN I SAW WHAT WAS GOING ON, I HAD TO RESPOND THE ONLY WAY I COULD. MY DECISION WAS NOT FOR ANY PERSONAL REASONS."
"I DIDN'T TRY TO STOP YOU WHEN YOU DENIED ME THE PRIVILEGE OF MARRYING THE WOMAN I LOVED."
"I DIDN'T STOP YOU WHEN MY FAMILY WAS IN DANGER."
KNOCK KNOCK
"I DIDN'T STOP YOU WHEN YOU SHUT DOWN MY SEMINARY OR HUMILIATED AND PERSECUTED MY STUDENTS- OR EVEN TOOK MY HOUSE."
"I CONTINUED TO APPEAL TO THE CONSCIENCE OF THE PEOPLE TO REMOVE YOU FROM OFFICE."
"BUT YOU DENIED ME EVEN THE OPPORTUNITY TO SPEAK OF THE EVILS YOU WERE DOING."

WHEN YOU SILENCED THOSE WHO SPOKE OUT FOR THE PRESERVATION OF LIFE, YOU CROSSED A LINE.

THAT IS NOT GOD'S WAY; THAT IS NOT THE WAY OF ALLOWING US TO BE TRULY HUMAN.

"I DID NOT TRY TO KILL THOSE WHO WERE YOUR INSTRUMENTS. I DID NOT GO AND KILL INNOCENT PEOPLE."

"I WOULD HAVE RATHER TRIED YOU IN THE COURTS, BUT YOU TOOK CONTROL OF THE COURTS."

"I WOULD HAVE RATHER APPEALED TO YOUR MORAL REASONING, BUT YOU REJECTED MORAL REASONING."

"I WOULD HAVE RATHER TRIED YOU BY THE LAW OF THE LAND, BUT YOU ABOLISHED IT AND MADE YOURSELF THE SUPREME LAW."

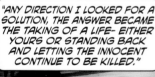

"ANY DIRECTION I LOOKED FOR A SOLUTION, THE ANSWER BECAME THE TAKING OF A LIFE- EITHER YOURS OR STANDING BACK AND LETTING THE INNOCENT CONTINUE TO BE KILLED."

"IT WAS NOT SO MUCH THAT THE CHOICE WAS EVIL BUT THAT TO LEAVE THE SITUATION UNCHECKED WAS EVIL."

"I SOUGHT THE CROSS EACH DAY AND WEPT FOR THE COURAGE TO DO WHAT WAS RIGHT."

"FOR WHAT WOULD GUARD THE SACREDNESS OF LIFE FOR ALL, AND TO BE FORGIVEN IF I WAS WRONG."

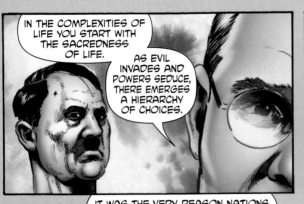

IN THE COMPLEXITIES OF LIFE YOU START WITH THE SACREDNESS OF LIFE.

AS EVIL INVADES AND POWERS SEDUCE, THERE EMERGES A HIERARCHY OF CHOICES.

I RESTED ON GOD'S POWER TO RAISE THE DEAD AND ON MY WILLINGNESS TO PROTECT HUMAN LIFE AS NOT MERELY A POLITICAL IDEOLOGY.

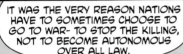

IT WAS THE VERY REASON NATIONS HAVE TO SOMETIMES CHOOSE TO GO TO WAR- TO STOP THE KILLING, NOT TO BECOME AUTONOMOUS OVER ALL LAW.

"THE WORLD WAS NOT COMING TO OUR RESCUE. THE WORLD LOOKED ON FOR TOO LONG. THE WORLD LOOKED ON WHILE MILLIONS SCREAMED IN GAS CHAMBERS."

"I COULD NOT LOOK ON ANY LONGER."

"I WOULD NOT GO ON A RAMPAGE."

"IT WAS ONLY YOU THAT NEEDED TO BE STOPPED."

"I WAS WILLING TO DIE FOR THAT CAUSE TO SAVE HUMANITY."

"WHEN YOU SENT ME TO THE GALLOWS I WAS NOT AFRAID."

"I HAD DONE WHAT WAS RIGHT, THE ONLY THING I COULD DO TO SAVE MILLIONS."

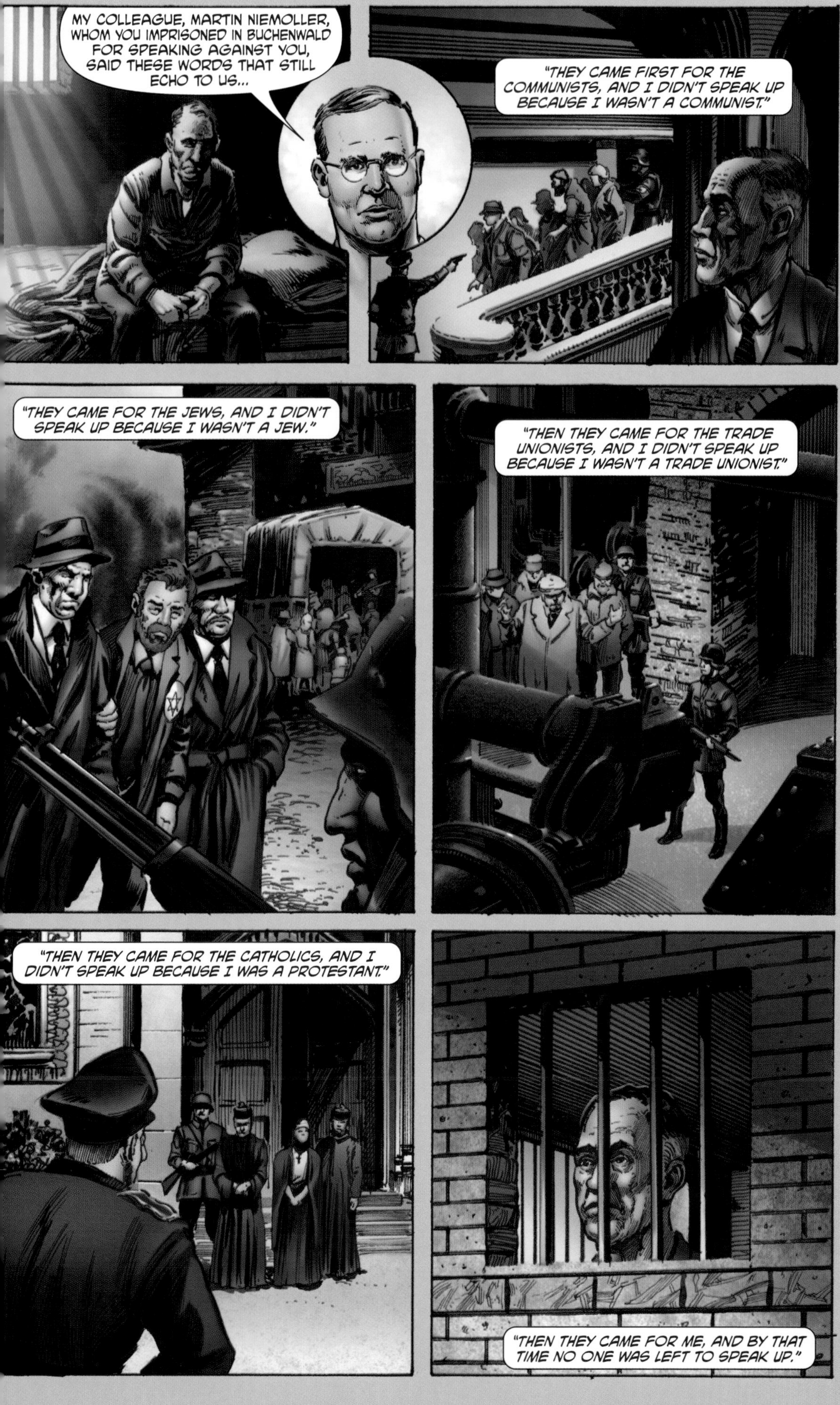
MY COLLEAGUE, MARTIN NIEMOLLER, WHOM YOU IMPRISONED IN BUCHENWALD FOR SPEAKING AGAINST YOU, SAID THESE WORDS THAT STILL ECHO TO US...
"THEY CAME FIRST FOR THE COMMUNISTS, AND I DIDN'T SPEAK UP BECAUSE I WASN'T A COMMUNIST."
"THEY CAME FOR THE JEWS, AND I DIDN'T SPEAK UP BECAUSE I WASN'T A JEW."
"THEN THEY CAME FOR THE TRADE UNIONISTS, AND I DIDN'T SPEAK UP BECAUSE I WASN'T A TRADE UNIONIST."
"THEN THEY CAME FOR THE CATHOLICS, AND I DIDN'T SPEAK UP BECAUSE I WAS A PROTESTANT."
"THEN THEY CAME FOR ME, AND BY THAT TIME NO ONE WAS LEFT TO SPEAK UP."

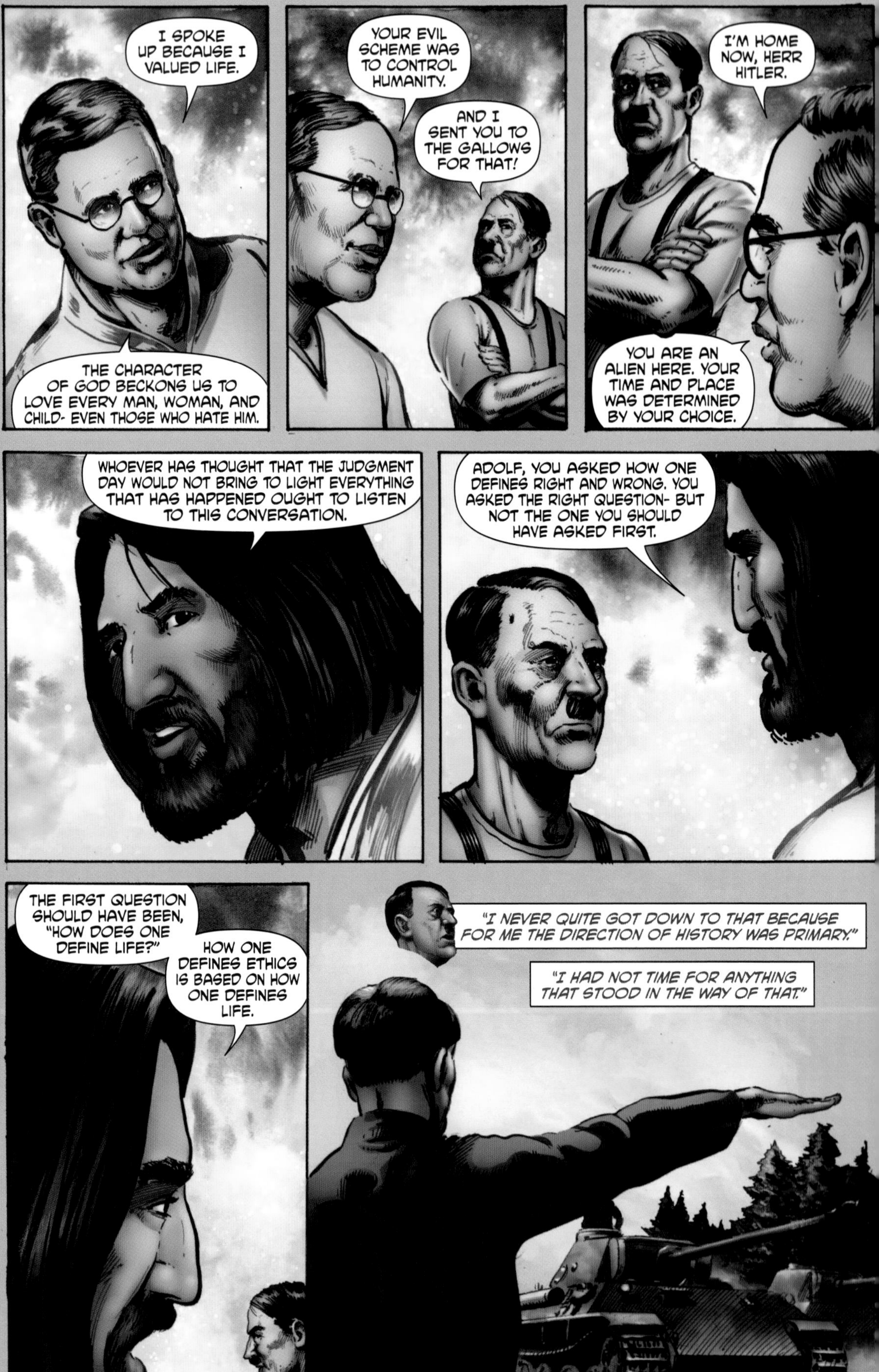

I SPOKE UP BECAUSE I VALUED LIFE.
THE CHARACTER OF GOD BECKONS US TO LOVE EVERY MAN, WOMAN, AND CHILD- EVEN THOSE WHO HATE HIM.
YOUR EVIL SCHEME WAS TO CONTROL HUMANITY.
AND I SENT YOU TO THE GALLOWS FOR THAT!
I'M HOME NOW, HERR HITLER.
YOU ARE AN ALIEN HERE. YOUR TIME AND PLACE WAS DETERMINED BY YOUR CHOICE.
WHOEVER HAS THOUGHT THAT THE JUDGMENT DAY WOULD NOT BRING TO LIGHT EVERYTHING THAT HAS HAPPENED OUGHT TO LISTEN TO THIS CONVERSATION.
ADOLF, YOU ASKED HOW ONE DEFINES RIGHT AND WRONG. YOU ASKED THE RIGHT QUESTION- BUT NOT THE ONE YOU SHOULD HAVE ASKED FIRST.
THE FIRST QUESTION SHOULD HAVE BEEN, "HOW DOES ONE DEFINE LIFE?"
HOW ONE DEFINES ETHICS IS BASED ON HOW ONE DEFINES LIFE.
"I NEVER QUITE GOT DOWN TO THAT BECAUSE FOR ME THE DIRECTION OF HISTORY WAS PRIMARY."
"I HAD NOT TIME FOR ANYTHING THAT STOOD IN THE WAY OF THAT."

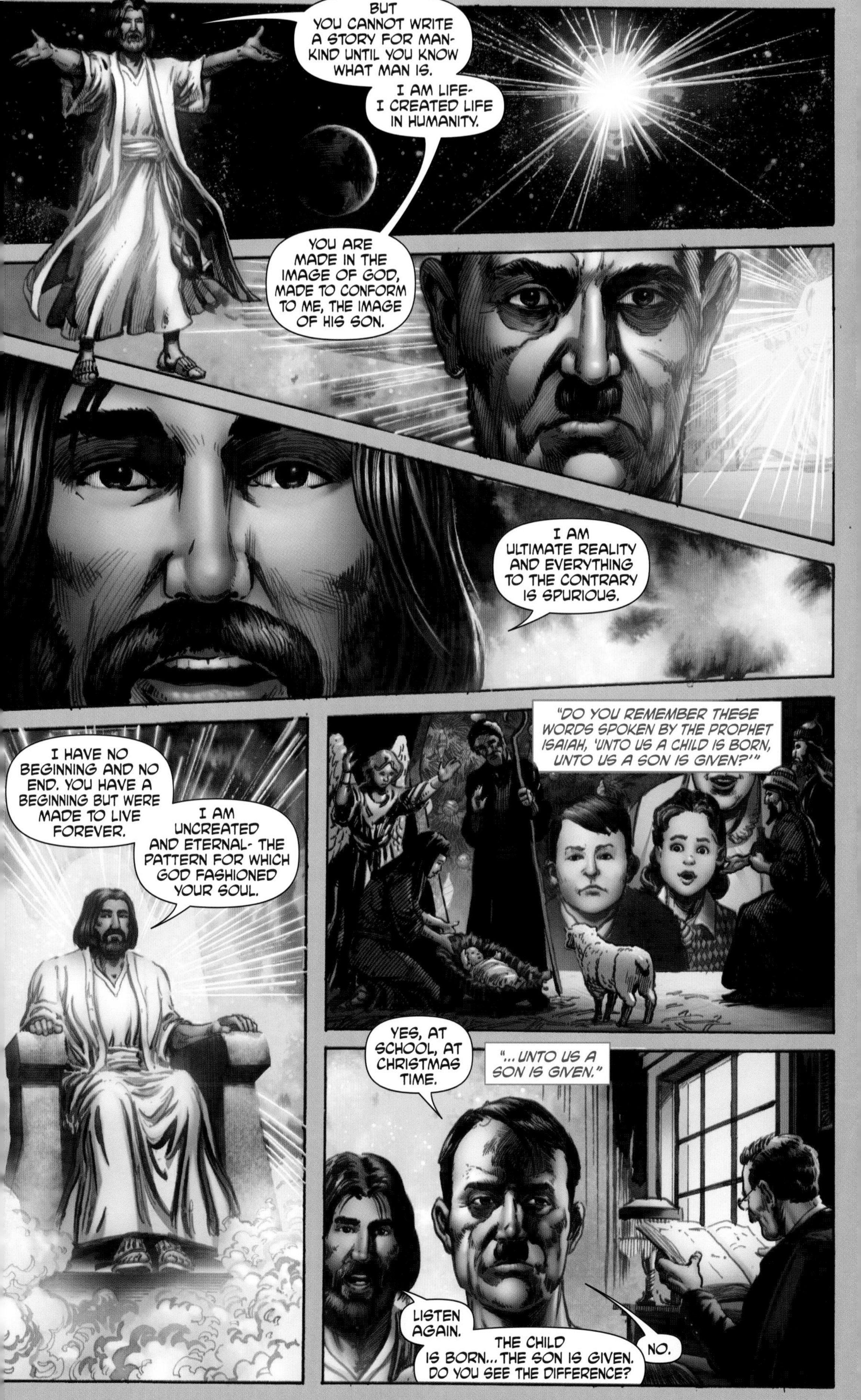
BUT YOU CANNOT WRITE A STORY FOR MAN-KIND UNTIL YOU KNOW WHAT MAN IS.
I AM LIFE- I CREATED LIFE IN HUMANITY.
YOU ARE MADE IN THE IMAGE OF GOD, MADE TO CONFORM TO ME, THE IMAGE OF HIS SON.
I AM ULTIMATE REALITY AND EVERYTHING TO THE CONTRARY IS SPURIOUS.
I HAVE NO BEGINNING AND NO END. YOU HAVE A BEGINNING BUT WERE MADE TO LIVE FOREVER.
I AM UNCREATED AND ETERNAL- THE PATTERN FOR WHICH GOD FASHIONED YOUR SOUL.
"DO YOU REMEMBER THESE WORDS SPOKEN BY THE PROPHET ISAIAH, 'UNTO US A CHILD IS BORN, UNTO US A SON IS GIVEN?'"
YES, AT SCHOOL, AT CHRISTMAS TIME.
"...UNTO US A SON IS GIVEN."
LISTEN AGAIN.
THE CHILD IS BORN... THE SON IS GIVEN. DO YOU SEE THE DIFFERENCE?
NO.

"THE SON WAS NOT BORN."

"I AM THE SON *AND* I ETERNALLY EXISTED IN RELATIONSHIP WITH MY FATHER."

"YOU *READ* THEM IN THE MONUMENT AT LINZ."

"IN MY WORD, THE BIBLE, YOU WILL READ THAT THERE IS ONENESS IN THE GODHEAD- THE FATHER, THE SON AND THE HOLY SPIRIT."

"GOD IS A BEING IN A RELATIONSHIP."

THIS IS SO UNIQUE AND SO TRUE THAT IT IS THE GREATEST MYSTERY IN ALL OF FAITH.

ISN'T THIS THE VERY TRUTH MOHAMMED DENIED?

YES, HE DENIED IT, AND HIS FOLLOWERS HAVE NEVER BEEN TAUGHT THE TRUTH ABOUT IT.

ADOLF, WHAT HAS BEEN THE GREATEST SEARCH IN PHILOSOPHY?

THE GREATEST SEARCH IN CULTURE?

THE GREATEST STRUGGLE WITHIN THE HUMAN HEART?

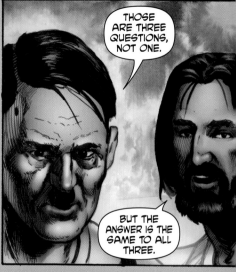

THOSE ARE THREE QUESTIONS, NOT ONE.

BUT THE ANSWER IS THE SAME TO ALL THREE.

I SAY THE GREATEST SEARCH IS FOR SELF-UNDERSTANDING. SOME, LIKE ME, ARE SUPERIOR IN THEIR SELF-UNDERSTANDING.

I WILL TELL YOU HOW YOU HAVE FAILED AND WHAT IS IN GOD'S HEART.

THE GREATEST SEARCH IN PHILOSOPHY, CULTURE AND THE HUMAN HEART IS FOR UNITY WITHIN DIVERSITY.

THE GREEKS SOUGHT THIS, DIDN'T THEY?

AND THAT IS WHY THE UNIVERSITY WAS FORMED, TO FIND UNITY IN DIVERSITY.

"I REMEMBER WHEN TEACHING IN NEW YORK, SEEING ON EVERY COIN 'E PLURIBUS UNUM'- OUT OF MANY, ONE- AND OFTEN WISHING THAT COULD BE TRUE FOR THE WHOLE WORLD."

"LORD, HOW DO YOU SPEAK TO THIS? MY HEART IS EAGER."

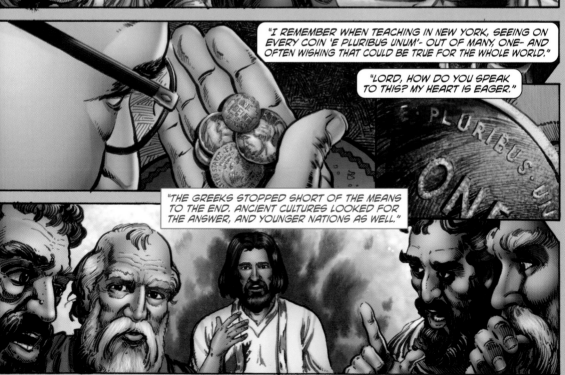

"THE GREEKS STOPPED SHORT OF THE MEANS TO THE END. ANCIENT CULTURES LOOKED FOR THE ANSWER, AND YOUNGER NATIONS AS WELL."

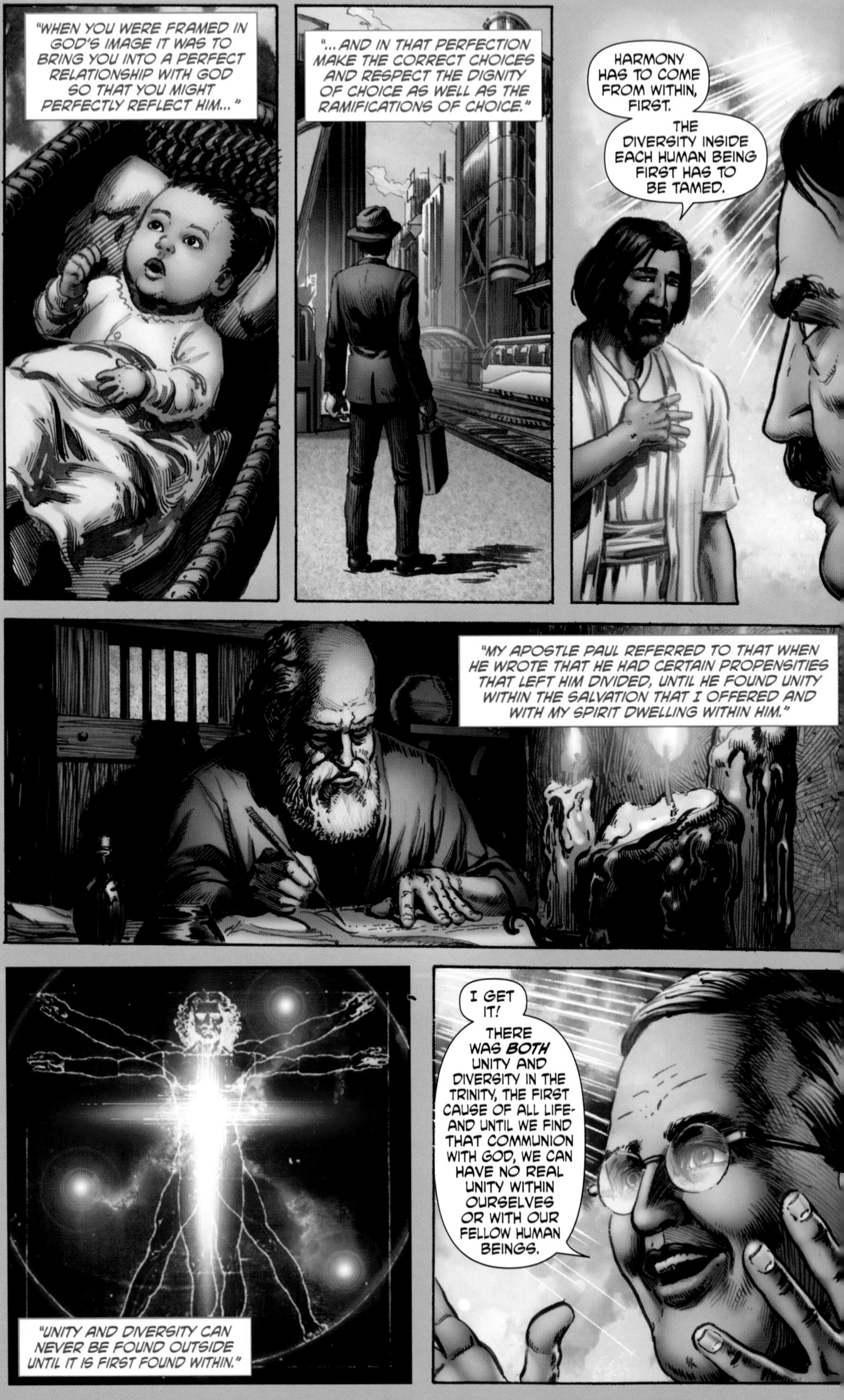
"WHEN YOU WERE FRAMED IN GOD'S IMAGE IT WAS TO BRING YOU INTO A PERFECT RELATIONSHIP WITH GOD SO THAT YOU MIGHT PERFECTLY REFLECT HIM..."
"...AND IN THAT PERFECTION MAKE THE CORRECT CHOICES AND RESPECT THE DIGNITY OF CHOICE AS WELL AS THE RAMIFICATIONS OF CHOICE."
HARMONY HAS TO COME FROM WITHIN, FIRST.
THE DIVERSITY INSIDE EACH HUMAN BEING FIRST HAS TO BE TAMED.
"MY APOSTLE PAUL REFERRED TO THAT WHEN HE WROTE THAT HE HAD CERTAIN PROPENSITIES THAT LEFT HIM DIVIDED, UNTIL HE FOUND UNITY WITHIN THE SALVATION THAT I OFFERED AND WITH MY SPIRIT DWELLING WITHIN HIM."
"UNITY AND DIVERSITY CAN NEVER BE FOUND OUTSIDE UNTIL IT IS FIRST FOUND WITHIN."
I GET IT!
THERE WAS ***BOTH*** UNITY AND DIVERSITY IN THE TRINITY, THE FIRST CAUSE OF ALL LIFE-AND UNTIL WE FIND THAT COMMUNION WITH GOD, WE CAN HAVE NO REAL UNITY WITHIN OURSELVES OR WITH OUR FELLOW HUMAN BEINGS.

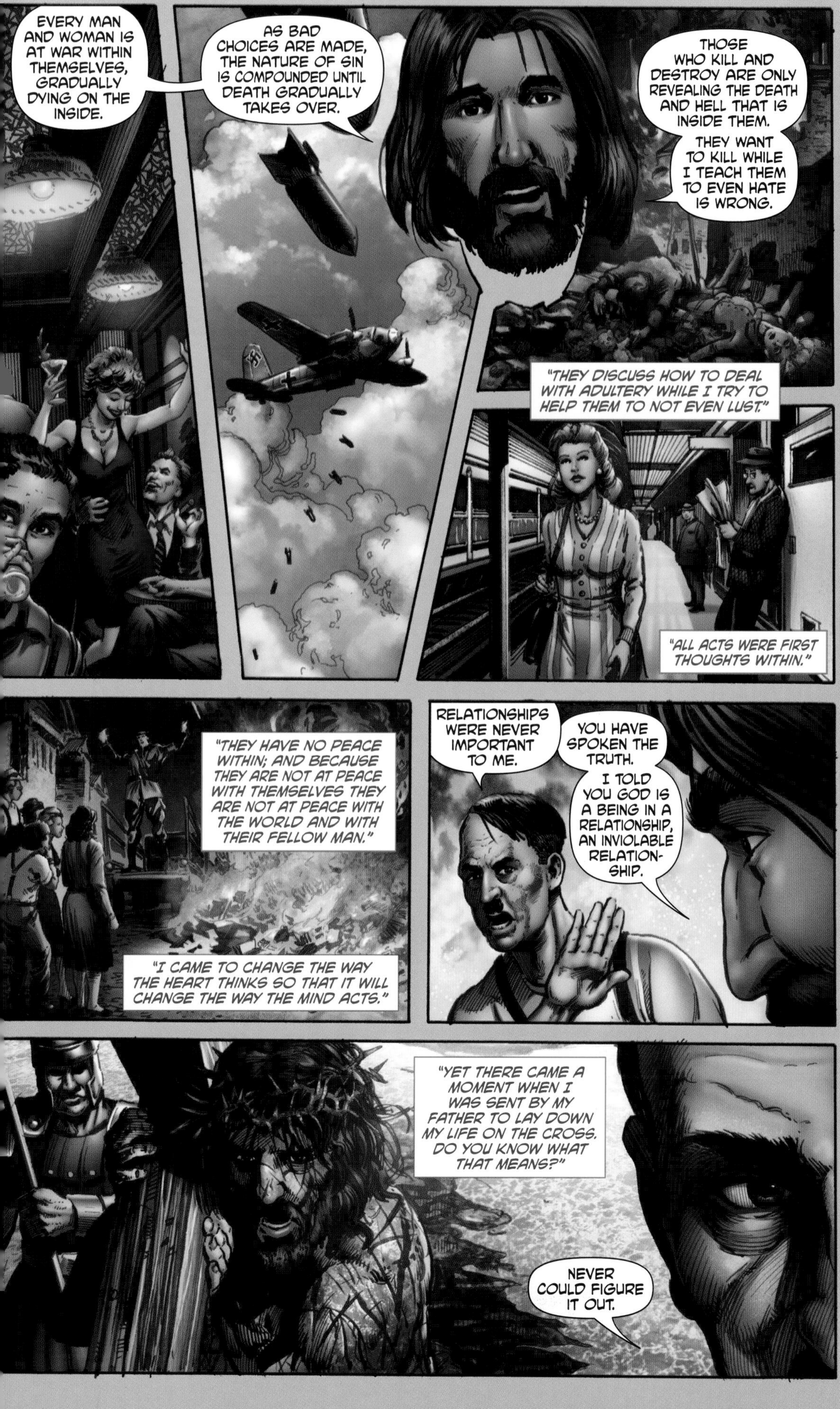
EVERY MAN AND WOMAN IS AT WAR WITHIN THEMSELVES, GRADUALLY DYING ON THE INSIDE.
AS BAD CHOICES ARE MADE, THE NATURE OF SIN IS COMPOUNDED UNTIL DEATH GRADUALLY TAKES OVER.
THOSE WHO KILL AND DESTROY ARE ONLY REVEALING THE DEATH AND HELL THAT IS INSIDE THEM.
THEY WANT TO KILL WHILE I TEACH THEM TO EVEN HATE IS WRONG.
"THEY DISCUSS HOW TO DEAL WITH ADULTERY WHILE I TRY TO HELP THEM TO NOT EVEN LUST."
"ALL ACTS WERE FIRST THOUGHTS WITHIN."
"THEY HAVE NO PEACE WITHIN; AND BECAUSE THEY ARE NOT AT PEACE WITH THEMSELVES THEY ARE NOT AT PEACE WITH THE WORLD AND WITH THEIR FELLOW MAN."
"I CAME TO CHANGE THE WAY THE HEART THINKS SO THAT IT WILL CHANGE THE WAY THE MIND ACTS."
RELATIONSHIPS WERE NEVER IMPORTANT TO ME.
YOU HAVE SPOKEN THE TRUTH.
I TOLD YOU GOD IS A BEING IN A RELATIONSHIP, AN INVIOLABLE RELATION-SHIP.
"YET THERE CAME A MOMENT WHEN I WAS SENT BY MY FATHER TO LAY DOWN MY LIFE ON THE CROSS. DO YOU KNOW WHAT THAT MEANS?"
NEVER COULD FIGURE IT OUT.

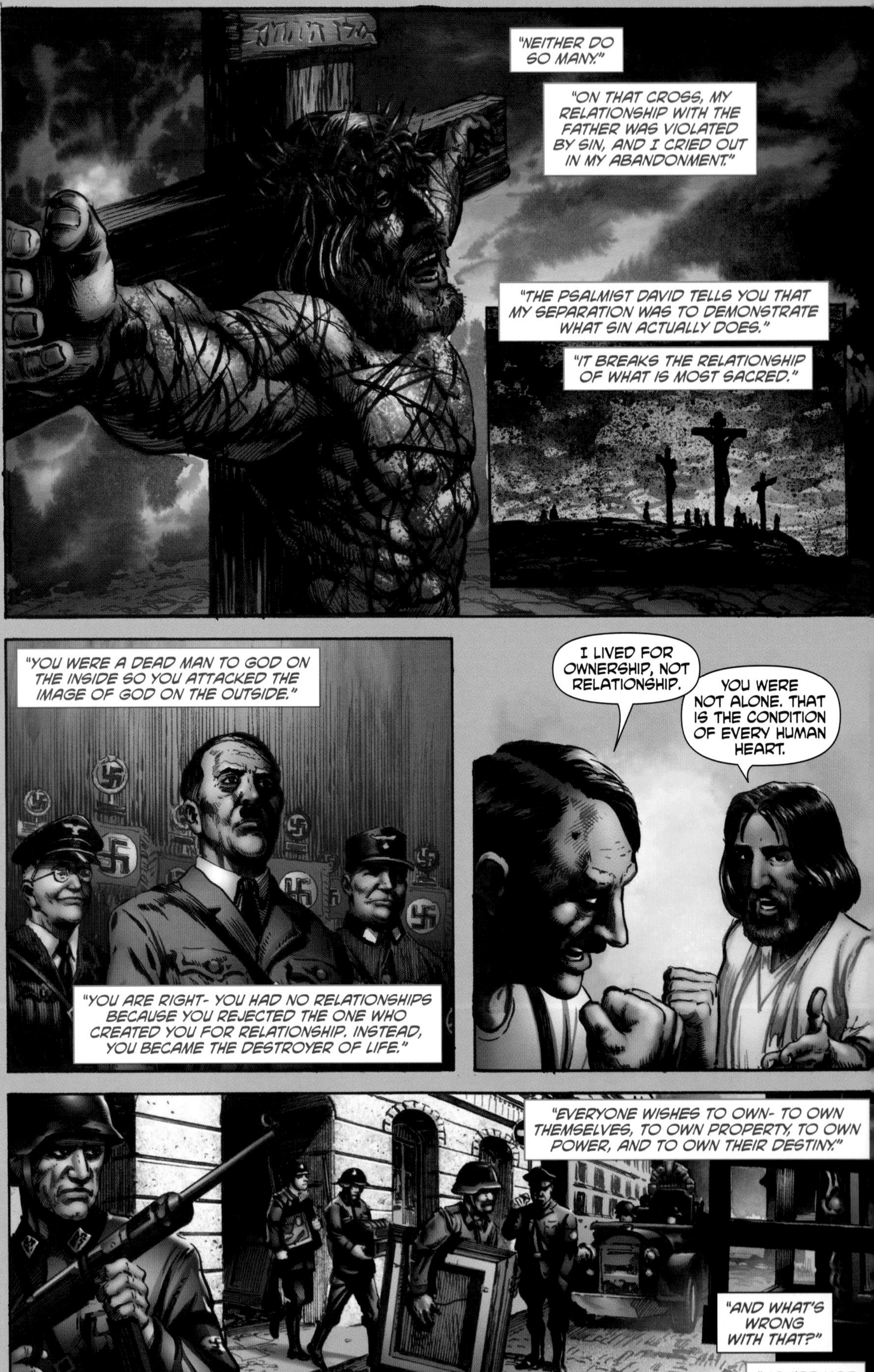
"NEITHER DO SO MANY."
"ON THAT CROSS, MY RELATIONSHIP WITH THE FATHER WAS VIOLATED BY SIN, AND I CRIED OUT IN MY ABANDONMENT."
"THE PSALMIST DAVID TELLS YOU THAT MY SEPARATION WAS TO DEMONSTRATE WHAT SIN ACTUALLY DOES."
"IT BREAKS THE RELATIONSHIP OF WHAT IS MOST SACRED."
"YOU WERE A DEAD MAN TO GOD ON THE INSIDE SO YOU ATTACKED THE IMAGE OF GOD ON THE OUTSIDE."
"YOU ARE RIGHT- YOU HAD NO RELATIONSHIPS BECAUSE YOU REJECTED THE ONE WHO CREATED YOU FOR RELATIONSHIP. INSTEAD, YOU BECAME THE DESTROYER OF LIFE."
I LIVED FOR OWNERSHIP, NOT RELATIONSHIP.
YOU WERE NOT ALONE. THAT IS THE CONDITION OF EVERY HUMAN HEART.
"EVERYONE WISHES TO OWN- TO OWN THEMSELVES, TO OWN PROPERTY, TO OWN POWER, AND TO OWN THEIR DESTINY."
"AND WHAT'S WRONG WITH THAT?"
"YOU'RE NOT LISTENING."

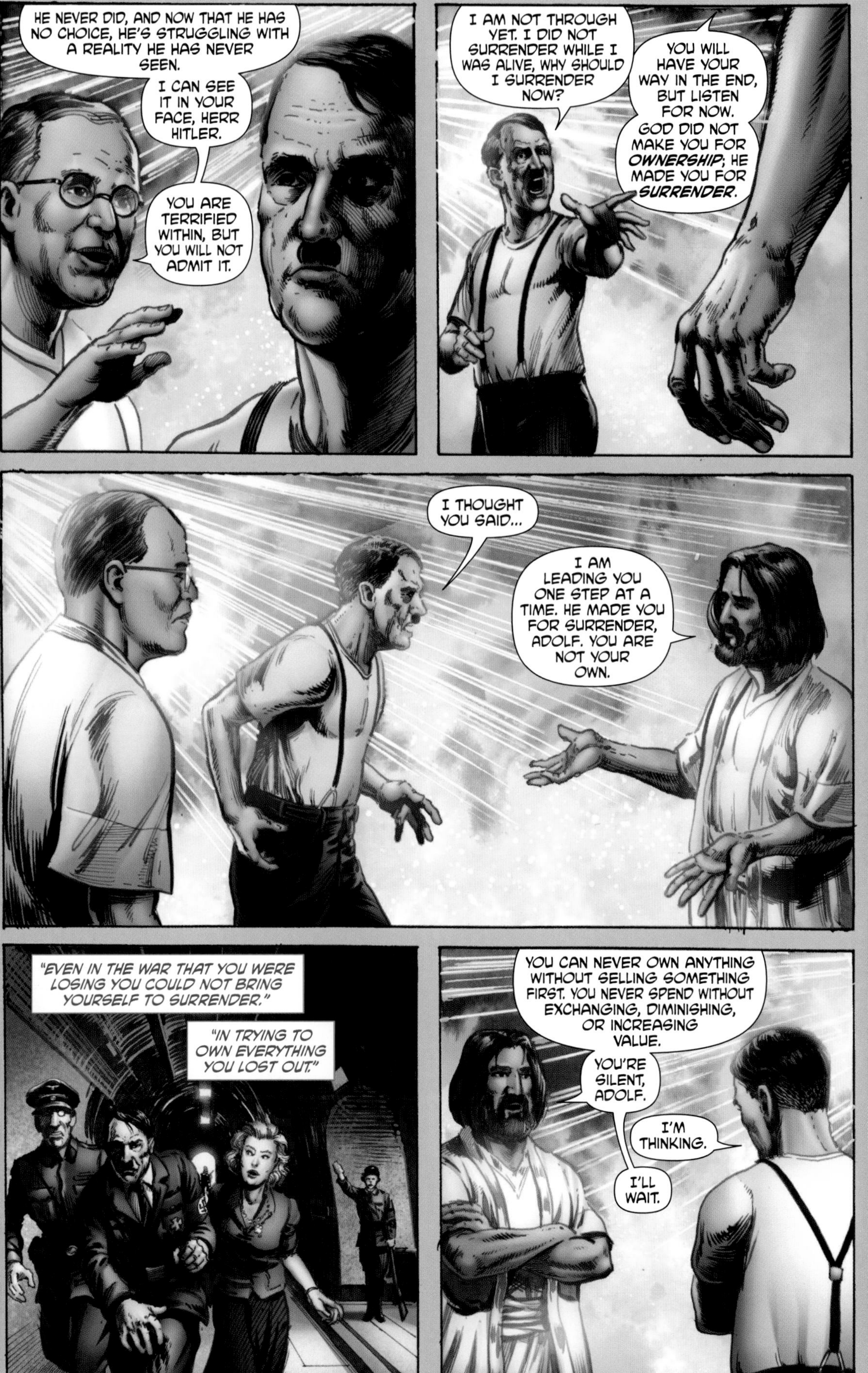
HE NEVER DID, AND NOW THAT HE HAS NO CHOICE, HE'S STRUGGLING WITH A REALITY HE HAS NEVER SEEN.
I CAN SEE IT IN YOUR FACE, HERR HITLER.
YOU ARE TERRIFIED WITHIN, BUT YOU WILL NOT ADMIT IT.
I AM NOT THROUGH YET. I DID NOT SURRENDER WHILE I WAS ALIVE, WHY SHOULD I SURRENDER NOW?
YOU WILL HAVE YOUR WAY IN THE END, BUT LISTEN FOR NOW. GOD DID NOT MAKE YOU FOR OWNERSHIP; HE MADE YOU FOR SURRENDER.
I THOUGHT YOU SAID...
I AM LEADING YOU ONE STEP AT A TIME. HE MADE YOU FOR SURRENDER, ADOLF. YOU ARE NOT YOUR OWN.
"EVEN IN THE WAR THAT YOU WERE LOSING YOU COULD NOT BRING YOURSELF TO SURRENDER."
"IN TRYING TO OWN EVERYTHING YOU LOST OUT."
YOU CAN NEVER OWN ANYTHING WITHOUT SELLING SOMETHING FIRST. YOU NEVER SPEND WITHOUT EXCHANGING, DIMINISHING, OR INCREASING VALUE.
YOU'RE SILENT, ADOLF.
I'M THINKING.
I'LL WAIT.

YOU NEVER SPEND WITHOUT EXCHANGING, DIMINISHING, OR INCREASING VALUE?

YES. AND LIFE IS OF ESSENTIAL VALUE.

THAT'S WHERE I THINK... THAT'S WHERE MY DEFINITIONS DEPART FROM YOURS.

"THAT IS EXACTLY THE TRUTH. YOU REDUCED THE VALUE OF HUMAN LIFE TO NOTHING MORE THAN MERE MATTER THAT STOOD IN YOUR WAY."

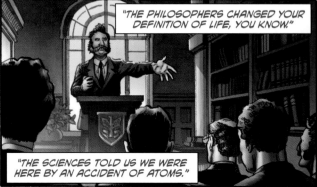

"THE PHILOSOPHERS CHANGED YOUR DEFINITION OF LIFE, YOU KNOW."

"THE SCIENCES TOLD US WE WERE HERE BY AN ACCIDENT OF ATOMS."

"I WAS PROUD OF MY FELLOW COUNTRYMAN NIETZSCHE— AND I PRESENTED HIS WORKS TO STALIN AND MUSSOLINI."

"YOU BOUGHT INTO A LIE."

"NIETZSCHE SAID THE WHOLE BUSINESS OF HUMAN BEINGS BEING EQUAL IS A LIE CONCOCTED BY INFERIOR PEOPLE."

"THE REAL TRUTH ABOUT 'OBJECTIVE TRUTH' IS THAT THE LATTER IS A FICTION."

HE FURTHER SAID THAT TRUTH MUST FIRST BE EXPRESSED IN LANGUAGE, AND LANGUAGE IS NOTORIOUSLY UNABLE TO GET US TO REALITY.

THAT'S NOT ALL HE SAID.

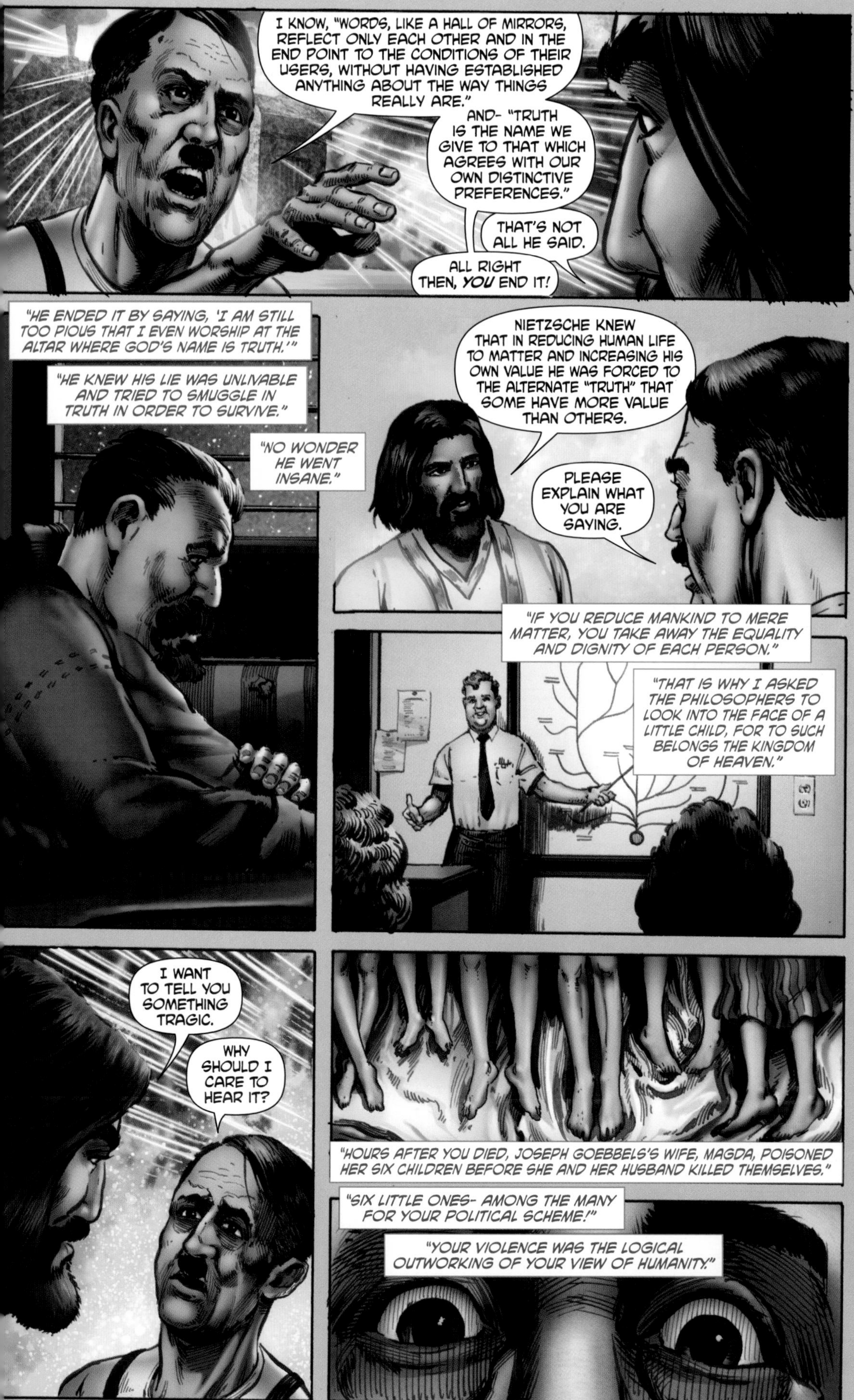
I KNOW, "WORDS, LIKE A HALL OF MIRRORS, REFLECT ONLY EACH OTHER AND IN THE END POINT TO THE CONDITIONS OF THEIR USERS, WITHOUT HAVING ESTABLISHED ANYTHING ABOUT THE WAY THINGS REALLY ARE."
AND- "TRUTH IS THE NAME WE GIVE TO THAT WHICH AGREES WITH OUR OWN DISTINCTIVE PREFERENCES."
THAT'S NOT ALL HE SAID.
ALL RIGHT THEN, *YOU* END IT!
"HE ENDED IT BY SAYING, 'I AM STILL TOO PIOUS THAT I EVEN WORSHIP AT THE ALTAR WHERE GOD'S NAME IS TRUTH.'"
"HE KNEW HIS LIE WAS UNLIVABLE AND TRIED TO SMUGGLE IN TRUTH IN ORDER TO SURVIVE."
"NO WONDER HE WENT INSANE."
NIETZSCHE KNEW THAT IN REDUCING HUMAN LIFE TO MATTER AND INCREASING HIS OWN VALUE HE WAS FORCED TO THE ALTERNATE "TRUTH" THAT SOME HAVE MORE VALUE THAN OTHERS.
PLEASE EXPLAIN WHAT YOU ARE SAYING.
"IF YOU REDUCE MANKIND TO MERE MATTER, YOU TAKE AWAY THE EQUALITY AND DIGNITY OF EACH PERSON."
"THAT IS WHY I ASKED THE PHILOSOPHERS TO LOOK INTO THE FACE OF A LITTLE CHILD, FOR TO SUCH BELONGS THE KINGDOM OF HEAVEN."
I WANT TO TELL YOU SOMETHING TRAGIC.
WHY SHOULD I CARE TO HEAR IT?
"HOURS AFTER YOU DIED, JOSEPH GOEBBELS'S WIFE, MAGDA, POISONED HER SIX CHILDREN BEFORE SHE AND HER HUSBAND KILLED THEMSELVES."
"SIX LITTLE ONES- AMONG THE MANY FOR YOUR POLITICAL SCHEME!"
"YOUR VIOLENCE WAS THE LOGICAL OUTWORKING OF YOUR VIEW OF HUMANITY."

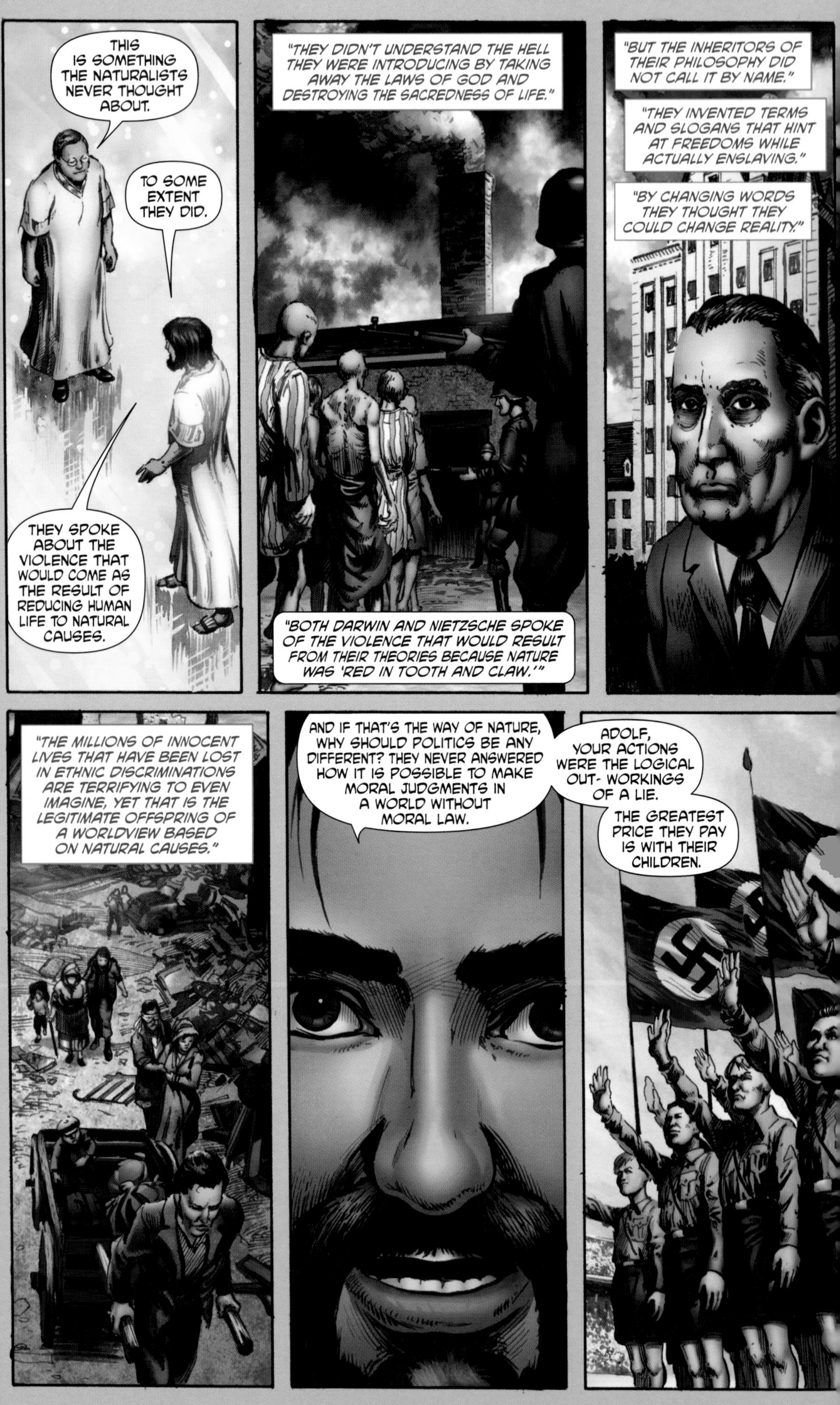
THIS IS SOMETHING THE NATURALISTS NEVER THOUGHT ABOUT.
TO SOME EXTENT THEY DID.
THEY SPOKE ABOUT THE VIOLENCE THAT WOULD COME AS THE RESULT OF REDUCING HUMAN LIFE TO NATURAL CAUSES.
"THEY DIDN'T UNDERSTAND THE HELL THEY WERE INTRODUCING BY TAKING AWAY THE LAWS OF GOD AND DESTROYING THE SACREDNESS OF LIFE."
"BOTH DARWIN AND NIETZSCHE SPOKE OF THE VIOLENCE THAT WOULD RESULT FROM THEIR THEORIES BECAUSE NATURE WAS 'RED IN TOOTH AND CLAW.'"
"BUT THE INHERITORS OF THEIR PHILOSOPHY DID NOT CALL IT BY NAME."
"THEY INVENTED TERMS AND SLOGANS THAT HINT AT FREEDOMS WHILE ACTUALLY ENSLAVING."
"BY CHANGING WORDS THEY THOUGHT THEY COULD CHANGE REALITY."
"THE MILLIONS OF INNOCENT LIVES THAT HAVE BEEN LOST IN ETHNIC DISCRIMINATIONS ARE TERRIFYING TO EVEN IMAGINE, YET THAT IS THE LEGITIMATE OFFSPRING OF A WORLDVIEW BASED ON NATURAL CAUSES."
AND IF THAT'S THE WAY OF NATURE, WHY SHOULD POLITICS BE ANY DIFFERENT? THEY NEVER ANSWERED HOW IT IS POSSIBLE TO MAKE MORAL JUDGMENTS IN A WORLD WITHOUT MORAL LAW.
ADOLF, YOUR ACTIONS WERE THE LOGICAL OUT- WORKINGS OF A LIE.
THE GREATEST PRICE THEY PAY IS WITH THEIR CHILDREN.

JESUS, I HAVE ONE QUESTION FOR YOU.

BY OFFERING HIM FORGIVENESS IF HE REPENTS, ARE YOU GIVING HIM A SECOND CHANCE?

YOU WILL SEE AND UNDERSTAND.

BEFORE I MAKE MY CASE, I MUST ASK A QUESTION.

YOU HAVE YOUR MOMENT NOW.

"YOU CLEARLY TOLD YOUR DISCIPLES THAT POLITICS AND RELIGION DON'T MIX."

"WHY DID YOU LET THE CLERGY PLOT AGAINST ME, THE POLITICAL LEADER?"

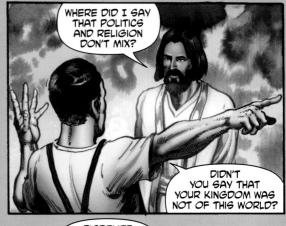

WHERE DID I SAY THAT POLITICS AND RELIGION DON'T MIX?

DIDN'T YOU SAY THAT YOUR KINGDOM WAS NOT OF THIS WORLD?

"I SAID THAT ANY POWER THAT PILATE HAD WAS ONLY TEMPORARY AND PART OF AN ETERNAL PLAN."

"KINGS AND LEADERS DO NOT UNDERSTAND THAT POLITICS AND TRUST IN GOD MUST SPEAK TO EACH OTHER."

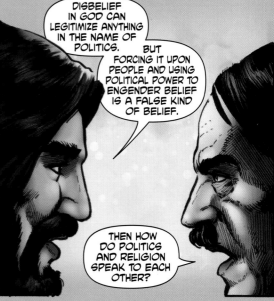

DISBELIEF IN GOD CAN LEGITIMIZE ANYTHING IN THE NAME OF POLITICS.

BUT FORCING IT UPON PEOPLE AND USING POLITICAL POWER TO ENGENDER BELIEF IS A FALSE KIND OF BELIEF.

THEN HOW DO POLITICS AND RELIGION SPEAK TO EACH OTHER?

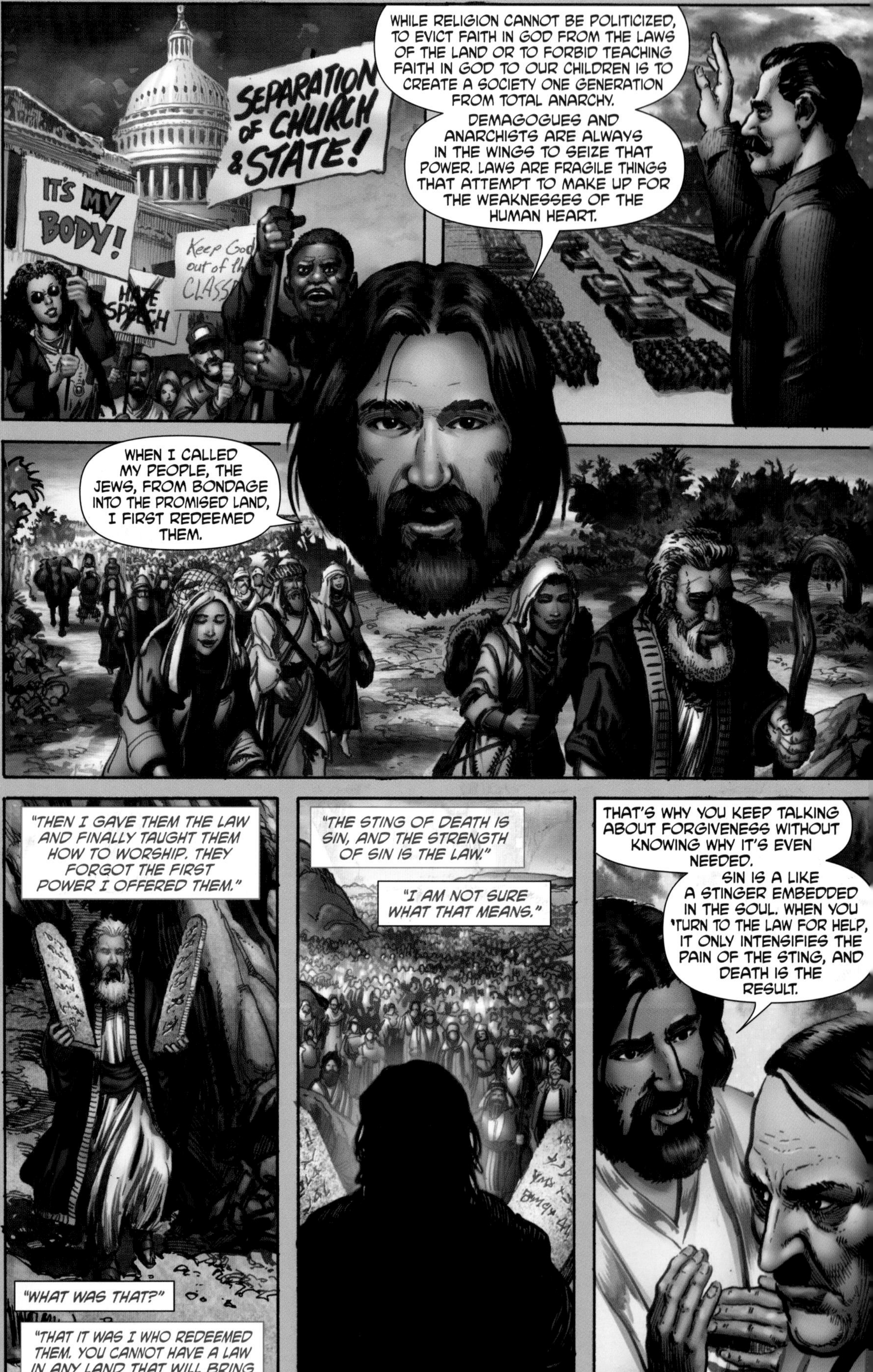
SEPARATION OF CHURCH & STATE!
IT'S MY BODY!
Keep God out of the CLASS
HATE SPEECH
WHILE RELIGION CANNOT BE POLITICIZED, TO EVICT FAITH IN GOD FROM THE LAWS OF THE LAND OR TO FORBID TEACHING FAITH IN GOD TO OUR CHILDREN IS TO CREATE A SOCIETY ONE GENERATION FROM TOTAL ANARCHY.
DEMAGOGUES AND ANARCHISTS ARE ALWAYS IN THE WINGS TO SEIZE THAT POWER. LAWS ARE FRAGILE THINGS THAT ATTEMPT TO MAKE UP FOR THE WEAKNESSES OF THE HUMAN HEART.
WHEN I CALLED MY PEOPLE, THE JEWS, FROM BONDAGE INTO THE PROMISED LAND, I FIRST REDEEMED THEM.
"THEN I GAVE THEM THE LAW AND FINALLY TAUGHT THEM HOW TO WORSHIP. THEY FORGOT THE FIRST POWER I OFFERED THEM."
"WHAT WAS THAT?"
"THAT IT WAS I WHO REDEEMED THEM. YOU CANNOT HAVE A LAW IN ANY LAND THAT WILL BRING PEACE UNTIL THE HEART HAS BEEN REDEEMED."
"THE STING OF DEATH IS SIN, AND THE STRENGTH OF SIN IS THE LAW."
"I AM NOT SURE WHAT THAT MEANS."
THAT'S WHY YOU KEEP TALKING ABOUT FORGIVENESS WITHOUT KNOWING WHY IT'S EVEN NEEDED.
SIN IS A LIKE A STINGER EMBEDDED IN THE SOUL. WHEN YOU TURN TO THE LAW FOR HELP, IT ONLY INTENSIFIES THE PAIN OF THE STING, AND DEATH IS THE RESULT.

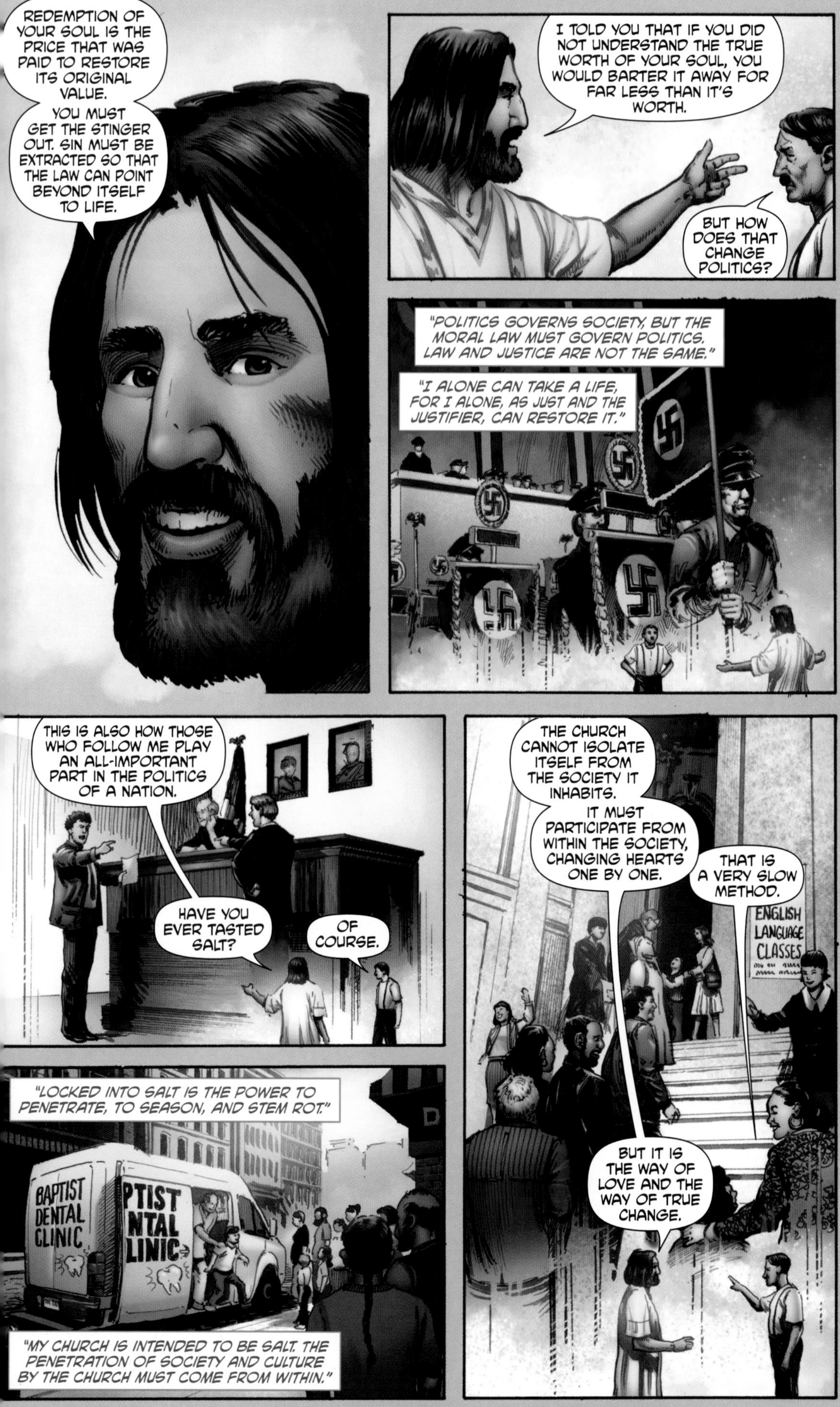
REDEMPTION OF YOUR SOUL IS THE PRICE THAT WAS PAID TO RESTORE ITS ORIGINAL VALUE.
YOU MUST GET THE STINGER OUT. SIN MUST BE EXTRACTED SO THAT THE LAW CAN POINT BEYOND ITSELF TO LIFE.
I TOLD YOU THAT IF YOU DID NOT UNDERSTAND THE TRUE WORTH OF YOUR SOUL, YOU WOULD BARTER IT AWAY FOR FAR LESS THAN IT'S WORTH.
BUT HOW DOES THAT CHANGE POLITICS?
"POLITICS GOVERNS SOCIETY, BUT THE MORAL LAW MUST GOVERN POLITICS. LAW AND JUSTICE ARE NOT THE SAME."
"I ALONE CAN TAKE A LIFE, FOR I ALONE, AS JUST AND THE JUSTIFIER, CAN RESTORE IT."
THIS IS ALSO HOW THOSE WHO FOLLOW ME PLAY AN ALL-IMPORTANT PART IN THE POLITICS OF A NATION.
HAVE YOU EVER TASTED SALT?
OF COURSE.
"LOCKED INTO SALT IS THE POWER TO PENETRATE, TO SEASON, AND STEM ROT."
BAPTIST DENTAL CLINIC
PTIST NTAL LINIC
"MY CHURCH IS INTENDED TO BE SALT. THE PENETRATION OF SOCIETY AND CULTURE BY THE CHURCH MUST COME FROM WITHIN."
THE CHURCH CANNOT ISOLATE ITSELF FROM THE SOCIETY IT INHABITS.
IT MUST PARTICIPATE FROM WITHIN THE SOCIETY, CHANGING HEARTS ONE BY ONE.
THAT IS A VERY SLOW METHOD.
ENGLISH LANGUAGE CLASSES
BUT IT IS THE WAY OF LOVE AND THE WAY OF TRUE CHANGE.

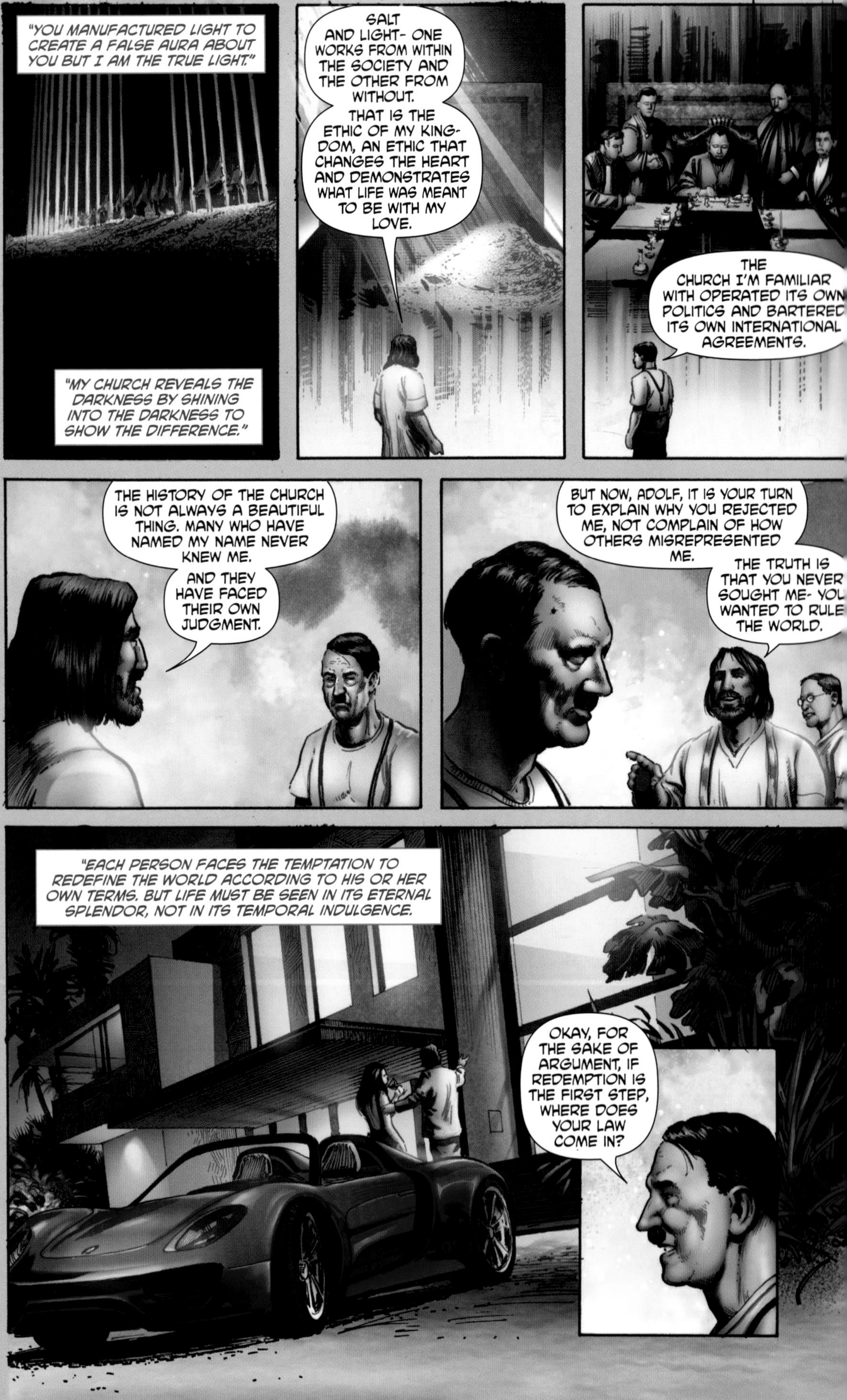
"YOU MANUFACTURED LIGHT TO CREATE A FALSE AURA ABOUT YOU BUT I AM THE TRUE LIGHT."
"MY CHURCH REVEALS THE DARKNESS BY SHINING INTO THE DARKNESS TO SHOW THE DIFFERENCE."
SALT AND LIGHT- ONE WORKS FROM WITHIN THE SOCIETY AND THE OTHER FROM WITHOUT.
THAT IS THE ETHIC OF MY KINGDOM, AN ETHIC THAT CHANGES THE HEART AND DEMONSTRATES WHAT LIFE WAS MEANT TO BE WITH MY LOVE.
THE CHURCH I'M FAMILIAR WITH OPERATED ITS OWN POLITICS AND BARTERED ITS OWN INTERNATIONAL AGREEMENTS.
THE HISTORY OF THE CHURCH IS NOT ALWAYS A BEAUTIFUL THING. MANY WHO HAVE NAMED MY NAME NEVER KNEW ME.
AND THEY HAVE FACED THEIR OWN JUDGMENT.
BUT NOW, ADOLF, IT IS YOUR TURN TO EXPLAIN WHY YOU REJECTED ME, NOT COMPLAIN OF HOW OTHERS MISREPRESENTED ME.
THE TRUTH IS THAT YOU NEVER SOUGHT ME- YOU WANTED TO RULE THE WORLD.
"EACH PERSON FACES THE TEMPTATION TO REDEFINE THE WORLD ACCORDING TO HIS OR HER OWN TERMS. BUT LIFE MUST BE SEEN IN ITS ETERNAL SPLENDOR, NOT IN ITS TEMPORAL INDULGENCE.
OKAY, FOR THE SAKE OF ARGUMENT, IF REDEMPTION IS THE FIRST STEP, WHERE DOES YOUR LAW COME IN?

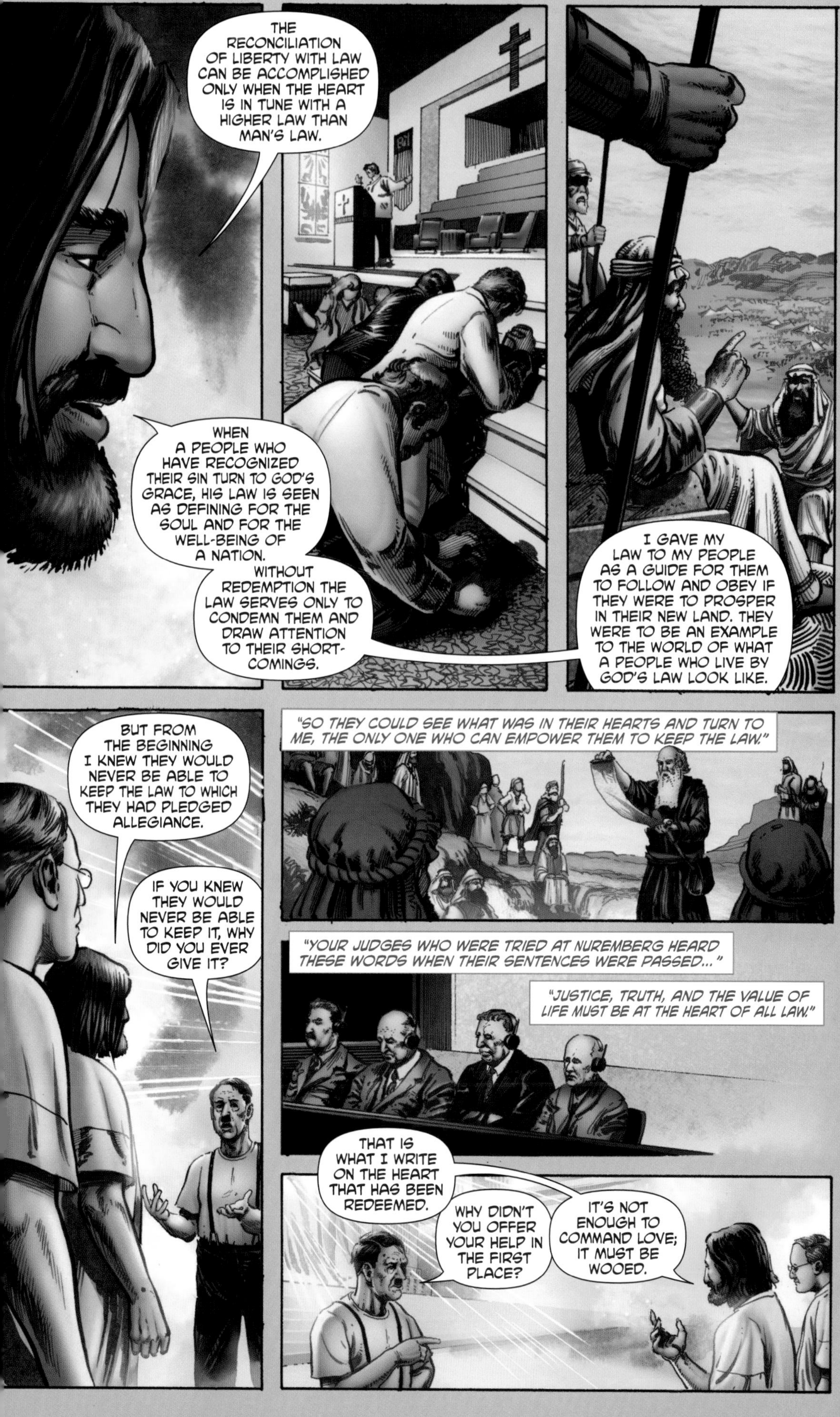
THE RECONCILIATION OF LIBERTY WITH LAW CAN BE ACCOMPLISHED ONLY WHEN THE HEART IS IN TUNE WITH A HIGHER LAW THAN MAN'S LAW.
WHEN A PEOPLE WHO HAVE RECOGNIZED THEIR SIN TURN TO GOD'S GRACE, HIS LAW IS SEEN AS DEFINING FOR THE SOUL AND FOR THE WELL-BEING OF A NATION.
WITHOUT REDEMPTION THE LAW SERVES ONLY TO CONDEMN THEM AND DRAW ATTENTION TO THEIR SHORT-COMINGS.
I GAVE MY LAW TO MY PEOPLE AS A GUIDE FOR THEM TO FOLLOW AND OBEY IF THEY WERE TO PROSPER IN THEIR NEW LAND. THEY WERE TO BE AN EXAMPLE TO THE WORLD OF WHAT A PEOPLE WHO LIVE BY GOD'S LAW LOOK LIKE.
BUT FROM THE BEGINNING I KNEW THEY WOULD NEVER BE ABLE TO KEEP THE LAW TO WHICH THEY HAD PLEDGED ALLEGIANCE.
IF YOU KNEW THEY WOULD NEVER BE ABLE TO KEEP IT, WHY DID YOU EVER GIVE IT?
"SO THEY COULD SEE WHAT WAS IN THEIR HEARTS AND TURN TO ME, THE ONLY ONE WHO CAN EMPOWER THEM TO KEEP THE LAW."
"YOUR JUDGES WHO WERE TRIED AT NUREMBERG HEARD THESE WORDS WHEN THEIR SENTENCES WERE PASSED..."
"JUSTICE, TRUTH, AND THE VALUE OF LIFE MUST BE AT THE HEART OF ALL LAW."
THAT IS WHAT I WRITE ON THE HEART THAT HAS BEEN REDEEMED.
WHY DIDN'T YOU OFFER YOUR HELP IN THE FIRST PLACE?
IT'S NOT ENOUGH TO COMMAND LOVE; IT MUST BE WOOED.

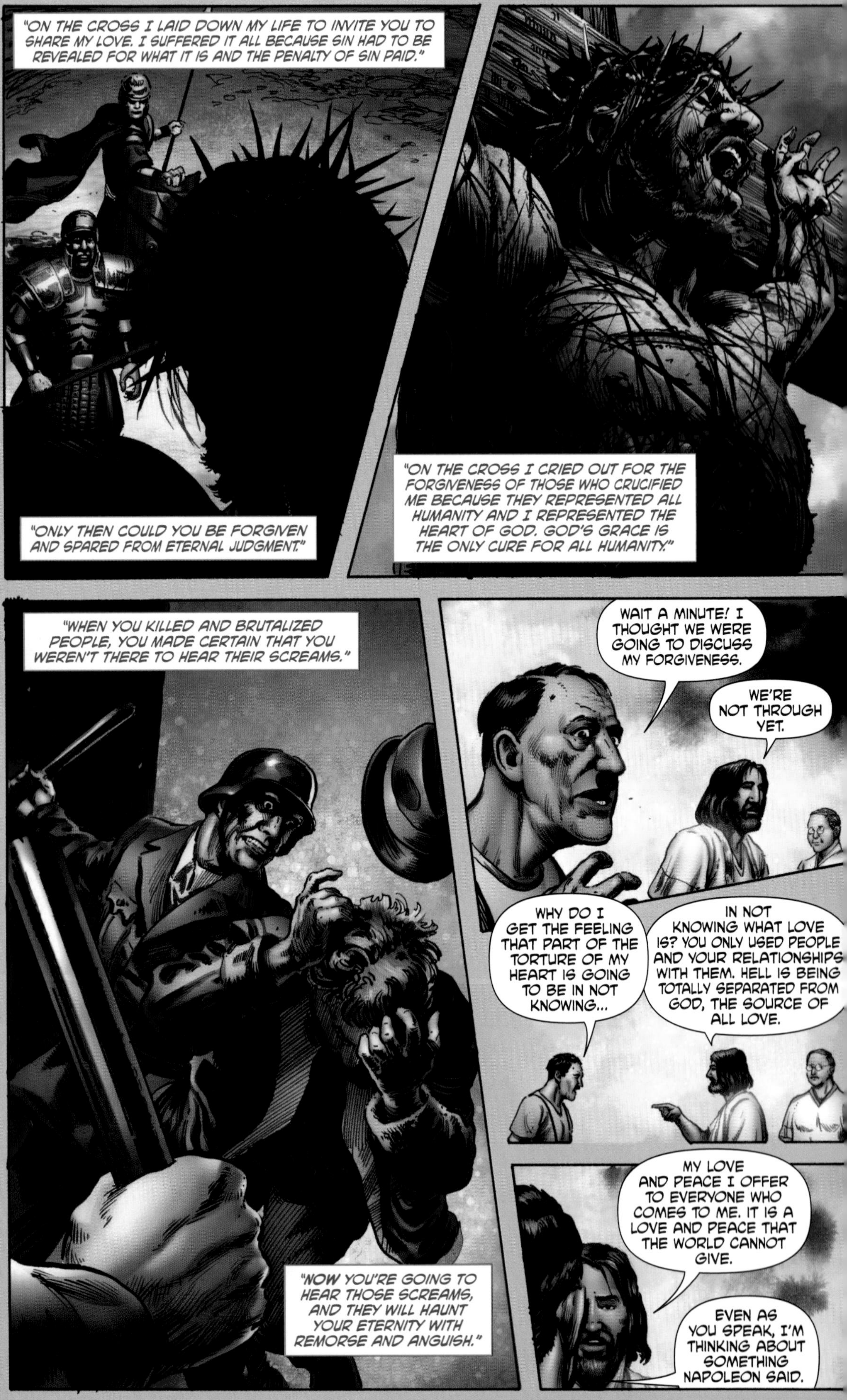
"ON THE CROSS I LAID DOWN MY LIFE TO INVITE YOU TO SHARE MY LOVE. I SUFFERED IT ALL BECAUSE SIN HAD TO BE REVEALED FOR WHAT IT IS AND THE PENALTY OF SIN PAID."
"ONLY THEN COULD YOU BE FORGIVEN AND SPARED FROM ETERNAL JUDGMENT."
"ON THE CROSS I CRIED OUT FOR THE FORGIVENESS OF THOSE WHO CRUCIFIED ME BECAUSE THEY REPRESENTED ALL HUMANITY AND I REPRESENTED THE HEART OF GOD. GOD'S GRACE IS THE ONLY CURE FOR ALL HUMANITY."
"WHEN YOU KILLED AND BRUTALIZED PEOPLE, YOU MADE CERTAIN THAT YOU WEREN'T THERE TO HEAR THEIR SCREAMS."
"NOW YOU'RE GOING TO HEAR THOSE SCREAMS, AND THEY WILL HAUNT YOUR ETERNITY WITH REMORSE AND ANGUISH."
WAIT A MINUTE! I THOUGHT WE WERE GOING TO DISCUSS MY FORGIVENESS.
WE'RE NOT THROUGH YET.
WHY DO I GET THE FEELING THAT PART OF THE TORTURE OF MY HEART IS GOING TO BE IN NOT KNOWING...
IN NOT KNOWING WHAT LOVE IS? YOU ONLY USED PEOPLE AND YOUR RELATIONSHIPS WITH THEM. HELL IS BEING TOTALLY SEPARATED FROM GOD, THE SOURCE OF ALL LOVE.
MY LOVE AND PEACE I OFFER TO EVERYONE WHO COMES TO ME. IT IS A LOVE AND PEACE THAT THE WORLD CANNOT GIVE.
EVEN AS YOU SPEAK, I'M THINKING ABOUT SOMETHING NAPOLEON SAID.

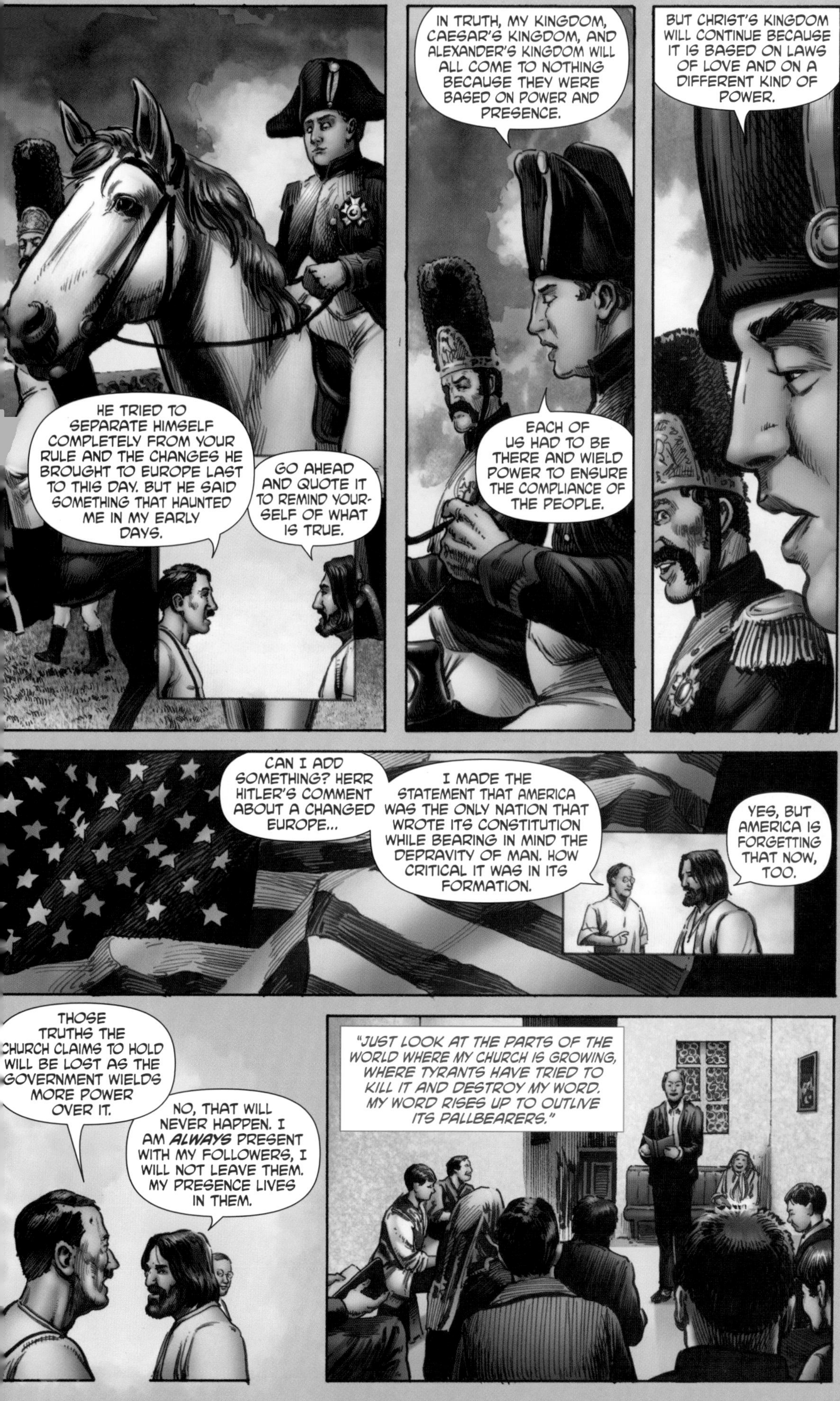
HE TRIED TO SEPARATE HIMSELF COMPLETELY FROM YOUR RULE AND THE CHANGES HE BROUGHT TO EUROPE LAST TO THIS DAY. BUT HE SAID SOMETHING THAT HAUNTED ME IN MY EARLY DAYS.
GO AHEAD AND QUOTE IT TO REMIND YOURSELF OF WHAT IS TRUE.
IN TRUTH, MY KINGDOM, CAESAR'S KINGDOM, AND ALEXANDER'S KINGDOM WILL ALL COME TO NOTHING BECAUSE THEY WERE BASED ON POWER AND PRESENCE.
EACH OF US HAD TO BE THERE AND WIELD POWER TO ENSURE THE COMPLIANCE OF THE PEOPLE.
BUT CHRIST'S KINGDOM WILL CONTINUE BECAUSE IT IS BASED ON LAWS OF LOVE AND ON A DIFFERENT KIND OF POWER.
CAN I ADD SOMETHING? HERR HITLER'S COMMENT ABOUT A CHANGED EUROPE...
I MADE THE STATEMENT THAT AMERICA WAS THE ONLY NATION THAT WROTE ITS CONSTITUTION WHILE BEARING IN MIND THE DEPRAVITY OF MAN. HOW CRITICAL IT WAS IN ITS FORMATION.
YES, BUT AMERICA IS FORGETTING THAT NOW, TOO.
THOSE TRUTHS THE CHURCH CLAIMS TO HOLD WILL BE LOST AS THE GOVERNMENT WIELDS MORE POWER OVER IT.
NO, THAT WILL NEVER HAPPEN. I AM *ALWAYS* PRESENT WITH MY FOLLOWERS, I WILL NOT LEAVE THEM. MY PRESENCE LIVES IN THEM.
"JUST LOOK AT THE PARTS OF THE WORLD WHERE MY CHURCH IS GROWING, WHERE TYRANTS HAVE TRIED TO KILL IT AND DESTROY MY WORD. MY WORD RISES UP TO OUTLIVE ITS PALLBEARERS."

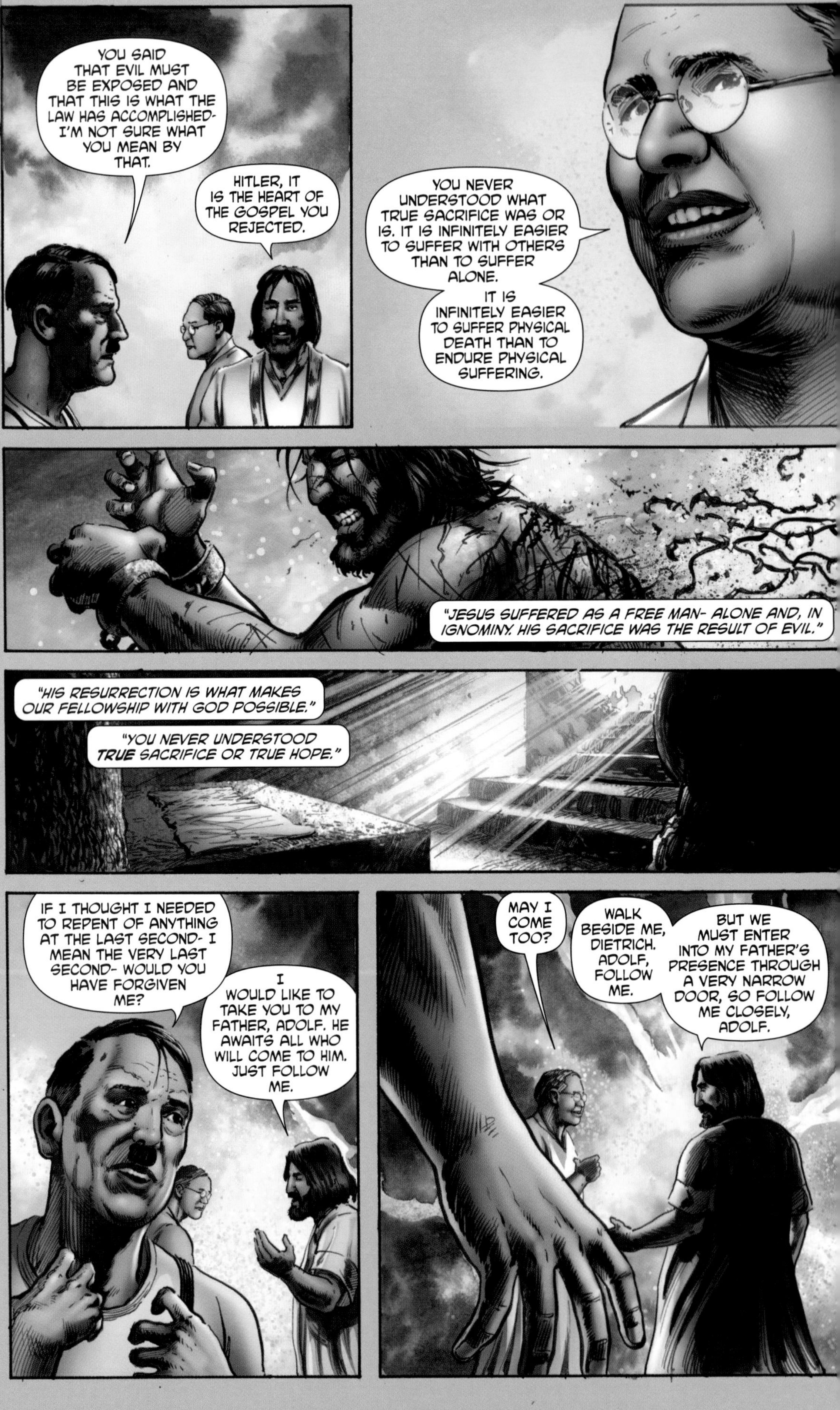

YOU SAID THAT EVIL MUST BE EXPOSED AND THAT THIS IS WHAT THE LAW HAS ACCOMPLISHED- I'M NOT SURE WHAT YOU MEAN BY THAT.
HITLER, IT IS THE HEART OF THE GOSPEL YOU REJECTED.
YOU NEVER UNDERSTOOD WHAT TRUE SACRIFICE WAS OR IS. IT IS INFINITELY EASIER TO SUFFER WITH OTHERS THAN TO SUFFER ALONE.
IT IS INFINITELY EASIER TO SUFFER PHYSICAL DEATH THAN TO ENDURE PHYSICAL SUFFERING.
"JESUS SUFFERED AS A FREE MAN- ALONE AND, IN IGNOMINY. HIS SACRIFICE WAS THE RESULT OF EVIL."
"HIS RESURRECTION IS WHAT MAKES OUR FELLOWSHIP WITH GOD POSSIBLE."
"YOU NEVER UNDERSTOOD **TRUE** SACRIFICE OR TRUE HOPE."
IF I THOUGHT I NEEDED TO REPENT OF ANYTHING AT THE LAST SECOND- I MEAN THE VERY LAST SECOND- WOULD YOU HAVE FORGIVEN ME?
I WOULD LIKE TO TAKE YOU TO MY FATHER, ADOLF. HE AWAITS ALL WHO WILL COME TO HIM. JUST FOLLOW ME.
MAY I COME TOO?
WALK BESIDE ME, DIETRICH. ADOLF, FOLLOW ME.
BUT WE MUST ENTER INTO MY FATHER'S PRESENCE THROUGH A VERY NARROW DOOR, SO FOLLOW ME CLOSELY, ADOLF.

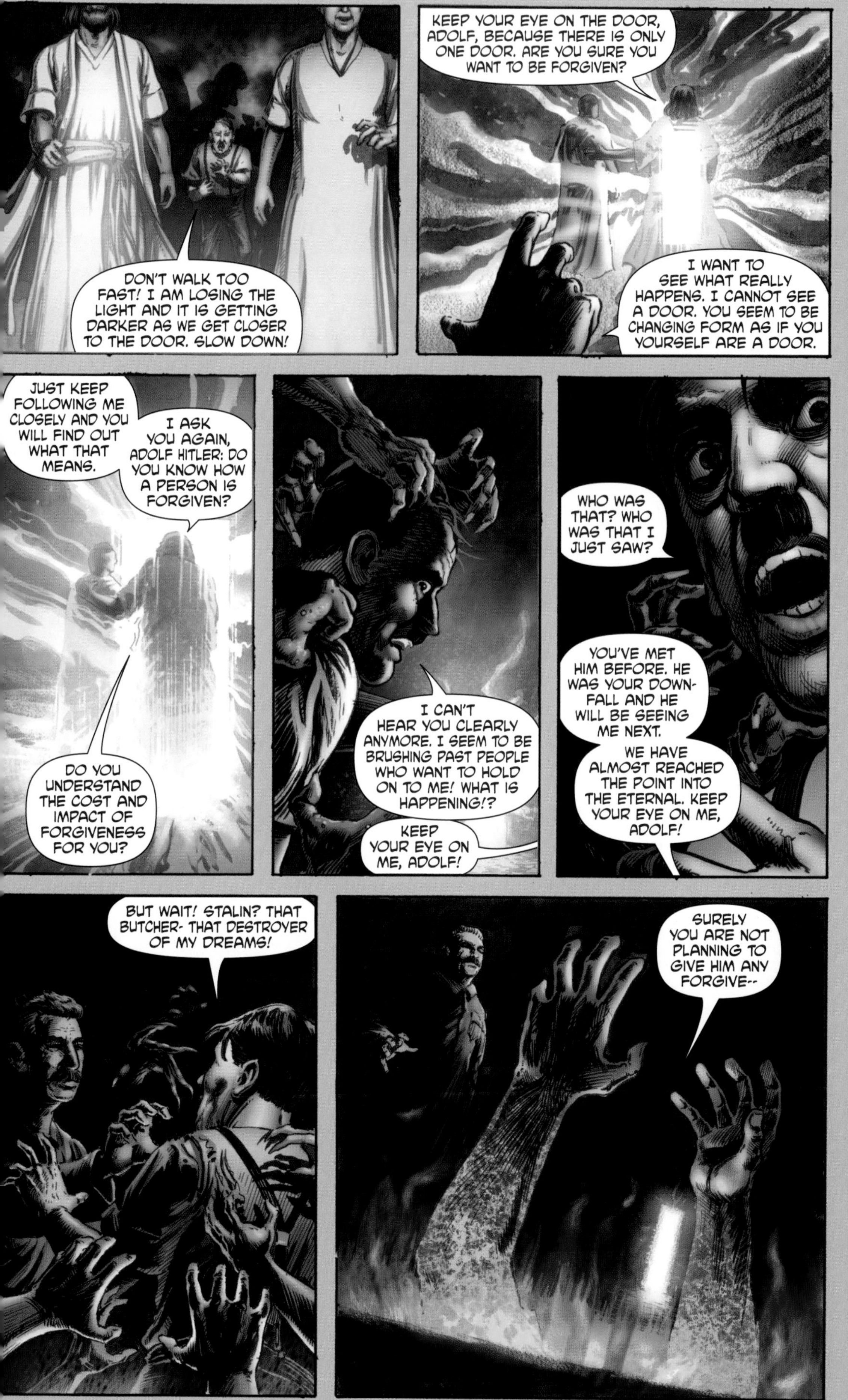
DON'T WALK TOO FAST! I AM LOSING THE LIGHT AND IT IS GETTING DARKER AS WE GET CLOSER TO THE DOOR. SLOW DOWN!
KEEP YOUR EYE ON THE DOOR, ADOLF, BECAUSE THERE IS ONLY ONE DOOR. ARE YOU SURE YOU WANT TO BE FORGIVEN?
I WANT TO SEE WHAT REALLY HAPPENS. I CANNOT SEE A DOOR. YOU SEEM TO BE CHANGING FORM AS IF YOU YOURSELF ARE A DOOR.
JUST KEEP FOLLOWING ME CLOSELY AND YOU WILL FIND OUT WHAT THAT MEANS.
I ASK YOU AGAIN, ADOLF HITLER: DO YOU KNOW HOW A PERSON IS FORGIVEN?
DO YOU UNDERSTAND THE COST AND IMPACT OF FORGIVENESS FOR YOU?
I CAN'T HEAR YOU CLEARLY ANYMORE. I SEEM TO BE BRUSHING PAST PEOPLE WHO WANT TO HOLD ON TO ME! WHAT IS HAPPENING!?
KEEP YOUR EYE ON ME, ADOLF!
WHO WAS THAT? WHO WAS THAT I JUST SAW?
YOU'VE MET HIM BEFORE. HE WAS YOUR DOWN-FALL AND HE WILL BE SEEING ME NEXT.
WE HAVE ALMOST REACHED THE POINT INTO THE ETERNAL. KEEP YOUR EYE ON ME, ADOLF!
BUT WAIT! STALIN? THAT BUTCHER- THAT DESTROYER OF MY DREAMS!
SURELY YOU ARE NOT PLANNING TO GIVE HIM ANY FORGIVE--

JESUS, WHAT HAPPENED? THE FLOOR GAVE WAY! IT'S AS IF THE EARTH ITSELF OPENED UP AND THE WEIGHT OF HIS OWN UNBELIEF--

THERE IS NO SECOND CHANCE HERE, DIETRICH.

THE ONLY THING THAT HAPPENS BEFORE THEY MEET THEIR DESTINY IS A CONFIRMATION THAT THEY DO NOT UNDERSTAND FORGIVENESS AND HOW A FORGIVEN PERSON LIVES.

NOR DO THEY WANT IT.

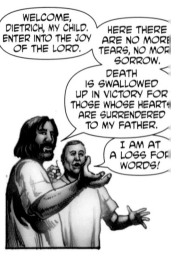

WELCOME, DIETRICH, MY CHILD. ENTER INTO THE JOY OF THE LORD.

HERE THERE ARE NO MORE TEARS, NO MORE SORROW.

DEATH IS SWALLOWED UP IN VICTORY FOR THOSE WHOSE HEARTS ARE SURRENDERED TO MY FATHER.

I AM AT A LOSS FOR WORDS!

AND *THAT* IS YOUR ONLY LOSS!

EPILOGUE
†

The Indian sage Acharya Vinoba Bhave said that in the premodern world, violence was relative. In the modern world, he said it would be absolute. That was quite a statement to have made decades ago. What does it mean, that violence is absolute? It means that violence would become the governing ethic for a world in which all seek ascendance. Hitler was just a representative of the human heart when violence has become absolute.

I urge the reader to see the two movies *Nuremberg* and *Judgment at Nuremberg*. In that microcosm the immensity and tragedy of the human predicament become evident: In denying the moral law, everything becomes a pathetic attempt to defend even the abominable. In our world today, struggling with Al Qaeda and those who try to justify their evil ways, there is little difference. Anytime a worldview seeks to govern by force, this is the result. Nor is there a difference in the devaluing of life that we see even in so-called free societies. The atrocities we commit in our civilized societies are only dressed up with law and language. The world is reeling with the tricks being played to justify the profane. Our ways today are only better than sixty years ago at the surface level. At the core we are in the same mess.

That is why Jesus never sought to bring in His kingdom by our means. His is neither a pure democracy nor an imposed autocracy. He sought to win the hearts of men and women who in turn will live their lives conformed to the image of God's Son, respecting the intrinsic dignity of each individual person and understanding true freedom. But that is not as simple as it may sound.

In the Bible, there is an interesting conversation between Jesus and the Pharisees. A group of them came to Jesus and said, "We know you're a man of integrity and you teach the way of God according to the truth. Tell us then what is your opinion? Is it right to pay taxes to Caesar or not?"

This was truly a trick question because they hated the yoke of Rome. But at the same time it was a real question. "Can you legitimize paying money to a pagan power?" "What do you do when your faith is violated by the powers that deny you the value of your own faith and of life itself?"

Jesus' answer was brilliant, but like many of His answers there was intentional subtlety so that only those who really sought the truth would find it. He asked for them to show Him a coin. "Whose image is on the coin?" he asked.

"Caesar's," they answered.

"Then give to Caesar what is Caesar's and to God what is God's," Jesus said.

If you ponder that answer, you have the answer to politics. The coin may have Caesar's image on it, but whose image does the person who asked the question bear? The Pharisees missed the point. So did the Nazi officers who justified everything by saying they were "giving to Caesar what belonged to Caesar."

Humanity was not made in the image of Caesar, but in the image of God. That is a uniquely Christian truth. When we understand that, we understand what it means to form a government and write laws that reflect that basic truth. No other worldview holds to that. We are made in God's image, but we have marred it. So those of us who castigate Hitler must realize that the castigation itself buys into the Judeo-Christian worldview that each human being has essential value because he or she has been made in the image of God. You simply cannot condemn Hitler without affirming the fundamental premise that life at its core is sacred.

And only in the person of God through His Son can we see the image we were meant to reflect. The hatred that tried Him and put Him to death was not accidental. Nor is the natural inclination in all of us throughout all ages to put Him away (or as the Bible says, to repeatedly crucify Him and put Him to open shame) accidental. For with Him out of the way, there is no absolute standard we can follow. And each person can then do and be what is right in his or her own eyes. But in His willingness to die by His own will, He has restored to us the unmarred image that we were meant to have. It took his death to show us our hearts, and it took His resurrection to rescue us from ourselves and show us the way out of our dilemma.

The Lamb talks to the Fuhrer to point the way back for all of us, for we have all killed God's image and find ways of hating while justifying it. The Lamb shows the way of loving by just means. Until we see in each one of us the same capacity for evil as Hitler had, we will never see the possibility of Jesus in all of us. The Third Reich meant control from the outside by fear. The Rule of God means peace on the inside by the incentive of love. Outside of Jesus Christ there is no possibility of true freedom and intrinsic worth. That is why He said, "I have come that you might have life."

For Hitler, who denied the image of God, the ends justified the means, and the ends were spelled by the supremacy of some men over others. That was his reich, his kingdom. Dietrich Bonhoeffer, who affirmed the image of God, knew that the means had to justify themselves because without that, any ends could be justified and any means employed to destroy the value of human life. That was the true reich, the true kingdom to be pursued. Jesus showed the only means to the ends for which we were made. Beginning with the poor in spirit and ending with the pure in heart, the kingdom is attained, for that is God's kingdom. Only in Jesus could both Hitler and Bonhoeffer have recognized the problem and found the solution. And so we pray, "Thy kingdom come, O Lord – in our hearts first before we see it in the world."